Extensive Reading in the Second Language Classroom

CAMBRIDGE LANGUAGE EDUCATION
Series Editor: Jack C. Richards

This series draws on the best available research, theory, and educational practice to help clarify issues and resolve problems in language teaching, language teacher education, and related areas. Books in the series focus on a wide range of issues and are written in a style that is accessible to classroom teachers, teachers-in-training, and teacher educators.

In this series:

Agendas for Second Language Literacy *by Sandra Lee McKay*

Reflective Teaching in Second Language Classrooms *by Jack C. Richards and Charles Lockhart*

Educating Second Language Children: The whole child, the whole curriculum, the whole community *edited by Fred Genesee*

Understanding Communication in Second Language Classrooms *by Karen E. Johnson*

The Self-directed Teacher: Managing the learning process *by David Nunan and Clarice Lamb*

Functional English Grammar: An introduction for second language teachers *by Graham Lock*

Teachers as Course Developers *edited by Kathleen Graves*

Classroom-based Evaluation in Second Language Education *by Fred Genesee and John A. Upshur*

From Reader to Reading Teacher: Issues and strategies for second language classrooms *by Jo Ann Aebersold and Mary Lee Field*

Extensive Reading in the Second Language Classroom *by Richard R. Day and Julian Bamford*

Language Teaching Awareness: A guide to exploring beliefs and practices *by Jerry G. Gebhard and Robert Oprandy*

Vocabulary in Language Teaching *by Norbert Schmitt*

Extensive Reading in the Second Language Classroom

Richard R. Day
University of Hawaii

Julian Bamford
Bunkyo University

PUBLISHED BY THE PRESS SYNDICATE OF THE UNIVERSITY OF CAMBRIDGE
The Pitt Building, Trumpington Street, Cambridge, United Kingdom

CAMBRIDGE UNIVERSITY PRESS
The Edinburgh Building, Cambridge CB2 2RU, UK
40 West 20th Street, New York, NY 10011–4211, USA
10 Stamford Road, Oakleigh, Melbourne 3166, Australia
Ruiz de Alarcón 13, 28014 Madrid, Spain
Dock House, The Waterfront, Cape Town 8001, South Africa

http://www.cambridge.org

First published 1998
Second printing 2000

Printed in the United States of America

Typeset in Times Roman

Library of Congress Cataloging-in-Publication Data
Day, Richard R.
Extensive reading in the second language classroom / Richard Day and Julian Bamford.
p. cm.
"Bibliography of language learner literature in English" : p.
Includes bibliographical references (p.) and index.
ISBN 0-521-56073-X (hb). – ISBN 0-521-56829-3 (pb)
1. Language and languages – Study and teaching. 2. Reading.
I. Bamford, Julian. II. Title.
P53.75.D39 1997
418′.4′07–dc21 97-24481
CIP

A catalogue record for this book is available from the British Library

ISBN 0 521 56073 X hardback
ISBN 0 521 56829 3 paperback

To the late Dr. Shigekazu Fukuyama

To Terry and Leanne Day, and Marion and Vincent Bamford

And to Harold Palmer and Michael West, the parents of second language extensive reading in modern times

Contents

Series editor's preface

Although a number of useful books are available on the teaching of reading in a second or foreign language, this is the first book to focus specifically on the nature of extensive reading and the development of extensive reading programs in foreign and second language teaching. Richard Day and Julian Bamford offer an informed and practical analysis of the nature and scope of extensive reading, argue convincingly for the need to give greater attention to extensive reading in language teaching, and provide a valuable guide to developing an effective extensive reading program within a second or foreign language curriculum.

In developing their rationale for extensive reading, the authors review a comprehensive body of research that demonstrates the benefits that can accrue from extensive reading. These benefits include not only the obvious improvements in students' reading skills and reading speed but changes in their general language proficiency and in their attitudes toward reading and language learning. For many language students, the ability to engage in fluent reading and to read both for important information and for pleasure is perhaps the most valuable benefit they will gain from language study; hence it is crucial that such an outcome is planned for in language teaching rather than left to chance.

The authors demonstrate, however, that there is far more to extensive reading than simply providing materials. They analyze the factors that need to be considered in planning and implementing a program, and how such a program can be effectively organized and administered. Detailed guidance is given concerning how to integrate extensive reading into the second or foreign language curriculum, what the goals for such activities are, what resources and planning are needed, the criteria for choosing suitable reading texts, how to evaluate the program, and important factors to consider in the day-to-day management of a program.

The authors emphasize that although extensive reading is a student-centered and student-managed activity – since students choose what, when, and how to read – teachers have a crucial role to play in ensuring the success of the program. Teachers need a thorough understanding of the nature of second language reading, of the nature of extensive reading materials, and of the strategies for developing reading skills and a love of reading through extensive reading.

Extensive Reading in the Second Language Classroom provides a comprehensive and stimulating account of these and other important issues in extensive reading and will be a valuable resource both for classroom teachers and for teacher educators preparing novice teachers for careers in second and foreign language teaching.

Jack C. Richards

Preface

> Students are unsure of what they have read; they feel that they do not have sufficient language to say what they want to say. They hesitate to admit that they are not sure what they just read. They are apprehensive about being evaluated by the teacher and their peers. They elect to sit silently and wait for the teacher to ask questions or for other students to speak.

This is a description of what Jo Ann Aebersold and Mary Lee Field (1997, p. 116) call "the world of real L2/FL reading classes." But students learning to read a second language do not have to act like that. Rather, they can be enthusiastic and confident about reading, and can leave the second language reading course as independent and lifelong readers in the target language.

This book can help make such a transformation possible. Although it is a book about the teaching and learning of reading in a second language, it differs from most books on the subject because of its focus – extensive reading. The purpose of this book is to provide a theoretical and pedagogical foundation for the premise that extensive reading should be an integral part of reading instruction in the second language classroom.

Extensive reading is an approach to the teaching and learning of second language reading in which learners read large quantities of books and other materials that are well within their linguistic competence. Extensive reading, however, is not just a matter of submerging students in a bath of print. As Albert Harris and Edward Sipay observe, "It takes superior materials, clever teachers who love to read themselves, time, and effort to develop the reading habit" (1990, p. 655).

The benefits of such an instructional approach are wide-ranging. If set up and carried out appropriately, extensive reading not only helps students learn to read in the second language, but also leads them to enjoy reading.

This encourages them to continue reading long after formal study of the second language is over. In addition, extensive reading, at the very least, consolidates students' learning of the second language and, at best, increases their proficiency. For all these reasons, we are firm advocates of the inclusion of extensive reading in *any* second language reading program.

Second languages are learned by different people for different reasons. Although these differences are important in some contexts, we see extensive reading as useful to anyone who reads or intends to read a second language. We also see extensive reading as appropriate for both a *second language* context – where the target language is learned in a community of its speakers, such as learning English in the United States – and a *foreign* language context, in which the target language is learned where that language is not spoken, such as learning English in Japan. For convenience, throughout the book we use the term *second language* to include both a second and a foreign language learning environment. When the term *foreign* is used, it is to refer specifically to a foreign language learning context.

An extensive reading approach does not assume that the students have any particular level of ability in the target language. In our view, extensive reading is appropriate at all stages of language learning; it is never too early – or too late – to learn to read a second language. At the same time, an extensive reading approach has nothing particular to offer the prereading stages of learning to read. Therefore, in this book it is assumed that students are already literate in their first languages and that they know the written form of the second language.

The book has three major sections. Part I provides a theoretical foundation for extensive reading. Part II is a critical examination of materials development in second language reading. Part III presents and discusses the practical aspects of conducting an extensive reading program.

Although we believe that extensive reading should be a part of every second language reading program, it is not our intention to evangelize. Rather, we present an alternative or additional way of approaching the teaching of reading. We are not so naive as to believe that an extensive reading approach can turn all students into independent, fluent readers. However, if used appropriately, an extensive reading approach can considerably improve second language reading instruction and the chances that students will enjoy reading in the second language. It would be an unusual extensive reading class that fit the description of the typical L2/FL reading class described by Aebersold and Field.

We would like to express our appreciation to Jack Richards, the editor of the series in which this book appears, for his encouragement and support; to David Hill and the Edinburgh Project on Extensive Reading for making available their research in the form of the bibliography in the Appendix; to Steven Brown, Marc Helgesen, David Hill, Ted Plaister, Joyce Taniguchi, Roberta Welch, and Cambridge's anonymous reviewers for their invaluable comments on earlier drafts of the manuscript; to the Bodleian Library, Oxford, and the CILT Library in London and their staff; to Judy Davis for her work on the index; and to Mary Vaughn and Mary Carson at Cambridge University Press. We are particularly grateful to editor Olive Collen and copy editor David Thorstad for their exceptional work on the manuscript.

We hope that the ideas presented in this book will stimulate readers to reflect on their own second language reading experiences, both as teachers and as students. We also hope that readers will enjoy reading it as much as we enjoyed writing it.

Richard R. Day
Julian Bamford

PART I: THE DIMENSIONS OF EXTENSIVE READING

This first section of the book endeavors to build a cast-iron case for broadening second language reading instruction so that it becomes more natural, more pleasant, and more effective than is often the case. Chapter 1 introduces extensive reading as an approach to the teaching of second language reading. Then Chapters 2, 3, and 4 build a case from theory and from research that extensive reading should be part of second language reading instruction. Chapter 2 does this by examining reading from a cognitive point of view; Chapter 3, by examining the affective dimensions of attitude and motivation in relation to second language reading; and Chapter 4, by reporting the results of a number of extensive reading programs. Part I concludes with suggestions in Chapter 5 for integrating extensive reading into second language reading programs.

1 *An approach less taken: Extensive reading introduced*

> The rather curious situation has arisen whereby, despite universal acceptance of the view that one becomes a good reader through reading, reading lessons where most time is actually spent on reading (as opposed to discussion, answering questions, etc.) are relatively rare.
>
> —Chris Moran and Eddie Williams (1993, p. 66)

The purpose of this chapter is to:

- Reexamine the purposes for second language reading instruction.
- Define extensive reading and introduce it as an approach to the teaching of second language reading.
- List the defining characteristics of successful extensive reading programs.

At the beginning of the 1950s American musical *The Music Man,* Professor Harold Hill blows into River City, Iowa, and startles the residents with the pronouncement that they have trouble. Being careful not to criticize them as parents, Professor Hill asks the good citizens of River City to think about their children: Do they dress badly when they go out? Do they use slang? Are there nicotine stains between their fingers? Do they keep sleazy novels hidden from view?

In the same rhetorical manner, we begin with a similar pronouncement: There is trouble in the second language reading classroom. Take a moment to consider any students you know who are learning to read a second language. Are they reluctant to read? Do they seem bored or under stress? Do they come to reading class with fear and trepidation? Do they read anything in the second language apart from their assignments?

In *The Music Man,* Professor Hill was in fact a con artist who stirred up the citizenry for his own unscrupulous ends. Our intentions, on the other hand, are honorable. We raise the possibility that there may be, if not trouble, then at least two good reasons to reexamine the second language reading classroom: In general, *students learning to read a second language do not read and they do not like reading.*

Students not reading and not liking to read is a problem. It is simplistic but nevertheless true that the more students read, the better they become at it. "Reading . . . must be developed, and can only be developed, by means of extensive and continual practice. People learn to read, and to read better, by reading," states David Eskey (1986, p. 21). In addition, students with negative attitudes toward second language reading are unlikely to be motivated to do the reading they need to do to become fluent readers.

In an ideal world, are there any reading teachers who would *not* want their students to *(a)* read a great deal and *(b)* enjoy reading? It is unlikely. But such aims may seem remote, unattainable, and even irrelevant to the job at hand. After all, the curriculum is filled to the brim already. Teachers' immediate priorities are making sure their students do well in their courses and pass the necessary examinations; indeed, their livelihoods depend on it. What is more, teachers already know how to achieve these immediate priorities. They rightly pride themselves on their accomplishments and abilities.

Formal education has a life of its own. For students, it is commonly something that must be gone through, revolving around fulfilling credit requirements and passing examinations rather than the learning of something that one wants or feels a need to learn. Pedagogical practices also have a life of their own to the extent that they become divorced from the real needs or goals of the students. Second language reading classrooms are no exception to this possibility. Carlos Yorio, in a paper titled "The ESL Reading Class: Reality or Unreality," notes that, if one is "to compare . . . classroom activities with real-life situations in which people are reading for various purposes or reasons . . . in most cases the degree of 'unreality' of the ESL reading classes is striking" (1985, p. 151).

The second language reading lesson can avoid being merely an empty ritual – come to class, read the texts, do the exercises, leave class, return to real life – by addressing the two aims of students reading a great deal and enjoying reading. Teachers rightly feel satisfaction when students pass examinations and meet the requirements of the class. But their satisfaction would be even greater if their students also left their classes reading and enjoying the process.

Can the two aims of reading in quantity and developing a reading habit be integrated with the immediate priorities of teacher and student without undermining successful classroom practices and methodologies? Or are such aims merely the lofty dreams of academics far removed from the classroom, the preachings of those who do not know what it is like to face the daily rigors and pressing demands of teaching? In response, we can say that the present volume derives from the experiences of teachers whose students do read and enjoy it. These are not extraordinary teachers with extraordinary students. They are ordinary people facing the same demands everyone else faces, teaching and learning in situations that range from the extreme (a wall-less secondary classroom in Zanzibar) to the conventional (a well-equipped university classroom in the United States). Our purpose in this volume, then, is to present theoretical and practical support for the premise that an extensive reading approach can be profitably integrated into any second language reading classroom.

Extensive reading

Louis Kelly, in his volume *25 Centuries of Language Teaching,* credits Harold Palmer with first applying the term *extensive reading* in foreign language pedagogy (1969, p. 131). Palmer was a pioneer of language teaching in modern times, and among his many talents was a genius for terminology. For his 1917 book *The Scientific Study and Teaching of Languages,* he selected "extensive" from the multitude of synonyms previously used to convey similar ideas – such as "abundant reading" used in the landmark 1900 *Report of the Committee of Twelve* (Modern Language Association of America, 1901), which suggested how languages be taught in secondary schools.

For Palmer, extensive reading meant "rapidly" (1921/1964, p. 111) reading "book after book" (1917/1968, p. 137). A reader's attention should be on the meaning, not the language, of the text. Palmer contrasted this with what he termed *intensive reading,* by which he meant to "take a text, study it line by line, referring at every moment to our dictionary and our grammar, comparing, analysing, translating, and retaining every expression that it contains" (1921/1964, p. 111). A "multiple line of approach" (p. 111) was one of Palmer's nine principles of language study, and he consequently saw the importance of both types of reading.

In Palmer's conception of extensive reading, texts were clearly being read for the purposes of language study, but, because attention was on the content and not the language, it could only be that the texts were also being read for ordinary real-world purposes of pleasure and information. And so it was that extensive reading took on a special sense in the context of language teaching: real-world reading but for a pedagogical purpose.

Other terms for extensive reading were used, even as its goals were being made explicit. Michael West, a teacher and materials writer working in India who more than anyone else established the methodology of extensive reading, called it "supplementary" reading (1926/1955, p. 26). This was also the term used by the New York City Board of Education for its 1931 *Syllabus of Minima in Modern Foreign Languages*. Here the goal of supplementary reading was "the development to the point of enjoyment of the ability to read the foreign language" (1931/1948, p. 301), and the methodology involved "taking care of individual differences and encouraging the reading habit" (p. 302).

Today, in language-teaching terms, extensive reading is recognized as one of four styles or ways of reading, the other three being skimming, scanning, and intensive reading. Eddie Williams and Chris Moran note that these four reading styles are recognized "on the basis of observable behaviour (notably speed of reading, degree of re-reading, 'skipping' of text)" (1989, p. 222).

However, the present volume is not primarily concerned with extensive reading as a style; rather, the focus is on extensive reading as an approach to second language reading instruction.

An extensive reading approach

An extensive reading approach aims to get students reading in the second language and liking it. Or, to put things more formally, as the *Longman Dictionary of Language Teaching and Applied Linguistics* does, extensive reading is "intended to develop good reading habits, to build up knowledge of vocabulary and structure, and to encourage a liking for reading" (Richards, Platt, & Platt, 1992, p. 133). As this definition implies, extensive reading also pays off in increased general second language competence. Although this will occasionally be referred to, the present volume mainly restricts itself to the impact of extensive reading on the ability to read in a second language.

William Grabe, in a 1991 *TESOL Quarterly* paper, discusses some of the benefits of extensive reading. "Longer concentrated periods of silent reading build vocabulary and structural awareness, develop automaticity, enhance background knowledge, improve comprehension skills, and promote confidence and motivation" (p. 396). In addition, as Aud Marit Simensen points out (echoing Harold Palmer 60 years earlier), extensive reading can counteract "a tendency among foreign language learners always to regard a text as an object for language studies and not as an object for factual information, literary experience or simply pleasure, joy and delight" (1987, p. 42).

This last point may be more important than it at first seems. Studies of both first and second language beginning readers in many countries have revealed telling connections between reading ability and the views students hold about reading. Readers of lower ability tend to see reading in terms of "schoolwork" (Bondy, 1990, pp. 35–36) or "as a serious, difficult process, requiring hard work and disciplined effort" (Elley, 1992, p. 77). Students of higher reading ability, on the other hand, take a meaning-centered approach (Devine, 1984). For them, reading is a "pleasant, imaginative activity" (Elley, 1992, p. 77), a way to learn things that is both a private pleasure and a social activity (Bondy, 1990, pp. 36–38). It is the latter views – the kind fostered by extensive reading – that are most often associated with successful outcomes when teaching reading.

As an approach to learning to read a second language, extensive reading may be done in and out of the classroom. Outside the classroom, extensive reading is encouraged by allowing students to borrow books to take home and read. In the classroom, it requires a period of time, at least 15 minutes or so, to be set aside for *sustained silent reading,* that is, for students – and perhaps the teacher as well – to read individually anything they wish to.

Some reading specialists – Stephen Krashen and Beatrice Mikulecky come immediately to mind – call extensive reading *pleasure reading.* As he told a 1995 colloquium audience, William Grabe is not particularly keen on either term: extensive reading being rather general, and pleasure reading too specific in that "lots of people . . . get turned on to all kinds of materials that someone wouldn't put in a pile called pleasure reading. . . . Extensive reading is people willing to engage . . . [with] a lot of extended texts for a variety of reasons." There is also a possibility that "pleasure reading" has frivolous overtones for students, parents, and administrators. Perhaps for these reasons, Krashen and his colleagues have used another term, *free voluntary reading* (as in his 1993 book *The Power of Reading*).

The characteristics of an extensive reading approach

Just as it is hard to find a name for extensive reading that satisfies everyone, it is hard to reduce it to a dictionary-type definition. For teachers, a more useful way of understanding the complexity of extensive reading is though a description of the characteristics that are found in successful extensive reading programs.

1. *Students read as much as possible,* perhaps in and definitely out of the classroom.

2. *A variety of materials on a wide range of topics is available* so as to encourage reading for different reasons and in different ways.
3. *Students select what they want to read* and have the freedom to stop reading material that fails to interest them.
4. *The purposes of reading are usually related to pleasure, information, and general understanding.* These purposes are determined by the nature of the material and the interests of the student.
5. *Reading is its own reward.* There are few or no follow-up exercises after reading.
6. *Reading materials are well within the linguistic competence of the students* in terms of vocabulary and grammar. Dictionaries are rarely used while reading because the constant stopping to look up words makes fluent reading difficult.
7. *Reading is individual and silent,* at the student's own pace, and, outside class, done when and where the student chooses.
8. *Reading speed is usually faster rather than slower* as students read books and other material they find easily understandable.
9. *Teachers orient students to the goals of the program, explain* the methodology, *keep track* of what each student reads, and *guide* students in getting the most out of the program.
10. *The teacher is a role model of a reader for students* – an active member of the classroom reading community, demonstrating what it means to be a reader and the rewards of being a reader.

These elements raise questions for both students and teachers alike. At workshops on extensive reading, teachers ask such questions as:

- What are the theoretical foundations of extensive reading?
- What are the benefits?
- Is there any empirical evidence for these alleged benefits?
- Do second language learners have the proper attitude toward reading to allow extensive reading?
- Are learners motivated to read outside the classroom?
- How much reading is meant by *extensive*?
- What materials are suitable for students at various ability levels in the second language?
- Are simplified materials for lower-level students inferior to authentic "real-life" materials?
- On what basis might students who read extensively be evaluated and grades be given?
- How might the success of an extensive reading program be evaluated?

Some of these issues have barely been dealt with in the professional literature, and one of the aims of this book is to remedy that deficiency.

Conclusion

Is there trouble in the second language reading classroom? Is it a problem that, as noted by Moran and Williams at the beginning of this chapter, students do not read much in reading class? Is it a problem that, as Yorio claims, reading classes bear little resemblance to the real world of reading? It is our position that these are problems and that they have a direct bearing on students' reading ability and attitude toward reading; further, that second language reading instruction can and should allow students to develop into fluent, independent, and confident second language readers; and, finally, that, to paraphrase Eva Mayne writing in 1915, reading classes can give students a love for reading in the second language, a thirst for it that will stay with them throughout their lives.

Further reading

Maxim Newmark's 1948 edited collection *Twentieth Century Modern Language Teaching: Sources and Readings* contains, along with other valuable material, excerpts from the major U.S. reports on modern language teaching from the first half of the twentieth century. If you can locate the volume itself, it is a convenient source of the even harder-to-find original documents that outlined goals and methods of second language reading instruction.

For more on Harold Palmer and Michael West, a good place to begin is A. P. R. Howatt's *A History of English Language Teaching* (1984). Chapter 16 covers Palmer's life, work, and methodology (pp. 230–244; see also pp. 325–327). "Altogether," says Howatt, "no other single individual did more to create the English language teaching profession in the present century" (p. 327). An outline of Michael West's work in India follows in Chapter 17 (pp. 245–250; see also pp. 335–336).

2 *A cognitive view of reading*

> To teach foreign or second language reading well, we need to know as much as possible about how the reading process works and how to integrate that knowledge effectively into our reading pedagogy.
> —Marva Barnett (1989, p. 1)

> There is nothing as practical as a good theory.
> —Anonymous

The purpose of this chapter is to:

- Examine first and second language reading as a cognitive process.
- Explain from a cognitive perspective the role of extensive reading in developing fluent second language readers.

Which of these statements best captures your view of the role of theory in the teaching of reading?

1. "To tell the truth, I really don't pay much attention to this whole theory business. I'm a teacher and I need to know what to do in class."
2. "Well, I get very confused. I hear them talking about top-down and bottom-up reading and terms like that; I don't understand it. I just teach from the books that the school orders each year."
3. "The reading course in my master's program was based on theory, so I understand the issues. But I really learned to teach reading in the practicum."
4. "It's important, no doubt about it. I mean, everything that we do has a theoretical foundation. Isn't that right?"

We have encountered versions of these four points of view about the value of theory in the teaching of reading from widely different types of reading teachers – from graduates of advanced-degree programs in English as a second language to teachers who have minimal competence in the second language and little formal training in language teaching. The position taken in this book is closer to number 4 than to any of the others. Theory is important.

When educators design second language reading programs, and when reading teachers order texts, select materials, and plan activities, assumptions are being made about the nature of reading, and how students learn to read a second language. These assumptions are in reality theories of reading, and it is not uncommon for them to go unexamined. If they are brought to the surface and compared to accepted theoretical models, however, serious contradictions and inconsistencies may emerge. A deeper understanding of the reading process and how students learn to read a second language can offer a stronger theoretical rationale for second language reading programs and instructional approaches.

In this chapter we set out the first of two justifications for the premise that an extensive reading approach has important benefits to offer a second language reading program. This first justification is based on the nature of reading as a cognitive process. The first half of the chapter is a consideration of cognitive interactive models of reading; the second half examines the role that extensive reading can play in developing second language students' reading ability.

Reading as a cognitive process

Reading takes many forms. Think for a moment of all the activities that can be labeled *reading.* They include serious academic reading (what you are doing now), reading the comics, scanning the television listings for your favorite program, skimming a magazine article to find out whether it merits close attention, settling into a new novel by your favorite author, reading aloud to your children, absorbing the subtitles as you watch a movie in a foreign language, and glancing at your notes as you give a speech. And this list does not begin to capture the entire spectrum of activities that can be called reading.

These varied activities that go by the name of reading can be viewed from a number of different perspectives, including sociocultural, physiological, affective, philosophical, educational, and cognitive. Although these perspectives are interrelated and interdependent (as Martin Gill points out, for example, "culture and cognition are strictly inconceivable without each other" [1992, p. 62]), there is also value in looking at each perspective individually in its own terms. An analogy might be that although a novel can be appreciated in its entirety, insights can be gained from a detailed scrutiny of the development of the main characters. The focus of this chapter is the support a cognitive perspective on the reading process offers an extensive reading approach to second language reading instruction.

Although there are many activities called *reading,* it is possible to offer a definition that most reading experts would accept as helpful in understanding reading from a cognitive point of view. This simple definition is that *reading is the construction of meaning from a printed or written message.* The construction of meaning involves the reader connecting information from the written message with previous knowledge to arrive at meaning – at an understanding.

Cognitive psychologists have long been interested in how it is that a reader is able to create meaning from the printed page. The activities of the brain, of course, can only be viewed unhelpfully as bursts of electrical energy. The detective work carried out by cognitive psychologists, therefore, is done in metaphorical terms. Over the past forty years, scores of models of the reading process have been produced. Although essentially works of imagination, models are based on what can be observed about reading. They seek to explain such phenomena as the mistakes and self-corrections people make when reading aloud, or the way the eyes dart along lines of print. These models, then, are reality-based speculations that "combine findings from many studies into a single, coherent system" (Adams, 1994, p. 842).

Interactive models of reading

The most widely accepted models of fluent first language reading posit an *interaction* of a variety of processes, beginning with the lightning-like, automatic recognition of words. This initial process of accurate, rapid, and automatic recognition of vocabulary frees the mind to use several simultaneous processes involving reasoning, knowledge of the world, and knowledge of the topic to construct meaning. Although the hypothetical constructs *bottom-up processing* (i.e., text-driven) and *top-down processing* (i.e., concept-driven) were useful heuristics in conceptualizing earlier models of reading, it is probably better to leave them behind lest they unhelpfully polarize a description of how mental processes interact with text features in fluent reading comprehension.

The following description of the reading process draws on a number of sources, including Adams (1990, 1994), Perfetti (1985), Samuels (1994), and Stanovich (1992).

- *Reading begins with the accurate, swift, and automatic visual recognition of vocabulary, independent of the context in which it occurs.*

Automatic word recognition is the basis of fluent reading; it is what allows skilled readers to read with apparent ease and lack of effort, rapidly breezing through material. Research has established that readers *fixate* (rest on) almost every word of text as their eyes move across the printed page.

Colin Harrison sums up the work of first language reading researchers reported in, for example, Rayner (1983), Just and Carpenter (1987), and Rayner and Pollatsek (1989) this way:

> We now know that, in normal reading, adults . . . fixate nearly all words (over 80 per cent of content words, and over 40 per cent of function words, such as *of* or *the*), and almost never skip over more than two words. Fixations on words generally last from a fifth to a quarter of a second (200–250 milliseconds). (Harrison, 1992, p. 9)

Words that readers are able to recognize automatically are often referred to as *sight vocabulary.*

This automatic, rapid, and accurate process of word recognition should not be confused with the strategy of slow, letter-by-letter, or syllable-by-syllable sounding out of words. That strategy, termed *phonemic decoding,* is used by fluent readers only when they encounter words that are not part of their sight vocabulary.

This view of the centrality of word recognition processing does not suggest that a large sight recognition vocabulary *causes* comprehension. As Keith Stanovich states, "Efficient word recognition seems to be a necessary but not sufficient condition for good comprehension" (1992, p. 4).

- *Automatic recognition of a word allows lexical access.*

Lexical access is the automatic calling up from memory of "the word's meanings and its phonological representation" (Stanovich, 1992, p. 4). Contextually appropriate meanings, both semantic and syntactic, are related to words. More specifically, awareness of the context in which the word occurs automatically "emphasizes those aspects of a word's total meaning that are relevant to its ongoing interpretation" (Adams, 1994, p. 849).

Lexical access, like word recognition, is below the level of consciousness, automatic and rapid. This is critical for, as Marilyn Jager Adams points out, "Only to the extent that the ability to recognize and capture the meaning of print is rapid, effortless, and automatic can the reader have available the cognitive energy and resources on which true comprehension depends" (1994, p. 840).

There is evidence to suggest that the role of instantaneous, automatic lexical access in reading is not restricted to languages that use an alphabetic writing system. Keiko Kuhara-Kojima, Giyoo Hatano, Hirofumi Saito, and Tomokazu Haebara investigated its role in reading Japanese hiragana (a phonetic syllabary) and kanji (Chinese characters). They conclude that the process might indeed be general across languages: "The general aspects [of reading theory] may include the automaticity of lexical access as a prerequisite of reading comprehension" (1996, p. 169).

If lexical access fails, the reader has to slow down and give conscious attention to linking the orthographic representation of the word (how it is spelled) with possible semantic and syntactic interpretations (Harris & Sipay, 1990, pp. 436–437). As Charles Perfetti explains, "Inefficient lexical access, slow and effortful, makes it more difficult for working memory to do [its] work" (1985, p. 113).

- *The phonological representations of the words in a sentence hold the words in working memory long enough for comprehension to occur.*

The phonological representations, held in working memory, are interpreted both "on the fly" while reading and while pausing briefly at the end of a clause or sentence (Adams, 1994, p. 856). Adams, who calls phonological representations *phonological translations* (pp. 854–857), writes that during this interpretive process readers "work out the collective meaning of the chain of words in memory and that meaning's contribution to their overall understanding of the conversation or text" (p. 857).

If the reader cannot hold the clause or sentence in working memory long enough to construct meaning, then comprehension is severely disrupted. This happens when a reader takes too long to recognize words in a sentence. As Adams phrases it, "the beginning of the sentence will fade from memory before the end has been registered" (p. 857).

- *Comprehension draws on the reader's prior knowledge of the language, of the world, of text types, and of the topic.*

Crucial to comprehension is the knowledge that the reader brings to the text. The construction of meaning depends on the reader's knowledge of the language, the structure of texts, a knowledge of the subject of the reading, and a broad-based background or world knowledge. First language reading authorities Richard Anderson and Peter Freebody posit the *knowledge hypothesis* to account for the contribution these elements play in the construction of meaning (1981, p. 81). Martha Rapp Ruddell refines their hypothesis when she claims that these various knowledge elements interact with one another to build meaning (1994, p. 416).

Many researchers point to the role that schema theory plays in understanding how these high-order comprehension processes work, since it describes how readers might organize and access knowledge. Readers need more than just a random collection of vocabulary knowledge, world knowledge, linguistic knowledge, and so on, in order to construct meaning. As William Nagy and Patricia Herman write, "Knowledge does not consist simply of an unstructured set of individual facts, but rather of organized, interrelated structures or schemata" (1987, p. 28). Schema theory provides one way of understanding how this organization of knowledge might be achieved.

In contrast to word recognition and lexical access, which by virtue of their speed, accuracy, and automaticity use little processing capacity, these high-order processes of comprehension are "usually costly in terms of demands on attention" (Samuels, 1994, p. 829). The mind has only a certain amount of processing capacity available at one time. Thus, when fluent readers have to slow down and pay conscious attention to recognizing words (i.e., employing the strategy of phonemic decoding, described earlier), they find it difficult to understand the meaning of the sentence or the paragraph in which the unknown or unfamiliar words occur. As Isabel Beck explains, "if attention is more than occasionally focused on getting through the words during reading, too much processing capacity will be taken up with decoding and that will interfere with the higher level components of the reading process (i.e., constructing meaning)" (1981, p. 75).

What is true for fluent readers – that slowing down and paying conscious attention to recognizing words interfere with the construction of meaning – is even more true for beginning readers. The disruption is such for beginners that the link between the decoding process and the comprehension processes may be severed. As S. Jay Samuels describes it, "if the reader's attention is on decoding and if attention can be directed at only one process at a time, the comprehension task is not getting done" (1994, p. 821). Samuels believes that beginning readers are forced to switch their attention back and forth from decoding to constructing meaning, which, in his words, is "slow, laborious, and frustrating" (p. 822).

In sum, the most widely accepted cognitive models of fluent reading emphasize the importance of accurate, automatic word recognition; this process is the precursor of a number of other interactive, concurrent processes that, together with high-level cognitive reasoning, result in the construction of meaning. Although these interactive, concurrent processes have been artificially separated in this section for the purposes of discussion, fluent reading is in fact a seamless whole.

Reading in a second language

From a cognitive viewpoint, are fluent first language reading and fluent second language reading different? Charles Alderson and Alexander Urquhart state at the beginning of their book *Reading in a Foreign Language,*

"We do not, and indeed find it difficult to, draw a clear distinction between first and foreign language reading" (1984, p. xv). In more technical terms, Catherine Wallace notes in her book *Reading* that "we draw on similar processing strategies in the reading of all languages, even where the writing systems are very different" (1992, p. 22). Thus, it can be said that the description of the cognitive interactive processes of fluent reading discussed in the previous section is also useful in capturing the essence of fluent second language reading.

The role of extensive reading in developing fluent second language readers

Extensive reading can – perhaps must – play an important role in developing the components upon which fluent second language reading depends: a large sight vocabulary; a wide general vocabulary; and knowledge of the target language, the world, and text types. The role of extensive reading in developing each of these components is examined below.

The development of sight vocabulary

The development of a large sight vocabulary can be seen as overlearning words to the point that they are automatically recognized in their printed form. The best and easiest way to accomplish this is to read a great deal. Beginning readers simply have to encounter repeatedly words with which they have some familiarity. As an individual word is met and understood again and again in various contexts, "all the sources of information about a word are consolidated into a single, highly cohesive representation. . . . Thus a printed word becomes a symbol for its phonological, semantic, syntactic, and orthographic information" (Harris & Sipay, 1990, pp. 435–436). As a result of multiple encounters, the word enters the reader's sight vocabulary. Familiarity breeds automaticity.

To reformulate Stephen Krashen's famous designation of second language comprehensible input (e.g., 1985, 1991), the materials for this "automaticity training" (Samuels, 1994, p. 834) must be at *"i minus 1"* where *"i"* is the student's current level of acquisition. This *i minus 1* is in contrast to Krashen's comprehensible input hypothesis, in which, for further acquisition to take place, the comprehensible input has to contain elements that are *slightly beyond "i"* – that is, *"i + 1."* The reason for *i minus 1* is that the goal of the automaticity training is developing a large sight vocabulary rather than the learning of new linguistic elements. Of course, *i minus 1* text is an ideal target when learning to read; inevitably, material includes *i minus 1* vocabulary and syntactic structures as well as *i* (the reader's current level of linguistic competence) and some *i + 1* (elements that the reader has not yet mastered). But as long as the bulk of the vocabulary and grammar is well within the reader's competence – *i minus 1* – without too many *i + 1* distractions, the development of a sight vocabulary is possible.

The development of general vocabulary knowledge

In first language reading, the overarching role of vocabulary in fluent reading has been well established. Simply put, the larger children's vocabularies are, the better their comprehension. For example, Jeanne Chall writes, "Every study of reading achievement points to the importance of vocabulary knowledge" (1987, p. 15). Nagy and Herman state it unequivocally: "Children who know more words understand text better" (1987, p. 27).

Given our position that, from a cognitive point of view, there is no essential difference between fluent first and second language reading, the need for a large vocabulary is equally true in fluent second language reading. Just how important it is can be gauged from the following observation by William Grabe, a second language reading expert not given to overstatement. Grabe points out that fluent readers need "a *massive* [italics added] receptive vocabulary that is rapidly, accurately, and automatically accessed" (1988, p. 63). The lack of such a vocabulary, says Grabe, "may be the greatest single impediment to fluent reading by ESL students" (p. 63).

Children learn large numbers of new words in their first language by guessing their meanings in context while they read. Nagy and Herman conclude, after a review of the research literature, "Incidental learning of words during reading may be the easiest and single most powerful means of promoting large-scale vocabulary growth" (1987, p. 27).

Can second language learners do the same – learn words incidentally while reading? Although the second language research is not as abundant or robust as it is in first language reading, it allows a similar, albeit qualified, conclusion: Second language readers who read masses of varied and interesting *i minus 1* material can increase their general vocabulary knowledge. James Coady, in a review of the relevant second language research, concludes, "The incidental acquisition hypothesis suggests that there is gradual but steady incremental growth of vocabulary knowledge through meaningful interaction with text" (1993, p. 18). But Coady points out that *how* readers – either first or second language – do this is not known.

Part of the qualification for the conclusion, in addition to its slim research base, is the nature of the differences between beginning first and beginning second language readers. Beginning second language readers are at the early stages of second language linguistic development, unlike their first language counterparts. Beginning second language readers also lack the large oral vocabulary that beginning first language readers bring to the task of learning to read. This means that vocabulary learning from context while reading is, as Thomas Huckin and Margot Haynes put it, "distinctly problematic" (1993, p. 290) for beginning second language readers.

But the process of incidental vocabulary learning becomes more efficient as second language reading ability improves. "Once a certain level of knowledge (and vocabulary) is achieved . . . ," say Fredricka Stoller and William Grabe, "students will then be able to apply the richer knowledge to learning new vocabulary" (1993, pp. 31–32).

To allow this initially difficult and problematic process of guessing, learning, and refining the knowledge of words from context, second language readers must read materials with a very low ratio of unknown to known words. In other words, texts should be essentially *i minus 1,* containing only a very small number of unknown words and difficult syntactic structures. And the reading of these easy texts must be plentiful because "a clear sense of a word's defining features can only be reached through repeated encounters in diverse contexts" (Huckin & Haynes, 1993, p. 290).

As Paul Nation and James Coady conclude, "In general the research leaves us in little doubt about the importance of vocabulary knowledge for reading, and the value of reading as a means of increasing vocabulary" (1988, p. 108). Second language students must read and read some more both to learn words from context through multiple encounters and to become better readers so that incidental vocabulary learning becomes easier. An extensive reading approach – in which second language readers read large amounts of easy, varied, and interesting material – ensures that students have the best possible chance to do this.

The development of different knowledge types

The final factor necessary for fluent reading is knowledge, for it is on knowledge that comprehension depends. Interestingly, it seems as though reading is an excellent source of the knowledge that is needed for reading comprehension. Albert Harris and Edward Sipay, in discussing first language reading development, state that "wide reading not only increases word-meaning knowledge but can also produce gains in *topical and world knowledge* [italics added] that can further facilitate reading comprehension" (1990, p. 533).

Given that cognitive processes of fluent reading are the same in both first and second languages, there is a parallel situation in second language reading: Second language readers need linguistic, world, and topical knowledge, and it appears as though they can acquire this knowledge through second language reading. Grabe asserts that "the more reading done, of the greatest informational variety and range of purposes, the quicker the reader will achieve . . . the capacity for creating, refining, and connecting diverse arrays of cognitive schemata" (1986, p. 36).

An extensive reading approach, in which students read fluently and focus on the meaning of what they read, can therefore play a key role in ensuring that students have the best possible chance of developing this knowledge.

Although the discussion in this section has separated the acquisition of sight vocabulary, general vocabulary knowledge, and linguistic, topical, and world knowledge, we suggest that their development is interrelated. It is difficult to imagine a student reading extensively and failing to have increases in all three of these knowledge types.

Conclusion

The goal of this chapter has been to show how a theoretical model can be instrumental in helping reading teachers clarify how they might help their students learn to read a second language. A number of insights about reading can be learned from viewing reading as an interactive cognitive process. One of these is the basic importance of a large sight vocabulary as a precondition for fluent reading. Moreover, second language students must develop a large general vocabulary. The reading of large amounts of comprehensible and interesting texts is an obvious way of bringing these about. Such reading also has an important role in developing the linguistic and world knowledge necessary for reading comprehension. In short, an extensive reading approach makes it possible for students to develop into fluent readers.

This cognitive examination of reading provides the first justification for the inclusion of extensive reading in the second language reading curriculum. The second justification is an affective one, and is the subject of the next chapter.

Further reading

The 1988 volume edited by Patricia Carrell, Joanne Devine, and David Eskey, *Interactive Approaches to Second Language Reading,* is an essential collection of papers that traces the development of thinking toward interactive models of the second language reading process.

Interactive models of reading owe much to the work and writings of Frank Smith and Kenneth Goodman in the 1970s. Colin Harrison, in his article "The Reading Process and Learning to Read" (1992), gives a lively, balanced account (from a first language perspective) of both the enduring importance of Smith and Goodman's insights into the reading process and the modifications that must be made in light of subsequent research.

For more information and details about the first language research that helped to establish the role that automatic, rapid, and accurate word recognition plays in fluent reading, see *The Psychology of Reading and Language Comprehension* by Marcel Just and Patricia Carpenter (1987) and *The Psychology of Reading* by Keith Rayner and Alexander Pollatsek (1989). Although technical, these books repay the investment of effort and time.

The learning of vocabulary through reading is discussed in the 1993 volume *Second Language Reading and Vocabulary Learning,* edited by Thomas Huckin, Margot Haynes, and James Coady. Since most research on this topic has been done with first language subjects, a chapter of particular interest is "Implications for L2 Vocabulary Acquisition and Instruction from L1 Vocabulary Research" by Fredricka Stoller and William Grabe.

3 *Affect: The secret garden of reading*

> Attitudes and perceptions color our every experience. They are the filter through which all learning occurs.
> —Robert Marzano (1992, p. 3)

> It is not that students cannot learn; it is that they do not wish to learn.
> —Mihaly Csikszentmihalyi (1990b, p. 115)

The purpose of this chapter is to:

- Provide an introduction to attitude and motivation in second language reading.
- Relate extensive reading to attitude and motivation.

Teachers have a deep respect for the role that attitude and motivation play in learning. They know from their classroom experiences that students with poor attitudes about school, the subject matter, and their classroom are often poorly motivated and thus present major teaching challenges.

However, even though teachers recognize their importance, concerns for the affective aspects of reading seldom find their way into reading instruction, whether in the first or a second language. Michael McKenna, writing about the teaching of first language reading, suggests a reason for this: "Poor conceptualization of what Athey (1985) has called the 'shadowy variables' of affect (p. 527) may reinforce the notion that school time is best devoted to the pursuit of reading proficiency" (1994, p. 18).

The situation is similar in second language reading instruction. Notwithstanding work on general motivation to learn a second language – few teachers are unfamiliar with Robert Gardner and Wallace Lambert's integrative and instrumental motivational orientations (e.g., 1959), for example – there has been comparatively little concern for attitude and motivation in learning to read a second language.

The lack of systematic and principled attention to the affective dimensions of second language reading is unfortunate. After all, when teachers design their reading courses, order texts, develop lesson plans, and set up reading tasks, exercises, and activities, they are in effect making statements about the role that attitude and motivation play in their teaching and the learning of their students. Perhaps, like theoretical assumptions about the nature of how students learn to read a second language, these statements are unexamined. They are often pushed into the background by the daily pressures of teaching and a justified concern for meeting the tangible, concrete aims and goals of the reading course. Nevertheless, a deeper understanding of attitude and motivation and how teachers can use them to their advantage can have immediate, practical benefits.

This chapter introduces and discusses a second justification for including extensive reading in a second language reading program – a justification based on the affective dimension of the reading process. We begin by throwing Athey's shadowy variables of affect into as sharp a relief as possible, and then relating them to extensive reading. The first affective variable to be examined is attitude; the second, motivation.

Attitude

Attitude is a complex, hypothetical construction, whose general definition usually includes some notion of evaluation. For example, Icek Ajzen states that "an attitude is a disposition to respond favorably or unfavorably to an object, person, institution, or event" (1988, p. 4). Similarly, Alice Eagly and Shelly Chaiken (1993, p. 1) write, "Attitude is a psychological tendency that is expressed by evaluating a particular entity with some degree of favor or disfavor." This evaluative aspect of attitude is its defining attribute, and sets it apart from other affective variables.

Another important point about attitudes is that they are subject to change – they are not set in concrete. This is good news for teachers, in that poor attitudes can be changed. But the good news is tempered by the fact that there are many variables associated with attitude change (e.g., other attitudes, the strength of the particular attitude, and its source) so that attempts to change attitudes may not always be successful. There is some research, however, indicating that an awareness of a negative attitude and its source may help compensate for or even eliminate the bias (Pratkanis, 1989, p. 82). A useful first step for teachers, therefore, can be to understand the sources of student attitudes – positive or negative – toward second language reading.

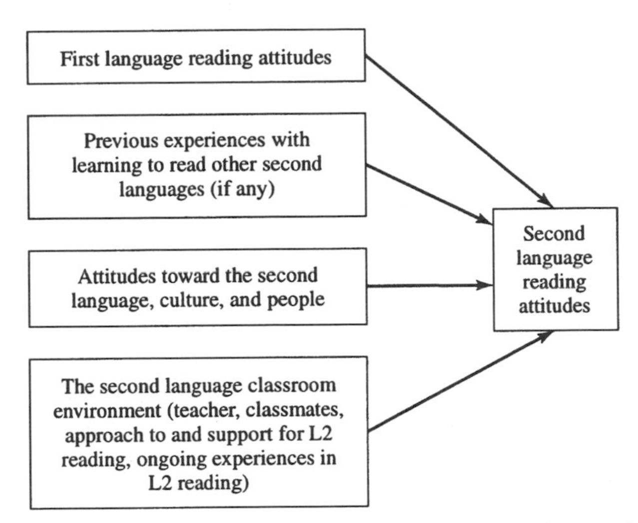

Figure 1 Model of the acquisition and development of second language reading attitudes.

Attitudes and second language reading

Some analysis of first language reading attitudes has been made, notably Grover Mathewson's 1994 "Model of Attitude Influence upon Reading and Learning to Read" and Michael McKenna's development of that model, published as "Toward a Model of Reading Attitude Acquisition" (1994). Figure 1 interprets this work from a second language perspective, and is a model depicting four sources of student attitude toward second language reading. These four sources – attitudes toward first language reading; previous second language reading experiences; attitudes toward the second language, culture, and people; and the second language classroom environment – are examined in turn below.

FIRST LANGUAGE READING ATTITUDES

Assuming that students are already literate in their first language, one source of attitudes toward second language reading is the attitude that students have toward reading in their native language. In short, students with positive attitudes toward reading in their own language are likely to begin with a positive attitude toward second language reading; students for whom first language reading is less attractive or important will come to second language reading with less than positive, or even negative, attitudes.

First language reading attitudes derive from the student's informal experiences with reading, instructional practices in the classroom, and the way reading is viewed within the first language culture. Albert Harris and Edward Sipay (1990, pp. 49–51) provide a helpful summary of research on the acquisition of reading attitudes. It is clear that early experiences with reading shape attitude, in addition to being the important first steps in learning to read. As Harris and Sipay note, "Seeing parents and older siblings read and being read to develop a favorable attitude toward reading, and help children to value reading" (p. 49).

Children fortunate enough to begin formal schooling with positive attitudes about reading may receive little subsequent reinforcement. Although the importance of fostering positive attitudes toward reading in students is widely recognized, actual practices may not follow. Betty Heathington explains that, "when forced to make a choice between promoting positive attitudes or emphasizing skill development, teachers seem to choose skill development. Their practices indicate that they believe that skills are more essential for their students than the attitudes their students have toward literacy" (1994, p. 199). Such practices, Heathington believes, can have disastrous consequences, because "forcing students to engage in activities they see as meaningless only drives them to adopt an attitude of hating those engagements and avoiding literacy activities once they leave school" (p. 200).

Interestingly, and perhaps contrary to common sense, these negative attitudes cut across reading proficiency, and can be held by students who are considered successes in terms of learning to read. In Frank Smith's words, "The real tragedy is that competent readers and writers as well as the less able leave school with a lifelong aversion to reading and writing, which they regard as purely school activities, as trivial and tedious 'work'" (1983, p. 115).

It is the hope of any second language reading teacher to have students who hold the attitude that reading is important and interesting. Even in a worst-case scenario, however, all is not lost, for first language reading attitudes are only one of four variables influencing the development of second language reading attitudes.

PREVIOUS EXPERIENCES WITH LEARNING TO READ SECOND LANGUAGES

If students have had experiences with learning to read other languages, these experiences will influence their attitudes toward reading in the new language. Prior successful experiences will predispose learners toward the new experience, whereas unsuccessful ones can turn them off even before the process of learning to read in the new language begins.

ATTITUDES TOWARD THE SECOND LANGUAGE, CULTURE, AND PEOPLE

Positive attitudes in this category can motivate students to read in the second language about its culture and people. It is not uncommon to find such favorable attitudes in communities where there are large numbers of people whose ancestors immigrated to the community. Their descendants are often eager to learn the language, to understand the culture, and to visit their ancestral homeland.

THE SECOND LANGUAGE CLASSROOM ENVIRONMENT

Favorable feelings for and experiences with the teacher, classmates, materials, activities, tasks, procedures, and so on, can forge positive attitudes toward reading in the second language. Unfavorable feelings and ongoing experiences can lead to negative attitudes.

Teachers know that learning to read a second language is no easy task for their students. They acknowledge this in various ways, for example, by building background knowledge prior to reading so as to make reading easier, or by providing appropriately simple tasks to accompany difficult readings.

At the same time, in spite of teachers' best efforts, it is probably a truism to say that in the majority of classrooms, students consider second language reading "difficult." Recall the description of "the world of real L2/FL reading classes" from Aebersold and Field (1997, p. 116) quoted at the beginning of the Preface, which characterizes students as "unsure of what they have read" and "apprehensive" about classroom practices.

A simple response would be that in many cases this cannot be helped; indeed, a goal of some reading courses, for example, in academic preparation programs, is to equip students to deal with reading passages that are in some ways beyond those students' linguistic ability in the second language. Such a response, however, ignores the inevitable affective toll that difficult or unpleasant reading experiences take.

The consequences of students leaving second language courses with negative attitudes toward reading are seldom discussed. The probable results can, however, be deduced from the first language students' aversion to reading referred to earlier in this chapter.

Extensive reading and attitude

What influence can an extensive reading approach to teaching second language reading be expected to have on student attitudes? Not all of the four sources of second language reading attitudes in Figure 1 can be influenced by extensive reading: First language reading attitudes and previous experiences with reading in other second languages both belong to the past and are beyond the reach of subsequent reading programs, extensive or otherwise. But as for the other two attitude sources, the impact of extensive reading can be substantial.

An extensive reading approach may influence attitudes toward the second language culture and people if the students, through their reading, come to view the second language culture and people in a favorable light. This, however, is only a possibility, as there is no guarantee that students will read about the target culture and people, since they are free to read what they want to.

On the other hand, because it includes individualized, free choice of reading material, an extensive reading approach makes it possible for individual students to follow their own interests in reading. It is therefore possible for them to enter the second language culture on their own terms, and even to enter it deeply. One of the authors of this book, for example, has students in an English language extensive reading program reading about (to cite four students) American major league baseball, important figures from the past such as Charlie Chaplin and Martin Luther King, holistic health and environmental activism, and contemporary cultural issues through American and British young adult fiction. Equally to the point, these individuals do not have to read about the other three topics, which interest them less or not at all. This flexibility is less available in classes in which students must read the same texts selected by the teacher.

Successful extensive reading programs also place great emphasis on positive classroom environment and ongoing reading experiences. Teachers take the role of active participant and model reader, lending prestige, example, and support to the activity. The individual, private nature of extensive reading also makes it easier for teachers to establish a noncompetitive, nonjudgmental community of readers. Fear of evaluation by teacher and peers is minimized because the emphasis is not on a right answer, but on students' personal reactions to the reading material. The individual variation inherent in any teaching and learning situation can also be catered to, for an extensive reading approach does not deal with students in a lockstep manner in which all learners have to read the same material at approximately the same rate.

It is indeed the ongoing experiences of extensive second language reading that have the most potential to establish positive attitudes toward second language reading. Students read material well within their linguistic ability, they have a choice of what to read, and they are not forced to read about topics in which they have no interest. In addition, they have the freedom to stop reading when they want to, with no questions asked. They read when and where they want to.

These elements of students' choosing what, when, how, and where to read are hallmarks of autonomy in learning. In a review of autonomy and second language learning, Leslie Dickinson (1995, p. 174) finds substantial evidence that learners taking responsibility for and being able to control their own learning helps them succeed in their second language learning.

Extensive reading is thus a powerful tool for teachers concerned with building and maintaining positive attitudes toward second language reading among their students. But the development of positive attitudes is not an end in itself, for attitude influences something equally important in reading: motivation.

Motivation

It is easy to confuse attitude and motivation. They have things in common: Neither can be directly observed; both must be inferred from behavior and actions. Both have degrees of intensity, ranging from strong to weak. But there are differences. Robert Franken (1988, p. 3) writes that the study of motivation has traditionally been concerned with the arousal, direction, and persistence of behavior. Simply put, motivation is what makes people do (or *not* do) something.

Psychological models of motivation are thick on the ground. One group of cognitive models particularly helpful from a teacher's point of view sees motivation as having two equal components – *expectations* and *value* (see Feather, 1982, pp. 1–5). The gist of these *expectancy + value* models is that people do what they expect to accomplish successfully and tend to avoid what they expect they cannot accomplish. This is balanced by people tending to undertake tasks that they value, and tending to avoid those things that have little value for them, even though they reasonably expect that they could do them.

Looking at expectancy + value in terms of reading, unless students have a reasonable expectation that they will be able to read a book with understanding, they will most likely not begin the undertaking: "I'd like to read that book, but I know that I can't, so I won't even try." But expectation of

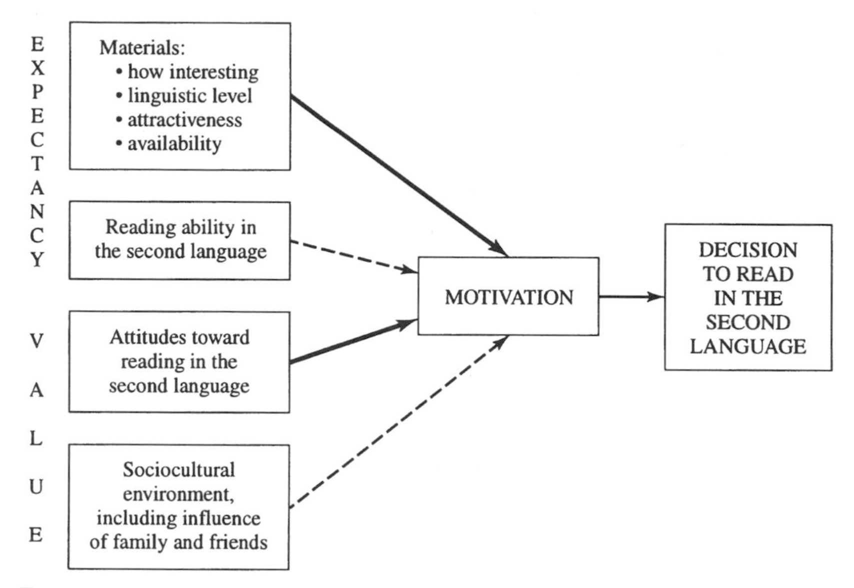

Figure 2 Model of the major variables motivating the decision to read in a second language (a solid line indicates a stronger influence than a broken line).

success or failure is only half of the picture. In an ideal classroom, students place a high premium on reading, believing it to be of value in learning to read and as a source of pleasure and information. They may consequently try to read difficult books because they value the result of the effort. In such cases, the value attached to the act of reading might outweigh the expectation that they will have a hard time reading.

Motivation and second language reading

Figure 2 is an expectancy + value model of motivation in the context of second language reading. Four major variables – materials, reading ability, attitudes, and sociocultural environment – are seen as motivating the desire to read a second language. Two of these variables – materials and reading ability – relate to the *expectation* of success in reading the second language, and two – attitudes and sociocultural environment – relate to the *value* attached to reading the second language.

Two of the variables in this model – materials and attitudes – are considered primary, and it is difficult to rank them. Rather than attempting to establish a case for either as more important than the other, it might be better to claim that they are of equal weight. A failure to have positive attitudes or the appropriate materials would result in a lack of the necessary motivation for a learner to decide to read the second language. What the model suggests is that either a low reading ability or an inappropriate sociocultural environment can be compensated for by positive second language reading attitudes and appropriate materials.

Extensive reading and motivation

An extensive reading approach to the teaching of reading has the potential to influence all of the variables in this motivation model.

MATERIALS

The reading materials used in extensive reading motivate positively the decision to read in the second language, as they are interesting, at the appropriate linguistic levels (i.e., predominantly *i minus 1*), and readily available. It is difficult to place too much emphasis on the role interesting material plays in the desire to read. Indeed, Ray Williams makes interesting texts the first in his top ten principles for teaching foreign language reading. As he puts it:

> In the absence of interesting texts, very little is possible. An obvious principle, but one which is often forgotten. Interest is vital, for it increases motivation, which in turn is a significant factor in the development of reading speed and fluency. (1986, p. 42)

READING ABILITY

Low-level reading abilities would normally lower expectations of success, and thus lower the motivation to read. This does not happen in an extensive reading approach, however, because the learners read at levels appropriate to their reading ability. They do not experience the frustration of having to read material beyond their reading capabilities. As there is a wide variety of materials that range from easy to difficult, students are able to select material they can read with ease.

ATTITUDE

That an extensive reading approach is likely to produce positive attitudes toward reading in the second language was discussed earlier in this chapter.

SOCIOCULTURAL ENVIRONMENT

The following anecdote might sound depressingly familiar: an American teenager, studying second-year German, is made fun of by his best friend for reading poetry in German. The student was reading poetry in the first place through the encouragement of his German teacher and his classmates who were making similar adventures in second language reading.

An extensive reading approach creates a classroom environment that values and encourages reading. Such an environment can counteract the influence of society, family, and friends if they are less than encouraging toward reading. It may even provide a safe haven for reading poetry away from the critical eyes of one's best friend.

The extensive reading bookstrap hypothesis

The extraordinary impact of extensive reading on both attitude and motivation can be explained by an extensive reading version of *bootstrapping,* an engineering concept describing a process in which the results of an action are fed back to achieve greater results more quickly with less effort. Given that the concern here is with reading, let us use the term *bookstrap. The extensive reading bookstrap hypothesis* works like this: Students' initial successful experiences in extensive reading result in the discovery that they can read in the second language and that it is rewarding and pleasurable. This stimulates the development of positive attitudes toward reading in the second language and the growth of motivation to read in the second language. These positive beginning experiences then feed back into subsequent extensive reading experiences and assignments, resulting in greater gains in reading ability and positive attitudes, and increases in motivation and enjoyment.

Eventually, bookstrapping may lead some students to become hooked on books. Peter Johnston and Richard Allington (1991) write that reading instruction that captures the student's interest and involvement may result in *flow experiences* – the losing of oneself in the activity (cf. Csikszentmihalyi, 1990a). Flow experiences are a powerful incentive to continue one's involvement with reading, and to make reading a part of one's life. Colin Harrison describes such readers. They

> pick up books, curl up with them on easy chairs, worry or get excited about what is going to happen to the characters in a story, and later talk spontaneously about what they have been reading to their parents or their friends. As children, many of us became so keen on books that we read under the bedclothes by

torchlight, risking the anger or concern of our parents and admonitions that we would ruin our sight. (1992, p. 13)

Imagine teaching students who had even a fraction of such motivation to read.

Conclusion

Frances Hodgson Burnett's *The Secret Garden* provides an apt metaphor for the role of affect in second language reading instruction. By most accounts, students find the learning of second language reading to be difficult and stressful. Second language reading teachers may accept a bleak, wintry classroom as inevitable, given the reality of the task to be accomplished. Nevertheless, out of sight is a garden where it is always spring. If students can enter that garden, that is, develop positive attitudes and a strong motivation to read in the second language, then the whole undertaking of learning to read is transformed. Extensive reading can be the key to the secret garden.

Further reading

Norman Feather's Introduction to *Expectations and Actions: Expectancy-Value Models in Psychology,* the volume he edited on expectancy + value models, has a helpful overview of motivational models (1982, pp. 1–5).

One of the few introductions to affect and reading is the volume edited by Eugene Cramer and Marrietta Castle (1994), *Fostering the Love of Reading: The Affective Domain in Reading Education.* Although the focus is first language reading development, much of the material will be of interest to those involved in second language reading, particularly the reports of research and helpful pedagogical suggestions. This volume also includes Michael McKenna's model of first language reading attitudes.

Another book that does not focus on second language reading but contains many insights into reading in general and extensive reading in particular is Victor Nell's *Lost in a Book: The Psychology of Reading for Pleasure.* It also boasts some of the best opening lines in academia:

> Reading for pleasure is an extraordinary activity. The black squiggles on the white page are still as the grave, colorless as the moonlit desert; but they give the skilled reader a pleasure as acute as the touch of a loved body, as rousing, colorful and transfiguring as anything out there in the real world. (1988, p. 1)

4 *The power of extensive reading: Insights from the research*

> The amount of free reading done consistently correlates with performance on reading comprehension tests, a result that confirms the hypothesis that we learn to read by reading.
>
> —Stephen Krashen (1988, p. 291)

The purpose of this chapter is to:

- Discuss empirical results of extensive reading programs.

The scene is a seminar of students enrolled in the master of arts degree program in English as a second language at the University of Hawaii. They are discussing their prior experiences in learning second languages. One of the participants, Mei Fung Elsa Shek, describes her learning of English in Hong Kong:

> I started learning English when I was three. We learned English at school, where they taught vocabulary. In primary school, we were taught more vocabulary, grammar, punctuation, and simple sentences. From secondary school on, I received bilingual education. Other than Chinese language and Chinese history, all the subjects were taught in English, though our teachers often switched between English and Cantonese.
>
> My English language as a subject was okay. I got good grades. However, my English really flourished when I started to read extensively while I was in senior high. My English teacher, Miss Wong, brought her collection of English novels and fiction to our classroom and set up a class library. She encouraged us to read whatever appealed to us. We had to read fifty pages a week and write a report on those fifty pages. At first it was really hard to finish fifty pages in a week, but later, I could read 200 pages in one day (8 hours). I remember I did not check every new word, but only those words which appeared frequently in the book or words that I wanted to learn. I understood the story and enjoyed reading tremendously. My vocabulary was enlarged and my writing grammar improved. Once, a fellow student commented after reading one of my essays, "Wow, you write like those authors (of the books)!" Since then, I have continued reading, and it continues to help me improving my English.

Is Ms. Shek's experience unusual? Can we expect other students to have similar results from reading extensively? Research on second language extensive reading programs indicates that her experience is an expected outcome; students can improve their second language reading ability, and develop positive attitudes toward reading and increased motivation to read. Moreover, reading extensively can result in gains in vocabulary and other aspects of second language learning.

The title of this chapter, "The Power of Extensive Reading: Insights from the Research," echoes the title of Stephen Krashen's 1993 book on free voluntary reading. This is to recognize the substantial contributions of Krashen and his associates to an understanding of the role that reading plays in language acquisition and learning to read.

Results of extensive reading programs

Table 1 is an overview of a number of investigations of extensive reading in both second and foreign language settings. With one exception, all were English as a second language (ESL) or English as a foreign language (EFL) programs. It is apparent from Table 1 that extensive reading in these programs had beneficial results. Students increased their reading ability in the target language, developed positive attitudes toward reading, had increased motivation to read, and made gains in various aspects of proficiency in the target language, including vocabulary and writing. These programs were in a variety of settings with diverse populations, from young children to adults.

One of the most comprehensive investigations of extensive reading was done by Warwick Elley and Francis Mangubhai in a rural area of Fiji in 1980. In a carefully controlled longitudinal investigation involving many schools, some students were "given a rich diet of books" while others had "little or no access to books" (1981, p. 4). The rich diet of books, labeled "book flood," featured "activities designed to encourage extensive reading" (p. 6). Eight months later, comparisons in a number of different categories were made with groups of similar ability and circumstances. The results were exciting. As Elley and Mangubhai write:

> The impact of the books is clearly positive, and, as one would expect, most marked in those English skills which the pupils had been practising – general reading and listening comprehension. However, the effect did spread to related skills, as shown by the greater progress made in learning written English structures, and the ability to recite complex English sentences correctly. (pp. 24–25)

Table 1. Summary of results of extensive reading programs

Report	*Population*	*Results*
Elley & Mangubhai (1981)	EFL; primary; Fiji	Gains in reading and general proficiency, including listening and writing; growth in positive affect
Janopoulos (1986)	ESL; university; USA	Gains in writing proficiency
Hafiz & Tudor (1989); Tudor & Hafiz (1989)	ESL; adolescents; England	Gains in reading proficiency, positive affect, and general linguistic competence, including writing; slight, nonsignificant increase in vocabulary base
Pitts et al. (1989)	ESL; adults; USA	Gains in vocabulary
Robb & Susser (1989)	EFL; university; Japan	Gains in reading proficiency and positive affect
Hafiz & Tudor (1990)	EFL; primary; Pakistan	Gains in vocabulary base and writing
Elley (1991)	EFL; primary; Singapore	Gains in reading proficiency and positive affect
Lai (1993a; 1993b)	EFL; secondary; Hong Kong	Gains in reading proficiency and vocabulary
Cho & Krashen (1994)	ESL; adults; USA	Gains in reading proficiency, vocabulary, positive affect, and oral skills
Rodrigo (1995)	Spanish; university; USA	Gains in positive affect; no statistically significant gains in vocabulary
Mason & Krashen (1997)	EFL; university; Japan	Gains in reading proficiency, positive affect, and writing

It is important to stress that these results were obtained in a culture in which reading for pleasure "is not a widely accepted custom" (p. 3). Another factor that mitigated against the benefits was that most of the children were unable to take books home because of school rules.

The remainder of this chapter describes the results of the studies listed in Table 1 in the following areas: second language reading ability; affect; vocabulary; linguistic competence; writing; and spelling.

Second language reading ability

Of the seven studies that investigated the impact of extensive reading on second language reading, all reported gains, from primary students in Fiji (Elley & Mangubhai, 1981) and Singapore (Elley, 1991) to secondary students in England (Hafiz & Tudor, 1989; Tudor & Hafiz, 1989) and Hong Kong (Lai, 1993a, 1993b). These results are strong confirmation of the position that second language students, like first language children, learn to read by reading.

An extensive reading approach seems to be effective in a wide variety of circumstances and with different types of students. Even when circumstances might be judged as less than favorable, the gains are nonetheless apparent. For example, Fung-Kuen Lai (1993a, 1993b) in Hong Kong discovered that in a four-week summer extensive reading program the students displayed gains in their reading performance in English. Beniko Mason and Stephen Krashen (1997) report that "reluctant" EFL readers at a Japanese university made statistically significant gains on a cloze test after a semester of reading extensively.

Affect

Gains in affect, like gains in reading ability, are impressive. Study after study shows how attitudes changed toward reading in the second language and how the students became eager readers.

- In Singapore, Warwick Elley reported that the students seemed to develop "very positive attitudes toward books as they raised their literacy levels in English" (1991, p. 397).
- In the United States, Kyung-Sook Cho and Stephen Krashen reported that the attitudes of their four subjects toward reading in English changed dramatically as a result of reading books from some of the popular *Sweet Valley* series written for young native speakers. The subjects quickly

became motivated to read, discovering the pleasure that reading can bring. Comments of the subjects include:

> "I never get bored reading the Sweet Valley series. This series of English books is the most interesting and understandable I have ever read." (1994, p. 665)
>
> "When I finished reading one volume of Sweet Valley Kids, I was looking forward to reading the next one. This was the first experience in which I wanted to read a book in English continuously." (p. 665)

- In a Spanish as a foreign language program in the United States, Victoria Rodrigo reported that the twenty-seven English-speaking university students developed "extraordinary positive reactions towards a reading program" (1995, p. 12). A sample of these reactions:

> "I do enjoy reading in Spanish very much."
>
> "Reading stimulated my interest in learning the language."
>
> "My first book, I felt it was an accomplishment." (pp. 12–13)

Vocabulary

Three of the five studies that looked specifically at vocabulary reported gains. In one of the studies that did not find an increase in vocabulary knowledge, Rodrigo (1995), the treatment groups did score higher than the control group on a vocabulary checklist test, but the gains were not statistically significant. However, Rodrigo explains that this was expected because of the "tiny sample size" of the control group (p. 10).

In the other study that did not report gains, Hafiz and Tudor (1989) found a small increase in vocabulary knowledge that was not statistically significant. They explained that the lack of a significant gain in vocabulary could have been due to the level of exposure that their subjects had to English. Because they were living in England and were relatively fluent in English, the subjects had extensive contact with the target language on a daily basis. Thus, Hafiz and Tudor concluded, the contribution of the extensive reading program to their vocabulary development was somewhat lessened (1990, pp. 36–37). In their other study (Hafiz & Tudor, 1990), the subjects were studying English in Pakistan and had a relatively lower level of proficiency in English. These subjects displayed significant gains in their vocabulary base, which Hafiz and Tudor defined as total number of lexical items and accuracy of usage.

Linguistic competence

Another variable positively related to extensive reading is second language ability. Every study that investigated this variable reports that their subjects increased their overall competence in the target language. For example:

- In the United States, Cho and Krashen (1994) reported that as a result of reading novels for pleasure, their four adult learners increased competence in both listening and speaking abilities.
- In England, Hafiz and Tudor found that "the experimental group shows statistically significant levels of improvement on all seven tests. . . . These results would appear to indicate that the extensive reading programme undertaken had effected a substantial improvement in subjects' linguistic proficiency" (1989, p. 8; see also Tudor & Hafiz, 1989).
- In Hong Kong, Lai wrote, "the extensive reading scheme designed for the present study, especially the summer reading programme, did satisfactorily facilitate students' English language acquisition" (1993a, p. 33).

Writing

The influence of extensive reading extends to writing, supporting the widely held notion that we learn to write through reading. In several of the programs reported in Table 1, gains were made in the students' writing abilities without any special instruction or focus on writing.

In Fiji, Elley and Mangubhai reported that the young children made significant improvement in "learning written English structures" (1981, p. 24). In England, Hafiz and Tudor (1989) were impressed by the gains their subjects made in writing in English, even though they were not given any particular writing tasks. In the United States, Michael Janopoulos, in an investigation of university ESL students, found a significant correlation between pleasure reading and proficiency in written English (1986, p. 767).

Spelling

Some studies indicate that reading extensively is linked to spelling proficiency. Krashen (1989) reviews the evidence for native speakers of English and establishes a rather strong case. But the empirical evidence for this relationship in second language learning is weak. There are only two studies, to our knowledge, on this topic: Polak and Krashen (1988) and Day and

Swan (1998). Although these two studies did not take place in the context of extensive reading programs (and are therefore not included in Table 1), they are discussed here because of their relevance to extensive reading.

Jeanne Polak and Stephen Krashen investigated the reading habits of community college ESL students in the United States and found a correlation with their spelling proficiency – the more the students read, the better their spelling. Richard Day and James Swan investigated the effect of reading for meaning on spelling by Japanese university EFL students. Their study revealed that the treatment group – subjects who read for pleasure a story that contained the target words – correctly spelled significantly more of the words on a posttest than the control group.

Conclusion

The outcomes of programs that used an extensive reading approach are impressive. Krashen expresses the benefits in these words:

> Reading is good for you. The research supports a stronger conclusion, however: Reading is the only way, the only way we become good readers, develop a good writing style, an adequate vocabulary, advanced grammar, and the only way we become good spellers. (1993b, p. 23)

And, equally exciting, students who learn to read through an extensive reading approach develop positive attitudes and become motivated to read in the second language.

If teachers and administrators are impressed by these outcomes, the next issue becomes how to integrate extensive reading into their second language curricula. There are many possibilities for this, as will be seen in the next chapter.

Further reading

Warwick Elley's comprehensive summary of the results of a number of "book flood" programs, "Acquiring Literacy in a Second Language: The Effect of Book-Based Programs," is well worth reading. It appears in the journal *Language Learning* (1991).

There are a number of sources for Stephen Krashen's work in extensive reading. For example:

- "Do We Learn to Read by Reading? The Relationship between Free Reading and Reading Ability," in Deborah Tannen's edited volume *Linguistics in Context: Connecting Observation and Understanding* (1988).

- "We Acquire Vocabulary and Spelling by Reading: Additional Evidence for the Input Hypothesis," in *The Modern Language Journal* (1989).
- "The Case for Free Voluntary Reading," in the *Canadian Modern Language Review* (1993a).
- A book-length treatment, *The Power of Reading: Insights from the Research* (1993b).

5 *Extensive reading and the second language curriculum*

One major way to round out a reading program is to introduce extensive reading material into the curriculum.

—William Grabe (1986, p. 43)

The purpose of this chapter is to:

- Discuss how extensive reading can be integrated into second language programs.
- Discuss reasons for including extensive reading in programs whose goal is the preparation of students for academic work in the second language.
- Present possible goals of an extensive reading program.
- Speculate as to why extensive reading is not a more common approach to the teaching of second language reading.

Most reading teacher resource books mention the important role extensive reading must play at all stages of the second language reading curriculum. For example, in their books on reading instruction, both Beatrice Mikulecky (1990) and Christine Nuttall (1982, 1996) include a chapter on extensive reading. Mikulecky states that "students must develop the habit of reading massive amounts" (1990, p. 13). Nuttall says, "We learn to read by reading. . . . We want students to read *better.* . . . To do this they need to read *more*" (1996, p. 128). And in the 1986 volume *Teaching Second Language Reading for Academic Purposes,* Fredricka Stoller's proposal for a low-level reading skills course has extensive reading as a built-in component, and Linda Jensen includes extensive reading as the third in a three-component advanced reading skills course.

Although such chapters are more or less detailed on the practical aspects of extensive reading, they seldom provide explicit guidance on how to integrate extensive reading into the curriculum. This chapter explores curricular issues in extensive reading and looks first at how extensive reading might be included in a variety of second language classrooms, courses, and programs, including academic preparation programs. This is followed by a discussion of goals that might be set when establishing an extensive reading program. Finally, we address the question that William Grabe asked at the 1995 TESOL Colloquium on Research in Reading in a Second Language: Given the overwhelming evidence for the importance of extensive reading in learning to read a second language, why isn't everybody doing it? Why does extensive reading continue to be the approach less taken when it comes to teaching second language reading?

Integrating extensive reading into second language programs

Extensive reading can be included in a second language curriculum in at least four broad ways:

- as a separate, stand-alone course
- as part of an existing reading course
- as a noncredit addition to an existing course
- as an extracurricular activity

These four ways are explained in turn.

As a separate course

Setting up an independent extensive reading course involves basically what the establishing of any other course does: a teacher, a syllabus, a classroom, materials, and a set time slot. And just as with other courses, the amount of time devoted to the extensive reading course has to be calculated in relation to the overall goals of the entire second language curriculum. It could vary, for example, from a single 50-minute period once a week to five times a week for 50 minutes each meeting.

As part of an existing reading course

This involves building into an existing course a certain amount of extensive reading (e.g., the reading of a certain number of books per week or per semester, both in class and for homework). The amount of credit to be given for the extensive reading assignments is calculated in relation to the percentage of curriculum time that extensive reading occupies. In addition to in-class reading, time is set aside in the reading class for extensive reading-related activities such as student oral book reports.

As a noncredit addition to an existing reading course

Students are encouraged to read according to their interests and for their own enjoyment. It is an optional assignment and not a formal part of the course. Although no credit is given for the purpose of awarding grades, extra credit that might help tilt a student's final grade could be given if the student were on the borderline between, say, an A and a B. Exactly how much attention is given to extensive reading as an optional supplement depends on the attitude of the teacher. If a teacher is firmly committed to extensive reading and promotes it actively, then students generally catch the teacher's enthusiasm and are drawn to doing it.

As an extracurricular activity

Optional extensive reading can also take the form of an extracurricular reading club, not connected to required courses in the curriculum. Such an extensive reading club can be open to anyone in the language program, regardless of level, and all can be encouraged to join. Like other extracurricular activities, the extensive reading club meets after school. The teacher in charge treats it like any other after-school activity. How much is accomplished depends entirely on the interests of the participants, including the teacher. It could range from a weekly or semimonthly activity to a more demanding activity in which the students meet two or three times a week for an hour.

These four possibilities for including extensive reading in a second language program are not mutually exclusive. Depending on the size of the program, two or three of these ways could be utilized at different levels or in different subjects of the language program. Further, for those educational institutions whose administrators and teachers do not wish to commit themselves to the first option (an independent, stand-alone extensive reading course), choosing one of the other three options can be a first step. In time, when the benefits of extensive reading are realized, consideration can be given to integrating extensive reading more fully into the institution's curriculum.

Just as there is no particular form that an extensive reading program must take, neither is there a particular way to go about setting up a program. One of the authors of this book, for example, approached the president of a private high school at which he was teaching and introduced the idea of extensive reading. The president was persuaded and, as a result, authorized the establishment of an elective extensive reading course. It is this sort of cutting through red tape that in part explains David Hill's comment that extensive reading programs require "official support at institutional level" (1992, p. 50). It is also possible, however, for a curriculum coordinator, group of teachers, or an individual teacher to include extensive reading in their classes without seeking an administrator's stamp of approval.

The particular circumstances of a school or institution will in part determine how extensive reading is integrated into the curriculum. The following brief scenarios illustrate how extensive reading can take different forms and produce different outcomes in different environments.

AN INTENSIVE LANGUAGE PROGRAM

In a full-time second or foreign language course, students have one 50-minute reading lesson per day. The program is reorganized so that the first 20 minutes of each reading lesson are devoted to sustained silent reading – the reading of individually selected materials by students. In addition, students are expected to read for homework, for at least an hour per day, books of their own choosing. At the end of the quarter, students have read more than a thousand pages each. Some students report that for the first time they feel they have been truly reading in the second language. Teachers, having observed students reading during the periods of sustained silent reading, report that they are more aware of each student's strengths and weaknesses as a reader, and are thus better able to give students individual guidance.

HIGH-SCHOOL FOREIGN LANGUAGE CURRICULUM

In this scenario, the focus is on a reading program in a foreign language situation – one in which the students are learning a language that is not used as an official language of the country (e.g., English in Japan). With a foreign language curriculum aimed at preparing for all-important examinations, the teacher feels that no class time can be spared for anything new: There is not even enough time to cover the examination curriculum. Nevertheless, the teacher decides that the students could read for about an hour a week on their own time. Apart from the benefits to the students' reading ability and confidence, the teacher considers that extensive reading, by nature relaxing and pleasurable, will be a good balance to the high-pressure cramming that characterizes most of the students' language study. The teacher replaces one of the weekly homework readings from the textbook with an extensive reading assignment: Students must select and read one short book and write a short report on it. Students are told that they must take no more than an hour to complete this: 40 minutes for reading and 20 minutes for writing. They are instructed to note at the bottom of their report how long they took to read and to write.

After a few weeks, several students say that they like this homework best of all because it is fun and easy. Several students read their books and write the reports during their lunch break. Others say that they read on the train on the way home from school or while waiting for dinner at home, thus freeing up their evening for their own pursuits or other study.

ADULT EDUCATION OR COMMERCIAL LANGUAGE SCHOOL

In a once-weekly adult education second language class held after working hours, students arrive one evening to find a small library of books on a shelf at the back of the classroom. The teacher invites students to select and take a book home to read. From then on, the teacher regularly devotes the first 10 minutes of the 90-minute class to short oral book reports by students, and designates the final 5 minutes of class as a time for students to select books from the library to take home. Reading is entirely voluntary; students may choose as many books as they wish, and they can read as little or as much as they feel like. After some weeks, students tell the teacher that they are reading anywhere from 20 minutes to several hours per week. For them, the reading does not feel like homework – homework has never been a part of this class anyway.

Extensive reading and second language academic programs

A first, understandable reaction to extensive reading from administrators and teachers in programs that prepare students for the stringent demands of academic work in a second language may be one of dismissal. University students need high-level reading skills in order to cope with the vast amount of reading often required of both undergraduates and graduates. What would a reading approach based on reading easy self-selected material have to offer such students?

There are sound reasons why extensive reading should be an integral, even major, part of preparing students for academic reading. Extensive reading, of course, has an essential role in developing the sight vocabulary, general vocabulary, and world knowledge on which fluent reading is based. It can also give students confidence and a positive attitude toward second language reading – of no small importance considering the fundamental role that reading so often plays in academic success. But the reasons for including extensive reading in academic preparation programs extend even further, and have to do with cognitive growth.

Extensive reading may play a role in developing the capacity for critical thinking so important for success in higher education. William Grabe, discussing the teaching of reading in an academic setting to students of English as a second language, writes:

> Discovery and creative thinking are emergent processes where the mind, almost of itself, makes nonobvious connections and relations between previously independent domains of knowledge in the mind of the person. It is always striking to note the inability of foreign students to discuss new or complex notions in English, even when their language abilities begin to allow for this. What is being noted is the rather formulaic thinking and expressions of opinions that often occur in advanced ESL classes. In short, second language students usually opt for "safe" responses. While there are many causes for this phenomenon, a chief one is the lack of background knowledge assumptions which form a basis from which to begin more speculative thinking, and which form the basis for many English language assumptions. The point is that prior reading experiences are crucial for having the information base to make nonobvious connections. (1986, p. 35)

Second language students in academic preparation programs must certainly master special skills for reading challenging academic texts. But unless they are also reading with fluency and confidence in the second language, they are unlikely to read broadly and deeply enough to achieve the mass of background knowledge on which speculative thinking depends. An extensive reading approach can make such reading possible for students.

Goals of an extensive reading program

When you are planning a new extensive reading program, some or all of the outcomes from extensive reading programs such as those discussed in the preceding chapter can be formulated as program goals. Having goals means that at the end of a program you can tell whether you have achieved what you wanted to achieve. Possible goals are that the students will

1. Have a positive attitude toward reading in the second language.
2. Have confidence in their reading.
3. Have motivation to read in the second language.
4. Read without constantly stopping to look up unknown or difficult words in the dictionary.
5. Have increased their word recognition ability.
6. Know for what purpose they are reading when they read.

7. Read at an appropriate rate for their purpose in reading.
8. Know how to choose appropriate reading materials for their interests and language ability.

The extent to which these goals are appropriate and will be successfully met depends in part on the intensity and duration of the extensive reading program. The more time allotted to the program, and the more the students read, the greater the likelihood that they will become effective and efficient readers. As Leo Schell states, "The amount of time spent in actual reading may be the most important factor in reading growth" (1991, p. 115). At the same time, it is important not to be discouraged by constraints or limitations. Remember that even Fung-Kuen Lai's students (1993a, 1993b) showed gains during a summer program.

Why is extensive reading the approach less traveled?

In light of the flexibility of incorporating an extensive reading approach into a second language curriculum, and the positive outcomes reported in the previous chapter, an obvious question to ask is why extensive reading is not more common in second language programs. Various reasons have been suggested, including

- cost
- the work required to set up a program
- the difficulty of finding time for it in the already-crowded curriculum
- the different role of the teacher
- the "light" nature of the reading material
- the dominance of the reading skills approach, especially in ESL academic preparation programs
- the belief that reading should be delayed until students can speak and understand the second language
- confusion between extensive reading and class readers

Although concerns such as these can seem to range from the irrelevant to the insurmountable depending on the situation, the fact that they have been raised at all means that they should be addressed.

Cost is indeed a major consideration. Money must be available to fund an adequate library. For programs on a limited budget, a solution is to start small.

The amount of attention and organization involved in setting up an extensive reading program is another real concern. Again, a solution is to start small and to let the positive results justify the expenditure of additional time and energy in expanding the program.

Finding time for extensive reading is a matter of priorities. If teachers and administrators support the notion of their students becoming fluent, independent readers in the second language, then time will be found, even if it is only an hour of homework a week.

The different role of the teacher in extensive reading can be a problem for teachers used to traditional roles. In extensive reading, teachers do not impart knowledge as much as guide students and participate with them as members of a reading community. As David Eskey has pointed out, this may seem "profoundly anti-pedagogical. Teachers like to teach; they like to feel they are doing something" (1995). Certainly, redefining the teacher's roles and responsibilities takes some getting used to. This is one of the challenges of an extensive reading approach, and it is a challenge that extends to the other side of the desk. Students, too, must become accustomed to new roles and responsibilities as learners.

The nature of the material used in extensive reading may be controversial. Stephen Krashen observes that "light reading" such the *Sweet Valley* series, magazines, newspapers, and comics may be regarded as lacking literary merit. Teachers, administrators, or parents may fear that the use of such light reading "will lead to a decline in taste, that it will detract from appreciation of the classics" (Krashen, 1993a, p. 80). As Krashen observes, the very opposite may be the case: The use of such light reading can be a springboard into the classics. He cites a 1992 study by James Davis, Lynn Gorell, Rebecca Kline, and Gloria Hsieh that found leisure reading in the foreign language as among the strongest predictors of positive attitudes toward literature.

The emphasis on the teaching of reading skills might contribute to the lack of attention given to extensive reading (Day, 1993, p. xi). A skills approach to the teaching of reading has achieved a sort of unstoppable momentum. The dominance of skills, especially in ESL academic programs, leaves little room for considering other approaches.

The belief that reading should be delayed until students have a solid ability to speak and understand the second language is still held by some teachers, and Grabe (1995) has suggested that this may be part of the explanation for extensive reading's low profile. The "speech-first" view was a characteristic of the audiolingual era of the 1950s and 1960s. It is now hard to justify withholding the written form of a second language on either theoretical or pedagogical grounds.

Confusion between extensive reading and class readers may have led to less attention for extensive reading. Colin Davis (1995, pp. 330–331) suggests that a program of class readers (in which each student reads the same book at the same time in class) may appear to be a way of avoiding the drawbacks of an extensive reading approach, such as the cost and the work involved in organizing it. However, a program of class readers has more in common with traditional forms of teaching reading and literature than with self-selected, individualized extensive reading. Class readers can supplement and support extensive reading, but they cannot replace extensive reading as a means of developing reading fluency and positive attitudes.

Davis, reviewing some of the problems associated with extensive reading, concludes:

> Ultimately, whether or not these problems are overcome is a matter of priorities. Teachers and educational planners first have to become convinced of the enormous boost such a programme can give to their pupils' command of the language in order to feel it worthwhile committing the resources required. (1995, p. 331)

Fortunately, as Davis also points out, "any teacher introducing extensive reading to his or her pupils will gradually become aware [of its benefits]" (p. 330). The most effective way to address the perceived problems associated with extensive reading may therefore be simply to introduce extensive reading, and let the proof of the pudding be in the eating.

Conclusion

As the discussion in this chapter makes clear, there is no dichotomy between the use of an extensive reading approach and other approaches to the teaching of second language reading. Extensive reading can be integrated into the second language curriculum in a variety of ways, from a standalone course to an extracurricular club activity. Appropriate goals for the extensive reading program should be set based on the results desired and the amount of reading that will be done.

There is no avoiding the fact that implementing extensive reading is challenging on many levels. In general, reservations about committing to extensive reading can be dealt with by starting small and letting extensive reading prove itself.

Further reading

The Edinburgh Project on Extensive Reading has always favored getting institutional and even governmental support for programs, on the grounds that this is the most effective means of introducing and ensuring the continuance of extensive reading. David Hill wrote the book on how to go about this: *The EPER Guide to Organising Programmes of Extensive Reading* (1992). This how-to guide to designing, preparing, and implementing a program is indispensable for such large-scale endeavors. It also has much to offer individual teachers and others introducing extensive reading in any context.

PART II: MATERIALS FOR EXTENSIVE READING: ISSUES IN DEVELOPMENT

The middle section of the book is a bridge between Part I, which lays the foundation and makes a case for extensive reading, and Part III, which gives practical advice for introducing extensive reading in the classroom. This bridge is necessary because confusion and controversy surround which materials are and which are not suitable for second language students to read.

Part II aims to breathe reason and logic into this debate. Chapter 6 covers the two major issues in the controversy, examining what *authenticity* means in relation to reading material, and what *simplification* of reading material for second language students involves. The different points of view concerning these two terms are reviewed, and a perhaps surprising conclusion is reached. Then, a brand-new concept in reading materials for language learners is introduced: *language learner literature.* Part II concludes with an in-depth look (in Chapter 7) at just what a literature for language learners entails.

6 *The cult of authenticity and the myth of simplification*

It is important to use authentic texts whenever possible.
—Françoise Grellet (1981, p. 7)

There is no such thing as authentic language data.
—Henry Widdowson (1976, p. 270)

Simplicity is difficult.
—Alan Davies (1984, p. 181)

The purpose of this chapter is to:

- Examine critically the concepts of authenticity and simplification as related to second language reading materials.
- Suggest the need for authentically simple texts that communicate to language learners.

It has been argued in this book that, for the purposes of developing reading fluency and confidence, second language students need to read interesting, understandable materials that are basically at the *i minus 1* level, that is, below their linguistic ability. Most second language books, newspapers, and magazines are, however, difficult for second language students to understand because the students have limited linguistic and background knowledge. The logical solution would appear to be to write texts for second language students that take into account their lack of linguistic ability and background knowledge. Such a solution, however, goes against the widely held assumption that authentic (real-life) materials should be used in language teaching. This chapter begins with a critical analysis of authenticity and then moves to a similar look at simplification. The final two sections discuss how second language material for extensive reading can combine the best features of both authentic and simplified materials while avoiding their problems.

The cult of authenticity

Developing texts for second language students that take into account their lack of linguistic ability and background knowledge is, regrettably, controversial. In language teaching, there is an enduring "cult of authenticity" that originated with the communicative language teaching (CLT) movement of the late 1970s. CLT argued that, for language teaching, authentic materials – those written by and for native speakers and not specifically for language teaching – were superior to materials especially written or simplified for language learners.

The appeal that authentic texts have for teachers and, as a consequence, for students, and the influence those texts have on students' ideas about reading, can be gauged from the "Introduction to the Student" in Catherine Walter's *Genuine Articles: Authentic Reading Texts for Intermediate Students of American English:*

> All of the texts in the book are real samples of written English. . . . None of them was written especially for foreigners. This means that some texts may be easier to understand than others; but *even the easier texts* [italics added] will help you read better. (1986, p. vii)

Part of the cult status of authenticity is the idea that it is the very difficulty of texts that makes them worthwhile as learning tools.

In spite of the widespread acceptance of the use of authentic materials, there is no consensus as to the meaning of *authentic.* Robin Scarcella and Rebecca Oxford note that, "generally, authentic language is considered unedited, unabridged text that is written for native . . . speakers" (1992, p. 98). Catherine Walter, on the other hand, includes texts both "shortened" and "slightly adapted" (1986, p. ix) in her *Genuine Articles* textbook. Yet another view is expressed by Henry Widdowson, who argues that authenticity is not a quality of text at all; instead, "authenticity . . . is achieved when the reader realizes the intentions of the writer" (1976, p. 264). Finally, Eddie Williams says simply that an authentic text is one "written to say something, to convey a message" (1984, p. 25).

Authentic texts – however defined – are used in language teaching because they are considered interesting, engaging, culturally enlightening, relevant, motivating, and the best preparation for reading authentic texts. (This latter reason can presumably be summed up in the axiom "We learn to read authentic texts by reading authentic texts.") As Williams explains, "if the learner is expected eventually to cope with real language outside the classroom, then surely the best way to prepare for this is by looking at real language inside the classroom" (1984, p. 25).

But, for many teachers, the most compelling argument for the use of authentic texts is that they are genuine discourse. Christine Nuttall, in the second edition of her influential book *Teaching Reading Skills in a Foreign*

Language, elaborates on this point. As she puts it, authentic materials not only motivate students but "exhibit the characteristics of true discourse: having something to say, being coherent and clearly organized" (1996, p. 177).

At the same time, authentic texts, for all their virtues, can actually set back reading development. Williams refers to the paradox that the use of authentic text with learners often has an effect opposite to that intended; instead of helping the reader to read for the meaning of the message, an authentic text at too difficult a level of language forces the reader to focus on the code (1983, p. 175). Wilga Rivers points out that "when average students encounter ungraded material too soon, they are usually forced back into deciphering with the aid of a dictionary, and valuable training in the reading skill is wasted" (1981, pp. 37–38). Nuttall, in her discussion of authentic materials, concedes that "linguistically difficult texts are unlikely to be suitable for developing most reading skills" (1996, p. 177).

In addition, there is the affective toll. Rivers observes that "rushing students too soon into reading material beyond their present capacity for fluent comprehension with occasional contextual guessing . . . destroys confidence" (1981, p. 260).

And yet, in spite of these drawbacks, authentic materials have become, in David Clarke's words, "almost a categorical imperative, a moral *sine qua non* of the language classroom" (1989, p. 73). As a colleague observed to one of us, "All I heard in graduate school ten years ago was the need to use authentic materials, whether in teaching reading or listening or whatever. But at the time, I knew from my own experiences both as a second language teacher and learner that simplified materials worked. So I was confused. And ever since then, I have felt guilty using them."

That he and other teachers use simplified materials at all points directly to the fatal flaw of authentic materials. Had Ambrose Bierce been a language teacher, he might well have added the following wonderfully cynical definition, courtesy of Andrew Cohen, to his *Devil's Dictionary:* "Authentic materials are those which are impossible or difficult for language learners to understand."

There was, in fact, some recognition of this problem in the writings of experts from the beginning, but often so indirectly stated that the point was lost. In *Developing Reading Skills,* when Françoise Grellet says "It is important to use authentic texts whenever possible" (1981, p. 7), it is the first part of the statement that makes the impact, not the last two words.

And so it is that teachers and students have come to see authentic materials as preferable to easy, simplified texts. For less-than-fluent second language readers, this is a dangerous view, for it can rob them of the most important source of the reading materials they need to become fluent readers.

The idea that simplified texts are to be avoided and that difficult texts are prestigious is equally pernicious in terms of attitude toward reading. In effect, it associates reading itself with difficulty. Students will *always* be able to find texts that are difficult for them, and they are liable to equate reading and learning to read with struggling through these texts. This is not the way to instill an appreciation for reading.

But the cult of authenticity did not arise in a vacuum. Part of its prominence can be traced to the nature of what may seem to be the only alternative to authentic texts: simplified materials.

The myth of simplification

To say that simplified texts have a bad name in language teaching is an understatement. If authentic texts are seen as natural, interesting, relevant, and pedagogically sound, texts-made-simple are generally considered to be just the opposite: stilted, unnatural, unreal, bland, and a pedagogical dead end. There is, to be sure, good reason for this point of view, but it is – pun not intended – simplistic. In Ronald Carter and Michael Long's words, "It is worth remembering that – as with all books – there are good, bad and indifferent simplified texts" (1991, p. 152). Why? Is it a matter of good and bad writing? Good and bad stories? Or is there more to it than that?

It is first necessary to be clear about what is meant by simplified texts, as the product of simplification goes by many names: *simplified, graded, abridged, adapted,* and *pedagogical.* This is unfortunate, because the numerous terms tend to cause confusion and mislead teachers and students.

Simplification can be used to develop at least two different types of second language reading materials: texts simplified from first language originals and texts written specifically for second language learners. The first type, text simplified from material originally written for an audience of first language readers, often uses classics whose copyrights have expired and that are therefore in the public domain. In English, there are literally hundreds of stories that have been simplified, such as *Black Beauty, The Adventures of Tom Sawyer, The Hound of the Baskervilles, Frankenstein, From Russia with Love, A Tale of Two Cities, Sinbad the Sailor,* and *The Great Gatsby.*

This rewriting or adaptation of texts written originally for an audience of first language readers is approached in one of two ways. The first is by entirely restating the ideas of the text in simpler form and language. Henry Widdowson, who has a sharp eye for dichotomies, christened this a *simple account* (1978, pp. 79, 89–91). The second way involves retaining in general terms the form and language of the original text, but abridging, replacing certain difficult words or structures with simpler ones, perhaps reordering certain parts for clarity, and sometimes elaborating on difficult concepts. Widdowson calls this a *simplified version* (1978, pp. 79, 88–89). The less proficient the language learner, the more limited the words and structures used to rewrite or adapt the original text.

The second type of simplified material is text written specifically for second language learners. Writing an original text from scratch for an audience of language learners has been termed a *simple original* by David Hill and Helen Reid Thomas (1988, p. 44). Just as in rewritten and adapted first language texts, the words, structures, and text types of simple originals are determined by the particular level of the students for whom the text is intended.

Whatever their origin – simple account, simplified version, or simple original – simplified materials are developed and used for second language reading for one inescapable reason: Beginning and intermediate second language students need them. And yet, reflecting the cult of authenticity, simplified materials are rarely considered for what they are – a positive contribution to reading instruction and language learning. They are generally seen in terms of what they are not, as when Christine Nuttall writes, "Authentic material is the ideal, but if you cannot find enough at the right level, you will have to use simplified or specially written materials to begin with" (1996, p. 178); or when she laments, "However good a simplification is, something is always lost; this is why some teachers refuse to use simplified versions" (1996, p. 178).

Certainly, criticism of simplified materials is justified, for they can be poorly written, uninteresting, and hard to read, and can lack normal text features such as redundancy and cohesion. Many of these shortcomings can be traced to two sources, one to do with language and the other content.

Because, for language learners, difficult language is the problem with authentic texts, simple language is sometimes considered the solution. Second language texts may be primarily written or adapted in terms of a linguistic formula based on lists of words and grammar patterns that learners are expected to know. Unfortunately for a writer, when working with a list of vocabulary and structures, "one's focus of attention is on lexis and syntax rather than on the discourse they are used to create" (Widdowson, 1978, p. 89).

Content problems can occur when attempts are made to simplify a complex original text. David Hill, reviewing the *Penguin Readers* series, gives one example: "In *Presumed Innocent,* 10 characters are introduced in the first chapter, three of them with nicknames, and incident follows incident in rapid staccato. The effect is often like a 33rpm record being played at 78rpm" (1995, p. 17).

Whatever the source of the problem, language or content, the result is the same. By focusing too much on simple language or the content of the original text, writers of simplified texts pay less attention to the essence of writing: communicating with an audience. This has led to the well-justified consensus that simplified material is not normal discourse (text written for communication), and is therefore less than good practice for learning to read.

This leaves teachers on the horns of a dilemma. For confidence building and developing reading fluency, authentic materials are not at the required *i minus 1* level, whereas simplified materials, with all their shortcomings, are. What second language readers actually need for extensive reading are texts that combine the desired features of authentic texts (their authenticity) and simplified texts (their simplicity) – in other words, texts that are both authentic and appropriately simple.

There are precedents for such texts. Native speakers have children's literature and young adult literature. Because these texts aim to communicate with their particular audiences, the discourse is natural. They are also, again by virtue of their aim to communicate, appropriately simple in language and concept.

Authenticity and simplicity reexamined

Can such a fusion of authenticity and simplicity be attained in second language texts? Closer examination of the concepts of authenticity and simplicity would suggest so. The definition of authenticity in the *Longman Dictionary of Language Teaching and Applied Linguistics* begins: "The degree to which language teaching materials have the qualities of natural speech or writing" (Richards, Platt, & Platt, 1992, p. 27). This is an insightful departure because, rather than being an appeal to author and audience (e.g., native speakers) or source (e.g., taken from newspapers or magazines), this definition highlights – without naming, however – those natural qualities that make a text authentic. Not only that, it allows that these "qualities of natural speech or writing" may be possessed by texts written or edited for language learners, that is, texts that are termed *simplified.*

In this view, simplified and authentic are not mutually exclusive opposites. Rather, simplified text can be judged in terms of whether it has the natural qualities of authenticity. It is therefore no paradox for Charles Alderson and Alexander Urquhart, in their collection *Reading in a Foreign Language,* to state: "We are committed to believing that simplified texts can be authentic" (1984, p. 198).

Others have reached the same conclusion. Sandra Silberstein, for example, in her volume *Techniques and Resources in Teaching Reading,* states that "reading texts, even those which are edited, can and should be authentic" (1994, p. 111). They

> should be authentic in the sense that they resemble the "real-world" texts students will encounter . . . in terms of . . . syntax, discourse structure, vocabulary . . . [and] content. . . . At all proficiency levels, we want students to be engaged with texts that are "authentically" similar to those which represent their reading goals. (p. 102)

How can fully authentic but simple texts be prepared? Is the answer, as Henry Widdowson once suggested, to "bring the language within the scope of what we suppose to be the learner's capacity for applying interpretative procedures on foreign language data" (1979, p. 190) – in other words, some kind of better linguistic simplification? This has been the thrust of most thought and research on the subject. John Klapper, for example, refers to work done by Ruth Berman (and reported in the aforementioned Alderson and Urquhart collection) on how complex syntax makes text "heavy" and harder to decipher. Klapper suggests that "Berman's (1984) concepts of textual density and heaviness . . . [should be used] as criteria for the process of simplification, and due note . . . taken of the important role played by redundancy in creating an adequate context for informed guessing" (1992, p. 53).

There have also been a number of studies of whether and under what circumstances linguistic manipulation can help second language learners understand a text. Patricia Johnson, for example, investigated the interaction of background knowledge and simplification of vocabulary and structure and concluded that foreign language students are helped by simplification only when they lack background knowledge (1981). Yasukata Yano, Michael Long, and Steven Ross (1994) compared three versions of a text: authentic (e.g., "Because he had to work at night to support his family, Paco often fell asleep in class."); simplified ("Paco had to make money for his family. Paco worked at night. He often went to sleep in class."); and elaborated ("Paco had to work at night to earn money to support his family, so he often fell asleep in class the next day during his teacher's lesson.") (p.

193). They found little difference in foreign language students' comprehension of the simplified and the elaborated versions, and concluded that elaboration is preferable to simplification as it helps inference and provides "the rich linguistic form [learners] need for . . . language learning" (p. 214).

What these suggestions and studies have in common is that they continue to see simplification in linguistic terms. Certainly, texts communicating with language learners will be written in simple language. It does not follow, however, that simple language is what makes a text communicate to language learners. As readability expert George Klare notes, "much more goes into writing than word and sentence considerations" (1984, p. 703), which is perhaps why Alan Davies and Henry Widdowson once asked, "Does the simplification of linguistic elements necessarily result in the simplification of a text as a piece of communication?" (1974, p. 183).

Communication

Is better simplification of linguistic elements the correct approach to the simplification of a text as a piece of communication? If not, what other approach to simplification might there be? A definition of authenticity by Janet Swaffar offers an answer:

> For purposes of the foreign language classroom, an authentic text . . . is one whose primary intent is to communicate meaning. In other words, such a text can be one which is written for native speakers of the language to be read by other native speakers (with the intent to inform, persuade, thank, etc.) or it may be a text intended for a language learner group. The relevant consideration here is not for whom it is written but that there has been an authentic communicative objective in mind. (1985, p. 17)

This characterization goes one step further than the *Longman Dictionary of Language Teaching and Applied Linguistics,* for it suggests that the "qualities of natural speech or writing" possessed by authentic text derive from the author's having a communicative objective.

Swaffar points out that, because textbooks aim to "teach language . . . rather than to communicate information . . . carefully edited short readings lack the essential features of authentic messages: repetition, redundancy, and discourse markers" (1985, p. 17). Apparently, then, it is the author's intention to communicate that endows text with the "essential features" that make it authentic. And so, to return to Sandra Silberstein's concern earlier in this chapter (that edited texts should be authentic) and the question this suggests (how can texts be edited so as to be authentic?), perhaps the answer is for the author/editor to intend to communicate.

This in turn suggests another interesting question: Does simplification exist? The bond between simplification and communication is made clear when Henry Widdowson defines simplification as "the process whereby a language user adjusts . . . language behaviour in the interests of communicative effectiveness" (1979, p. 196). And so it is that Christopher Brumfit is moved to ask if indeed "simplification deserves its special status, or whether in practice it is simply another way of referring to fundamental communication" (1993, p. 2). Alternatively, as Alderson and Urquhart wryly state, "If simplification is defined as making a text appropriate to the audience, then perhaps *any* text may be considered a simplification" (1984, p. 196).

Either way, it is suggested that, in second language teaching, simplification is no more than a term – even a somewhat insulting term – to refer to writing for language learners; and that any simplicity detected in such writing is not something gained at the expense of authenticity but is the very expression of authenticity itself.

Conclusion

First language children's literature and young adult literature are especially written to provide what children and young adults need in terms of entertainment and information. These texts, written on a wide variety of topics for a wide variety of age groups, also provide material with which to learn to read and to become hooked on books.

For all the same reasons – entertainment, information, learning to read, and becoming hooked on books – second language learners need a variety of excellent material written especially for them. Because of its communicative intent, such material would be authentic and appropriately simple in language and concept. Such material might properly be called *language learner literature,* and this is the subject of the next chapter.

Further reading

Breen, Davies, and Widdowson provide the generally accepted seminal discussions of authenticity: Michael Breen considers the subject in a 1982 paper "Authenticity in the Language Classroom" (reprinted in 1985 in the journal *Applied Linguistics*). Alan Davies discusses authenticity in his chapter "Simple, Simplified and Simplification: What Is Authentic?" in J. Charles Alderson & A. H. Urquhart's classic collection *Reading in a Foreign Language* (1984). Henry Widdowson's reflections on authenticity include:

1. "The Authenticity of Language Data," in Fanselow and Crymes's *On TESOL '76,* reprinted in Widdowson's *Explorations in Applied Linguistics* (1979).
2. The early part of a chapter titled "Comprehending and Reading," in Widdowson's *Teaching Language as Communication* (1978). The most relevant pages are 79–82.
3. "Reading and Communication," in Widdowson's *Explorations in Applied Linguistics 2* (1984a), also included in Alderson and Urquhart's *Reading in a Foreign Language.*

A well-known examination of the shortcomings of simplified texts is John Honeyfield's 1977 *TESOL Quarterly* article "Simplification."

William Lee was an early critic of the concept "authenticity." In "Some Points about 'Authenticity'" (*World Language English,* 1983), he takes a different approach from the one used in this chapter to reach essentially the same conclusion: that "authenticity" is another word for "communication."

7 *Language learner literature*

> In future years, the absence of imaginative content in language teaching will be considered to have marked a primitive stage of the discipline.
>
> —John McRae (1991, p. vii)

The purpose of this chapter is to:

- Introduce the concept of language learner literature.
- Examine techniques of writing for an audience of language learners.

In his history of language teaching, Louis Kelly traces the development of simplified texts back to the late fifteenth century, when they were written for learners of Latin (1969, p. 141). But the modern version of such books, often termed *readers,* is, historically at least, synonymous with the name of one man. As Alan Maley relates with relish, "Shortened, simplified, abridged and adapted – Readers have been with us from the dim mists of primeval English Language Teaching . . . where the wraith of Michael West can still be seen flitting through the swamps" (1988, p. 3). West, teaching English in India in the 1920s, wrote folktales and adapted literature for his students. Combining meticulous care for simple but natural language with storytelling flair, he single-handedly invented the contemporary version of the simplified reader. A number of his books are still in print today (see the Appendix).

West's pioneering work has led to books for learners in many different languages, and in almost every genre: thriller, biography, romance, horror, general fiction, science fiction, to name but a few. It is this body of work that is introduced and examined in this chapter.

Language learner literature introduced

One of the hallmarks of good writing is that it speaks to an intended audience. Writing is an act of communication, regardless of who the intended audience might be, or the author's particular purpose. In order to write successfully, an author must bear in mind the characteristics of the audience. This is not an option, but a prerequisite for all writing. The intended audience might be the readers of popular newspapers, children, or the readers of books such as this one, for example. Or it might be second language learners.

Language learners are an audience on a par with any other. To write material for an audience of second language learners is no less an act of communication than other forms of writing. Since there is an identifiable audience, since the terms *authentic* and *simplified* are ambiguous and inaccurate and carry unsatisfactory connotations, and since it is not simplification or elaboration but communication that is the issue, we suggest an alternative term for reading material that has been written with an audience of second language learners in mind: language learner literature.

We see the term *language learner literature* as analogous to the terms *young adult literature* and *children's literature* – established genres in their own right. It includes fiction and nonfiction, original writing, and texts adapted for language learners. But whatever form it takes, language learner literature presupposes the integrity that marks all genuine writing: that it be not a lesser version of something else but a fully realized, complete-in-itself act of communication between author and audience. The basis for judging the success or failure of language learner literature is therefore identical to that of other writing: the response of its readers – the sense they make and the experiences they have.

Writing for an audience of second language learners

In general terms, an author writing for an audience of second language learners must bear in mind three special characteristics of these readers. One is limited language ability, and consequent fatigue and limited attention span when reading. The second is unfamiliarity with concepts and topics that are common knowledge in the target-language culture. Third, second language readers may be unfamiliar with particular culture-specific text types. They may not understand the way such texts are organized – their rhetorical conventions – and how people normally react to such texts. These three general factors are most pronounced for beginner language learners/readers and gradually lessen in importance as learners make progress in the second language.

Beyond these three things held in common, second language learners are of various ages, have various interests, and come from a wide variety of cultures. There are still generalizations that can be made, however. With music, fashion, movies, and TV circling the globe, it is, as Keith Morrow and Marita Schocker observe, "fair to assume, for example, that 17-year olds in Britain are interested in much the same sort of thing as are 17-year olds in Germany" (1987, p. 253). Thus, writers who focus on the interests and mentality of a particular group of language learners with which they are familiar will almost certainly be communicating to a vast worldwide audience of similar learners.

Communicating with language learners involves considerations of both content and language, and in practice the two are inseparable. In all teaching, as Henry Widdowson points out, "concepts . . . are *organized and expressed* [italics added] so as to make them congruent with the learner's experience" (1979, p. 200). He could have been talking about all communication.

This integrated content and language perspective is an interesting one from which to look again at both the Johnson (1981) and the Yano et al. (1994) studies discussed in the preceding chapter. These and other studies considered linguistic simplification apart from content, and produced results that have been used to discredit linguistic simplification. Johnson reported that learners who lacked background knowledge benefited from simplification of language. This result serves to illustrate the interdependence of content and language when text is an act of communication. Yano et al. compared simplified and elaborated prose. In terms of communication, however, the point is not whether the author uses fewer words and shorter sentences ("simplification") or more words in embedded sentences, making explicit any background suppositions ("elaboration"). The point is to express – without being patronizing, terse, or verbose – the content in a way that communicates to the audience.

Because writing for language learners has generally been considered a matter of using simple language, writers use lists of easy words and simple structures, or apply readability formulas that judge the difficulty of a text in terms of how long the sentences and words are. The idea is that simple language aids communication. But this order of priorities is the opposite of true writing.

When an author communicates with an audience, the means of expression – the language – is normally intuitive. When an author focuses on the message and the audience, that is, focuses on the communication, the language suggests itself. As George Klare puts it, "most estimates of readability are . . . made by writers in the process of writing – in most cases subjectively and perhaps even unconsciously" (1984, p. 702). Charles Alderson and Alexander Urquhart make this further observation:

> The evidence . . . suggests that when a competent writer produces a 'simplified' version of a text, without explicit reference to the formulae, then the simplified version is not only easier to read, but also rates easier according to the formulae. The interesting question is what writers do in order to produce such texts. (1984, p. 196)

Answers have been offered from a variety of sources, including the editors of successful and highly regarded series of books for English language learners. John Milne, editor of *Heinemann Guided Readers,* explains that texts in his series are written "based on the writers' and editors' experience of what vocabulary students can cope with at a particular level. . . . We have thus used an intuitive approach to vocabulary control rather than relying on controls based on mechanical word counts or rigid word lists" (1977, p. 16).

As with almost all English language series, *Heinemann Guided Readers* are marked for level by using both a name and the number of basic vocabulary words within which the books are written – for example, beginner level/600 words, or elementary level/1,100 words. Interestingly, however, these vocabulary figures were arrived at *after* the books were written. As John Milne explains, "At each level a number of manuscripts were prepared. . . . Then an estimate was made of the number of basic words used across these manuscripts. By 'basic' we mean words not peculiar to the story" (p. 17). Structure is approached in the same way:

> Writers are not asked to apply structure controls rigidly and automatically. Instead, writers are expected to have constant . . . [recourse] to their intuitive feeling for language and hold a balance between those structures which may be necessary for the telling of a particular story and those which might cause students insurmountable difficulty. (p. 12)

Before writing, it is a basic necessity to, in Christopher Brumfit's words, "clarify in your own mind the type of learner you are writing for, as precisely as possible" (1985, p. 98). Then, as Tricia Hedge advises in her guidelines to writers of the *Oxford Bookworms* series for language learners, it is "useful to write the first part of your story intuitively, with a certain level of language learner in mind, and then see which level in the series it fits" (1988, p. 5).

Lists of words that learners probably know (or ought to know) can still be of great assistance to a writer – if used properly. Christopher Brumfit, in a review of the *Cambridge English Lexicon,* offers this advice: "Write your text as clearly and appropriately as you can, without any reference to the lexicon. . . . The lexicon . . . [can] inform and sensitize your judgement . . . [if] used negatively by writers, not positively. Only in this way will . . . writing . . . remain writing" (1985, p. 98). In other words, do not weave text from words known to learners, or automatically exclude words unknown to learners. Instead, use the lexicon *after* writing to alert you to words you used that learners may not know. That information can help you to judge better the use of a word in terms of the effect it will have on the intended readers.

To suggest that writers write intuitively does not necessarily mean writing without conscious attention to language as such. Certain authors may be hyperconscious of this aspect of communication, weighing every word for its contribution to the flow of the text. In the end, what all authors are hopefully aiming for is that elusive quality of good writing. When John Milne suggests that "each sentence has to be well balanced internally, running on smoothly from the sentence which preceded it and leading on naturally to the one which follows" (1977, p. 5), he is talking as much about style as cohesion. Tricia Hedge is also concerned with style when she urges authors to "develop a text with 'light and shade' by focussing information in different ways" (1988, p. 3).

All this is not the icing on the cake. It must be the essence of writing for language learners, for, as Milne points out, "a book which is badly written will not be easy to read" (1977, p. 5). Christopher Brumfit, therefore, is making an important point when he states that books for language learners "*above all* [italics added] need to be written by people who can write well" (1985, p. 99). Here Brumfit echoes Michael West, the teacher and writer who single-handedly brought language learner literature into being. West felt that books for language learners were best written by people "able to write an original short story or novel. . . . What is required is a person who can write with some inspiration" (1960, p. 28).

So far in this chapter, writing for language learners has been considered mainly in terms of the technical. But just as truly making love goes beyond a how-to manual like *The Joy of Sex,* communicating with language learners takes place on a different plane than, let us say, conjoining content and language. It is time, therefore, to consider language learner literature on its own merits, as a genuine art form.

An ideal way to begin to do this is to look at some examples of language learner literature. We conclude this section, therefore, with six extracts in English written or adapted for learners at progressively higher levels of language abilities. These samples were chosen by Tricia Hedge and Jennifer Bassett, editors of the *Oxford Bookworms* series, as illustrations for potential authors. So settle back now and enjoy a taste of the genre called language learner literature.*

* The excerpts on pp. 68 to 74 are reproduced by permission of © Oxford University Press.

Sample Text for Level One

The Phantom of the Opera by Jennifer Bassett

The Opera House in Paris is a very famous and beautiful building. It is the biggest Opera House in the world. Work on the building began in 1861, finished in 1875, and cost forty-seven million francs.

It has seventeen floors, ten above the ground, and seven under the ground. Behind and under the stage, there are stairs and passages and many, many rooms – dressing-rooms for the singers and the dancers, rooms for the stage workers, the opera dresses and shoes . . . There are more than 2,500 doors in the building. You can walk for hours and never see daylight, under the Paris Opera House.

And the Opera House has a ghost, a phantom, a man in black clothes. He is a body without a head, or a head without a body. He has a yellow face, he has no nose, he has black holes for eyes . . .

This is the true story of the Phantom of the Opera. It begins one day in 1880, in the dancers' dressing-room . . .

CHAPTER 1: THE DANCERS

'Quick! Quick! Close the door! It's him!' Annie Sorelli ran into the dressing-room, her face white.

One of the girls ran and closed the door, and then they all turned to Annie Sorelli.

'Who? Where? What's the matter?' they cried.

'It's the ghost!' Annie said. 'In the passage. I saw him. He came through the wall in front of me! And . . . and I saw his face!'

Most of the girls were afraid, but one of them, a tall girl with black hair, laughed.

'Pooh!' she said. 'Everybody says they see the Opera ghost, but there isn't really a ghost. You saw a shadow on the wall.' But she did not open the door, or look into the passage.

'Lots of people see him,' a second girl said. 'Joseph Buquet saw him two days ago. Don't you remember?'

Then all the girls began to talk at once.

'Joseph says the ghost is tall and he wears a black evening coat.'

'He has the head of a dead man, with a yellow face and no nose . . .'

'. . . and no eyes – only black holes!'

Then little Meg Giry spoke for the first time. 'Don't talk about him. He doesn't like it. My mother told me.'

'Your mother?' the girl with black hair said. 'What does your mother know about the ghost?'

Sample Text for Level Two

The Death of Karen Silkwood by Joyce Hannam

CHAPTER 1: THE ACCIDENT

It was dark. Nobody saw the accident. The small white car was found on its side by the bridge. A river ran underneath the road there, and the car was lying next to the bridge wall, below the road. Inside the car was a dead woman. Her name was Karen Silkwood and she was twenty-eight years old. It was November 13th, 1974.

How did the car come off the road? Why was it on the wrong side of the road? Why was it so far from the road? There was nothing wrong with the car. Karen Silkwood was a good driver. Everybody knew that.

The police thought that there was an easy answer to these questions. Karen was tired after a long day, so she fell asleep while she was driving. It could happen to anyone very easily. They took the car to a garage and they took Karen's body to a hospital.

But some people were not happy about the accident. First of all, her boyfriend, Drew Stephens. Also a newspaper journalist from the *New York Times* and a Union official from Washington. These three men were waiting for Karen on the night of the accident. She was bringing them some papers and some photographs in a big brown envelope. The papers were very important. The men were waiting for Karen in a hotel room a few miles from the accident. But she never arrived. When they heard about the accident, the men looked for the brown envelope at once. They looked for it inside the white car. They looked for it at the hospital and at the police station. The next morning they looked all around the wall and in the river, but they never found it. Nobody ever found that brown envelope.

Sample Text for Level Three

'Sredni Vashtar' from *Tooth and Claw*
Short stories by Saki, retold by Rosemary Border

Conradin was ten years old and was often ill.

'The boy is not strong,' said the doctor. 'He will not live much longer.' But the doctor did not know about Conradin's imagination. In Conradin's lonely, loveless world, his imagination was the only thing that kept him alive.

Conradin's parents were dead and he lived with his aunt. The aunt did not like Conradin and was often unkind to him. Conradin hated her with all his heart, but he obeyed her quietly and took his medicine without arguing. Mostly he kept out of her way. She had no place in his world. His real, everyday life in his aunt's colourless, comfortless house was narrow and uninteresting. But inside his small, dark head exciting and violent thoughts ran wild. In the bright world of his imagination Conradin was strong and brave. It was a wonderful world, and the aunt was locked out of it.

The garden was no fun. There was nothing interesting to do. He was forbidden to pick the flowers. He was forbidden to eat the fruit. He was forbidden to play on the grass. But behind some trees, in a forgotten corner of the garden, there was an old shed.

Nobody used the shed, and Conradin took it for his own. To him it became something between a playroom and a church. He filled it with ghosts and animals from his imagination. But there were also two living things in the shed. In one corner lived an old, untidy-looking chicken. Conradin had no people to love, and this chicken was the boy's dearest friend. And in a dark, secret place at the back of the shed was a large wooden box with bars across the front. This was the home of a very large ferret with long, dangerous teeth and claws. Conradin had bought the ferret and its box from a friendly boy, who lived in the village. It had cost him all his money, but Conradin did not mind. He was most terribly afraid of the ferret, but he loved it with all his heart. It was his wonderful, terrible secret. He gave the ferret a strange and beautiful name and it became his god.

Sample Text for Level Four

A Tale of Two Cities by Charles Dickens, retold by Ralph Mowat

CHAPTER 1: THE ROAD TO PARIS – 1775

It was the best of times, it was the worst of times. It was the season of light, it was the season of darkness. It was the spring of hope, it was the winter of sadness. It was the year one thousand seven hundred and seventy-five.

In France there was a King and a Queen, and in England there was a King and a Queen. They believed that nothing would ever change. But in France things were bad, and getting worse. The people were poor, hungry, and unhappy. The King made paper money and spent it, and the people had nothing to eat. Behind closed doors in the homes of the people, voices spoke in whispers against the King and his noblemen; they were only whispers, but they were the angry whispers of desperate people.

Late one November night, in that same year 1775, a coach going from London to Dover, stopped at the top of a long hill. The horses were tired, but as they rested, the driver heard another horse coming fast up the hill behind them. The rider stopped his horse beside the coach and shouted:

'I want a passenger, Mr Jarvis Lorry, from Tellson's Bank in London.'

'I am Mr Jarvis Lorry,' said one of the passengers, putting his head out of the window. 'What do you want?'

'It's me! Jerry, Jerry Cruncher, from Tellson's Bank, sir,' cried the man on the horse.

'What's the matter, Jerry?' called Mr Lorry.

'A message for you, Mr Lorry. You've got to wait at Dover for a young lady.'

'Very well, Jerry,' said Mr Lorry. 'Tell them my answer is – CAME BACK TO LIFE.'

It was a strange message, and a stranger answer. No one in the coach understood what they meant.

Sample Text for Level Five

King's Ransom by Ed McBain, retold by Rosalie Kerr

CHAPTER 1: 'WE WANT YOUR VOTING STOCK, DOUG'

Outside the window boats sailed up and down the River Harb. In the clear October air, orange and gold leaves screamed their colour against the cold blue sky.

The room was full of cigarette smoke. It hung over the five men like the breath of ghosts. The room was enormous, but it was full now, full of the dirty ash-trays, used glasses and empty bottles left at the end of a long and difficult discussion. The men themselves were as exhausted as the smoky air.

Tired but determined, the men sitting opposite Douglas King hammered out their argument. King listened to them silently.

'We're asking you to think about profit, Doug, that's all,' George Benjamin said. 'Is that a lot to ask?'

'Think of shoes, yes,' Rudy Stone said. 'Don't forget shoes. But think of profit. Granger Shoe is a business, Doug, a business. Profit and loss. The black and the red.'

'And our job,' Benjamin said, 'is to keep Granger in the black. Now take another look at these shoes.'

A thin man, he moved fast and silently to a glass table, which was covered with women's shoes. He picked one up from the pile and gave it to King.

'What woman wants to buy a shoe like this?' he asked.

'Don't misunderstand us,' Stone said quickly. He was a muscular blond man who looked much younger than his forty-five years. 'It's a good shoe, a fine shoe, but we're thinking of profit now.'

'The red and the black,' Benjamin repeated. He turned to an older man sitting beside him. 'Am I right, Frank?'

'One hundred per cent,' Frank Blake said, in a thick Southern accent. He blew cigarette smoke at the high ceiling.

'The American housewife,' Benjamin said, 'can't afford this shoe. But even if she *could* afford it, she wouldn't want it. Mrs America, our customer. The stupidest little woman in the world.'

Sample Text for Level Six

Pride and Prejudice by Jane Austen, retold by Clare West

CHAPTER 1: THE BENNETS' NEW NEIGHBOUR

It is a truth well known to all the world that an unmarried man in possession of a large fortune must be in need of a wife. And when such a man moves into a neighbourhood, even if nothing is known about his feelings or opinions, this truth is so clear to the surrounding families, that they think of him immediately as the future husband of one or other of their daughters.

'My dear Mr Bennet,' said Mrs Bennet to her husband one day, 'have you heard that someone is going to rent Netherfield Park at last?'

'No, Mrs Bennet, I haven't,' said her husband.

'Don't you want to know *who* is renting it?' cried Mrs Bennet impatiently.

'You want to tell me, and I don't mind listening.'

Mrs Bennet needed no further encouragement. 'Well, my dear, I hear that he's a very rich young man from the north of England. It seems he came to see Netherfield on Monday and was so delighted with it that he arranged to rent it at once. Of course, it *is* the finest house in the area, with the largest gardens. His servants will be here by the end of the week, and *he* will be arriving soon afterwards!'

'What is his name?' asked Mr Bennet.

'Bingley.'

'Is he married or single?'

'Oh, single, my dear, of course! A single man of large fortune – he has an income of four or five thousand pounds a year. How wonderful for our girls!'

'Why? How can it affect them?' Mr Bennet asked.

'My dear Mr Bennet,' she replied, 'how can you be so annoying! You must realize I'm thinking of his marrying one of our daughters.'

'Is that his purpose in coming to the area?'

'His purpose? No, of course not. But it's very likely that he'll fall in love with one of them. And I want him to see the girls as soon as possible, before our other neighbours introduce themselves. So you must visit him as soon as he arrives.'

'I really don't see why I should,' said Mr Bennet. 'You and the girls can visit him, or perhaps you should send them by themselves. Yes, that might be better, as you're as attractive as any of them, and Mr Bingley might like you best.'

'My dear, you flatter me,' replied his wife, 'I certainly have been called beautiful in the past, but I think a woman with five adult daughters should stop thinking of her own beauty. Mr Bennet, I beg you to visit him. You know it's correct for the gentleman of the family to visit new neighbours first. I simply cannot take the girls to see him unless you have already met him.'

'Surely you worry too much about the rules of polite society. I'm sure Mr Bingley will be delighted to see you all. And I'll write him a few lines, which you can give him, agreeing gladly to his marrying any of the girls, although I must especially recommend my dear little Lizzy.'

'Oh no, Mr Bennet!' gasped Mrs Bennet, horrified.

(Hedge and Bassett, forthcoming)

Language learner literature as art

Monica Vincent states that simplified texts "are qualitatively different" (1986, p. 210) from genuine literature. But do they really have to be?

What is literature? Ronald Carter and Michael Long, in their excellent and practical book *Teaching Literature,* suggest that it is written to "create an effect through words" (1991, p. 105). John McRae in his book *Literature with a Small 'l'* sees it as text that "will stimulate reaction and response" (1991, p. vii). McRae elaborates on these notions, taking as his starting point George Orwell's choice of the word "grimy" to describe London in the novel *Nineteen Eighty-Four* rather than the simpler "dirty."

> Literature *is* the difference between 'dirty' and 'grimy.' The very unfamiliarity and, frequently, the unexpectedness of the author's choice of words or of structures is what makes an imaginative text different from a purely referential piece of language use. . . . There is a clear relation between how the writer sees what he is writing about and how he or she wants the reader to see the same thing. The choices an author makes – *what* to write about and *how* to write about it – are fundamental to the text the reader receives. And what might be called 'desired effect' – . . . the impact the text has on its reader – depends very much on these authorial choices. (1991, p. 42)

This does not mean that *grimy* would be the better choice for language learners – or that *dirty* would be the right choice, either. It depends on the desired effect intended by an author *sensitive to a particular audience.* One is reminded of John Milne's observation in the preceding section, that writers need to use "their intuitive feeling for language and hold a balance between . . . [language] which may be necessary for the telling of a particular story and . . . [that] which might cause students insurmountable difficulty" (1977, p. 12).

McRae's assertion that literature depends on the unfamiliarity and unexpectedness of the author's choice of words would seem to back up Vincent's claim that simplified texts cannot be literature. *Dirty,* after all, is a word suitable for language learners, whereas *grimy* would probably just confuse: language learners cannot understand or appreciate such vocabulary. And yet, for learners whose linguistic world is smaller, words commonplace to native speakers can possess all the unfamiliarity, unexpectedness, and impact of a word such as *grimy.* Clever authors can exploit this to great effect.

There are examples of careful and effective choice of words of language learner literature in the passages in the previous section. Rosemary Border is a writer wonderfully sensitive to the nuances of language. Adapting Saki's short story "Sredni Vashtar" for pre-intermediate students of English, she uses the word *forbid* rather than the more common *say somebody cannot* or *not let/allow. Forbid* is far beyond the approximately 1000-word level at which Border is writing, but it has the sense of prohibition by someone in authority, thus emphasizing the powerlessness felt by Conradin in his aunt's world. *Forbid* is a word almost certain to cause difficulty to less than skilled readers who have precious little cognitive processing capacity available to devote to unfamiliar words. Yet Border chooses to include it precisely for its desired effect on the reader. She probably felt that it would not cause insurmountable difficulty, for it is placed so that its meaning can be guessed from context. She also repeats the word no less than three times in as many lines, thereby rendering it maximally salient. For a pre-intermediate language learner, it is arguable that the impact of this word ("He was forbidden to pick the flowers. He was forbidden to eat the fruit. He was forbidden to play on the grass.") is as powerful and literary in describing Conradin's world as George Orwell's use of the word *grimy* is in describing London.

It is clear that authors of language learner literature can communicate with impact and affect – if they are allowed to. But, as Christopher Brumfit – speaking as a writer of English language texts – relates with frustrated bitterness,

Most of us have our favourite horror stories of publishers' editors rejecting anything interesting in favour of anything dull ('she was coming to the evening of her life' becomes 'she was very ill') on the assumption that learners of English come to reading as blank and unliterary and inhuman as the computers on which the prevalent information transfer metaphor is based. (1985, p. 96)

Fortunately, sensitive editors exist, as evidenced by the flexible approach to vocabulary and the unexpurgated poetic and figurative expressions in the sample texts: In "Sredni Vashtar," Conradin's aunt is "locked out" of his world of imagination; in *A Tale of Two Cities,* Dickens's evocative paradox "It was the best of times, it was the worst of times" remains; and in *King's Ransom,* the mood is set by autumn leaves that "screamed their colour" and by cigarette smoke hanging in the air "like the breath of ghosts." The authors include – and the editors retain – these expressions in texts written for language learners beyond the beginning stage. These learners already have a sight vocabulary, albeit limited in development, and thus some cognitive capacity available to work out and appreciate such use of language.

The importance of content

"Unfortunately," notes David Hill with measured restraint, "the content of readers has not exercised writers and editors of graded readers nearly as much as the writing and application of grading schemes" (1997, p. 59). It appears that publishers and editors view a graded reader primarily as part of a series and only then as an individual creation. With such an order of priorities it is no wonder that the content of the books tends to take the back seat. Writers and editors appear to forget that, above all else, it is the appeal of a book in and of itself that matters to the person reading it.

For language learner literature to flower, it will probably need to break free of the confines of monolithic graded series presided over by editors whose apparent main concern is with the mechanics of producing a linguistically appropriate product. Publishers, editors, and authors must take seriously the idea of communicating with language learners as readers with their own interests, desires, and tastes. Then popular writers, characters, and series will appear for language learners, driven by the marketplace, just as they have in children's and young adult literature.

To give but one example of what might be, writer Stephen Rabley and illustrator Inga Moore have created a courageous (if stereotypical) French mouse detective called Marcel. Because he is a mouse, his exploits go unnoticed by the humans he helps, and therein lies his charm. Three or four Marcel stories have been published by Longman in its English-language

Easystarts and *Longman Originals* series (see levels F and G in the Appendix). Learners who love Marcel and Céline, his partner in solving mysteries, would gladly read more of their adventures. But as long as Marcel books are mere items within a graded series, the publisher is unlikely to consider them as works in their own right and unlikely to publish enough titles to satisfy demand.

Language learner literature should include all genres, even books that are, to echo John McRae, literature with the smallest "l" of all. In other words, for adult learners and if culturally appropriate, language learner literature should include what B. M. Z. Murphy, writing in *Modern English Teacher,* calls "bad books and dirty books" (1987, p. 23) – "pulp-style fiction" (p. 22) with all the steamy eroticism that drives that genre to the top of native-language best-seller lists.

Language learners are an audience like any other, deserving not just reading matter but a varied literature that speaks to them. There is cause for hope when Julie Stone, ELT secretary for a major publisher, talks in the following terms. Books for language learners

> should be as accessible as possible without patronizing the reader – above all – they should be enjoyable. . . . Stories must be strong on plot with a modest number of characters and sub-plots. Characters should have motivation and there should be a strong theme as well as drama and tension. Reading 'fodder' will soon deter and disappoint even the most energetic student. (1994, p. 15)

When Stone talks of books being accessible, she is alluding to a final consideration in producing language learner literature: the support offered to students to make reading easier. This is a matter, no less than communication and content, in which editors must decide their priorities.

Support for reading

If editors of language learner literature appear reluctant to think in terms of the content of their books, they seem positively set against providing assistance to the reader. A few series offer introductions that help the reader appreciate the context of the work, but these are the exception, not the rule. The only support most editors give the reader is the questions on the main points of the story at the end of the book, *after* reading is finished. This is a strong indication that editors are thinking of the needs of the teacher, not of the learner/reader. David Hill lucidly makes the case for more helpful aids to reading.

> In my judgement, learners need pre-reading support to help them overcome the difficulty of 'getting into' a book. They also need while-reading support, either in the form of a summary of the salient points so far, or as a note of the points

to look out for while reading the next section, or both. 'Jane Eyre has left school and obtained a job as a governess to the ward of a rich gentleman. How will she be treated by her new employers? How will she get on with her pupil?' Such an insertion between chapters would confirm the learners' understanding of what they had read, and provide them with a clear signpost through the next section. It would also take account of the fact that learners leave a book for a few hours or days, and can easily lose the thread.

This sort of support may be considered interfering and patronizing, and for learners who are competent and experienced readers in their own language, this may be so. But they need not use them, and graded readers should cater for those who are unskilled in reading long texts. (1997, pp. 64–65)

But the most difficult aspect of reading for language learners is vocabulary. Students need help both in understanding unknown words and in building their vocabularies. Few series offer such assistance. Those that do, rarely do it effectively, as Hill points out:

Some mark 'difficult' words in the text but do not put them in a glossary, others provide a glossary but do not mark the words in the text, while others mark the word and put them in a glossary. Editors are ready to go to the barricades in defence of their policy, but the only one that makes any sense to me is to mark the text and have a glossary. I hate looking up a word [at the back of a book] only to find it is not there, or reaching the end of a book before discovering that there is a glossary. (1997, p. 65)

Writing for and communicating with language learners means anticipating how they will respond. Measuring the effect a text will have on a reader should include consideration of support to ensure that reading is a pleasant and fruitful experience rather than a difficult and mystifying one. Glossaries and other aids to reading are valuable and appropriate tools for language learners and novice readers. Just as bold illustrations and big print characterize children's literature, and short chapters and colloquial language characterize young adult literature, difficult words marked in the text, glossaries, summaries, and guide questions should characterize a true literature for language learners.

Conclusion

Learning to read in a second language is a formidable task, involving time and effort on the part of student and teacher alike. Both deserve the best possible tools, in this case reading materials.

There is a need for a strong and varied language learner literature in as many second languages as possible. Teachers, students, and others interested in second language reading must ask for language learner literatures that are inherently interesting and well written, and that offer appropriate supports for reading. It is not an impossible demand. Until it is met, teachers who wish their students to develop reading ability and a love of reading in a second language will continue to have a tough row to hoe.

Further reading

In Chapter 4, "Comprehending and Reading," of his 1978 volume *Teaching Language as Communication,* Henry Widdowson examines the process of writing text that is both comprehensible for language learners and helpful for learning to read. See especially pages 77–93.

David Hill, who has almost certainly read more graded readers than any other human being living or dead, has distilled his experience into "Survey Review: Graded Readers" (1997), a state-of-the-art analysis of these books that is useful for teacher and writer alike. Also useful for potential writers of language learner literature are John Milne's *Heinemann Guided Readers Handbook* (1977) and the revised edition of *Oxford Bookworms: Guidelines for Authors* by Tricia Hedge and Jennifer Bassett (forthcoming).

It is always interesting to compare an adaptation with its original, and several authors have done this.

- Alan Davies and Henry Widdowson (assisted by Julian Dakin) compare the famous "Please, sir, I want some more" passage from Charles Dickens's *Oliver Twist* with two simplified versions, with thought as to what the simplifiers might have been trying to do in each case. See pages 176–177, 182–185, and 190–195 of their chapter "Reading and Writing" (pp. 155–201) in Allen and Corder's 1974 *Techniques in Applied Linguistics.*
- Ronald Carter and Michael Long compare lengthy passages from the original and simplified versions of George Eliot's *Adam Bede* in their book *Teaching Literature* (1991, pp. 148–153), clearly showing the differences between an excellent simplification and its literary original.
- Tricia Hedge juxtaposes an original and a simplified passage from Aldous Huxley's *Brave New World,* followed by careful comparison, in her book *Using Readers in Language Teaching* (1985, pp. 16–20).

David Hill and colleagues at the Edinburgh Project on Extensive Reading (EPER) have long been separating language learner literature from reading fodder. The EPER database ranks English language graded readers, both in print and out of print, on a quality scale. An EPER listing of the best of graded readers appears in the Appendix.

PART III: THE PRACTICE OF EXTENSIVE READING

This final section of the book – occupying more than half its length – details the process of setting up (Chapters 8–10), carrying out (Chapters 11–13), and finally evaluating (Chapter 14) an extensive reading program.

Chapter 8 is concerned with preparations for an extensive reading program, beginning with questions such as how much students will read and on what basis their reading will be evaluated. The next two chapters focus on reading materials: the various types that can be used for extensive reading (Chapter 9) and how to assemble them into a working library (Chapter 10).

The extensive reading program itself begins with a student orientation, covered in Chapter 11, and continues with classroom activities (Chapter 12) and activities used as a follow-up to reading (Chapter 13). At the end of the term or year, the program is analyzed in terms of its success and failure (Chapter 14).

Part III concludes by looking, in Chapter 15, at the conditions necessary for extensive reading to flourish. One of these conditions is the development of language learner literature. Both to encourage that process and to make the book as practical as possible (at least for teachers of English as a second language), a bibliography of the best language learner literature in English is included in the Appendix.

8 *Setting up a program: Curricular decisions*

> Teachers have to create the right conditions for reading to become a valued part of every student's life.
> —Christine Nuttall (1996, p. 127)

The purpose of this chapter is to address these curricular questions:

- How much material should students read?
- How can teachers evaluate students?
- Should students read in class or for homework or both?
- At what level of difficulty should students read?
- Should students use dictionaries while reading?

When teachers or administrators decide that students would benefit from extensive reading, they are most likely entering uncharted territory. Extensive reading belongs in an educational world different from the one that administrators, teachers, and students usually inhabit. For one thing, the major activity, reading, is not confined to the four walls of the classroom. For another, growth in positive attitude may be as important a goal as growth in reading ability. In the end, teachers may discover that they are not so much teaching a class in reading as building a community of readers.

Mapping extensive reading onto the template of compulsory education is not always straightforward. In school, students often find themselves studying subjects that do not, on the surface, seem to fit their immediate needs and interests. Although the ideal envisions a classroom in which students are eager and ready to take on all assignments willingly, the reality is different. Therefore, the pedagogical suggestions in this chapter are couched in terms of the reality of the everyday classroom: grades; requirements; rules and regulations.

This chapter is basically an orientation for teachers and administrators who are considering implementing an extensive reading approach. The five questions at the head of the chapter frame the major issues that teachers need to resolve when setting up an extensive reading program. We will consider each question in turn.

How much material should students read?

Extensive reading means reading a large amount in the second language. This is the very essence of the procedure, and all benefits are based on it. At the same time, there is no particular amount of reading that qualifies for the term *extensive*. How much students read is relative to their circumstances and abilities. The answer is therefore that, if their goal is to become fluent readers, students should read as much as is reasonably possible.

The major consideration is how much class and homework time the students have for reading. Are reading classes once a week or daily? How much time can students reasonably be expected to devote to homework reading per day or per week?

Another consideration is how long the students can read pleasurably before losing interest. Beginners obviously cannot read for as long as more advanced learners. It is not only that they read more slowly, they get tired more quickly. A beginner will perhaps have had enough after 20 minutes, whereas a more advanced student may not feel like stopping reading for an hour or more.

Reading expectations

Once all of the considerations have been discussed, the amount of reading expected of students can be expressed as a reading target. As William Grabe says:

> Progress in reading is only recognizable over a period of time. . . . Teachers must be willing to believe in the process. . . . One clear indication of faith and commitment is to demand performance. Reading is a personal experience and the teacher cannot peer over the shoulder of the student. But the teacher can . . . place expectations on the students. Most students rightly interpret such behavior as commitment and involvement on the teacher's part. (1986, pp. 44–45)

Reading targets – whether expected or required – and measuring progress toward them are very important in extensive reading. They are part of what keeps students reading in their own time, and even motivated students can be assisted by them. Students have many calls upon their time that can make it difficult for them to accomplish everything that they wish to. Establishing reading expectations ensures that they keep moving toward their goal of becoming fluent readers.

Reading targets can be expressed in terms of the material (number of books or pages read) or time (number of hours spent reading), or a combination of both. Bernard Susser and Thomas Robb, in an overview of extensive reading instruction, surveyed the literature to determine how much reading was suggested, and how quantity of reading was measured (1990, pp. 165–166). They found such suggestions as:

- 30 pages an hour (Hill & Reid Thomas, 1988, p. 50)
- 50 pages per week (Paulston & Bruder, 1976, p. 202)
- 60 books a year (Bright & McGregor, 1970, p. 69)

Regardless of the quantity and how it is expressed, however, an important consideration is that the reading assignments be long enough to discourage intensive study or translation. Alternatively, and to the same end, a time limit can be introduced within which students must finish reading. This was why the high-school teacher in Chapter 5 insisted that students complete their homework reading within a set time limit.

David Hill's rule of thumb – a book a week if the books are short and simple – is a good point of departure when formulating reading targets. One book of language learner literature at the lowest level can perhaps be read by a beginning-level student in about 15 minutes. Such a book contains about 16 pages of text. An intermediate-level book (60–70 pages) might take about 2 hours to read, and an advanced-level book (80+ pages and smaller print) about 3 hours. Books written for native speakers can be read by suitably advanced students at the rate of approximately 30 pages per hour (1 page of text has about 300 words, and students may read at an average of 150 words per minute, including pauses). From these figures, and by surveying your own students about how long it takes them to read, it is possible to work out how much to expect students to read in the time available. Students can then be expected to read a certain number of books per week, semester, or year.

Teachers are sometimes frustrated by watching students select library books "because they're short." Shouldn't students be encouraged to care more about the content of the books themselves? Some teachers have created "weighted pages" formulas, in part as a way of preventing lazy or unambitious students from reading easy or short books in order to avoid homework. Formulas also give teachers a reasonably objective criterion to better calculate exactly how much each student has read during the school year.

Formulas work like this. Each book in the library is examined and given a weighted pages value above or below a standard. Bernard Susser and Thomas Robb, for example, teaching English at Japanese universities, created a formula based on words per page, area of white space and illustrations, and readability level as indicted by a readability formula. Books in their libraries "ranged from 0.70 for some intermediate-level graded readers . . . to 2.30 for standard, adult novels" (1989, p. 9). (See "Further reading" at the end of this chapter for exact details of their formula.)

And yet, the ideas of "short" or "easy" are among the natural criteria used in selecting what to read, and they are not always a mark of laziness. A teacher told us that one of her students purposely selected short books so as to be able to read them during her train ride to school, for example. Teachers have the choice of letting such things be part of the book selection process or legislating against them. Needless to say, letting books be books without imposing special formulas on them is less complicated for teacher and students alike. It also avoids the possibility that teacher and student come to see reading as a matter of number of (weighted) pages per week rather than as the appreciation of individual books. There are always other forces that encourage students away from short, easy books. If students are exposed to the opinions of their classmates, for example, they tend to read what is recommended to them, regardless of length. And if all else fails, there will come a time when students will have read most of the shorter books in the library, and they will have to start selecting longer ones.

Whether to count quantity in terms of time spent reading or in terms of books, pages, or weighted pages – and whether to have any reading quotas at all – is finally up to the teacher. In smaller programs, where teachers can guide students individually, the amount and level of reading expected or required can be applied flexibly to individual students. In larger programs, when such close, individual attention is difficult, more rigid requirements may have to be imposed.

How can teachers evaluate students?

There is nothing about extensive reading that says that requirements cannot be set, records kept, or grades given as in other forms of instruction. Students can also be required to demonstrate understanding of their reading through written reports or answers to questions. The progress of individual learners can therefore be tracked, achievements can be recognized and rewarded, and assistance can be given as necessary to learners who are having difficulties.

One way of evaluating students is in terms of the reading targets, as discussed in the preceding section. Specifically, credit can be given for books read and reports turned in. A standard way of doing this is to assign the reading of a certain number of books or pages (for example, a book a week) in order for students to pass the class or to receive a certain grade.

Higher grades or extra credit can be offered to a student for reading over and above the minimum required to pass the class. This usually provides an incentive for students to challenge themselves to greater achievements.

Methods of record keeping and evaluation

READING NOTEBOOK

Using reading targets to evaluate students requires some way of keeping track of how much students are reading. This can be accomplished through a variety of record-keeping activities done by the students themselves. The most basic is a reading notebook. Students keep their own notebooks in which they write the names of the books and other materials they read. They add the dates on which they read the material, for how long they read on each date, and whether they enjoyed it. Teachers can look at these notebooks periodically, and use them as a basis for evaluation.

WEEKLY READING DIARY

A variation of the reading notebook in intensive reading programs is the weekly reading diary. Preprinted forms can be used: Students write their names at the top and fill in the forms daily, noting down what they read that day and for how long. They should record all reading in the second language, including newspapers and magazines. If these diary forms are turned in at the end of each week, teachers can see at a glance how much reading each student did over the previous seven days. Figure 1(a) is an example of a reading diary form, and 1(b) a completed diary form.

BOOK REPORTS

Another activity that can be part of evaluation and record keeping is written book reports. This is a simple procedure, as it involves only the students writing brief summaries of or personal reactions to the books they read. Written book reports make record keeping easy, although they will not reflect incidental reading of newspapers or magazines and so may give a less than complete picture of the reading habits of the students. Teachers can keep track of how many reports were submitted before handing them back to the students. Alternatively, students can be instructed to resubmit their portfolio of reports at the end of the course.

Name: ____________________________

Date	Material	Target: _____ per day
Monday		I read for minutes
Tuesday		I read for minutes
Wednesday		I read for minutes
Thursday		I read for minutes
Friday		I read for minutes
Saturday		I read for minutes
Sunday		I read for minutes

Figure 1(a) Weekly reading diary. Copyright © Cambridge University Press.

READING TESTS

Some teachers may wish to try to measure growth in reading ability. Beniko Mason and Tom Pendergast offer a holistic means of evaluating intermediate and advanced students' vocabulary, grammar, and general reading ability (1993, pp. 16–17). The following is a simplified form of their procedure.

Name: Shuichi

Date	Material	1 hr. Target: per day
Monday 11/25	Gandhi	I read for 60 minutes
Tuesday 26	Gandhi The Wonderful Wizard of Oz	I read for 60 minutes
Wednesday 27	The Wonderful Wizard of Oz APRIL IN MOSCOW THE NEW ROAD	I read for 60 minutes
Thursday 28	HERCULES ANNA and the Fighter	I read for 50 minutes
Friday 29	ANNA and the Fighter Death of a ~~Sod~~ Soldier The Long Tunnel	I read for 60 minutes
Saturday 30	The long Tunnel Grace Darling	I read for 20 minutes
Sunday 1		I read for 0 minutes

Figure 1(b) Weekly reading diary (filled out).

Choose a text (of about 1,500 words) of the type and difficulty that you expect students to be able to read at the end of the year. Leave the first paragraph intact, and then delete every tenth word of the rest of the text for a total of 100 deleted items. Ask several native speakers to take the test. From this information, compile a master list of acceptable words for each deletion.

Give the test to the students at the beginning of the course. It can be completed in about an hour. Do not tell the students that they will be doing the same test as a posttest. After giving the pretest, collect all materials so that the test remains secure. Ask a native speaker to look at the students' papers to see whether there are any more acceptable words for the deletions – add these to the master list of acceptable answers. The average score for this pretest should be less than 35 points out of 100. Give the same test at the end of the course.

Mason and Pendergast's cloze test can be reused with different students year after year and can thus repay the initial investment of preparation time.

NEGOTIATED EVALUATION

A different approach to evaluation is offered by Beatrice Dupuy, Lucy Tse, and Tom Cook. In their 1996 *TESOL Journal* article, "Bringing Books into the Classroom: First Steps in Turning College-Level ESL Students into Readers," they relate their experiences with "negotiated evaluation," a process by which students choose how they wish to be evaluated for their reading. As Dupuy, Tse, and Cook write, "Teachers may expect that students would choose easy assessments, but in our experience, if the students take the responsibility seriously, they often exceed teacher standards" (p. 14). Examples of ways students chose to be evaluated included "forming book promotion teams to introduce books to other classes, [and] writing sequels to stories or books" (p. 14).

A negotiated approach to evaluation is closer to the spirit of extensive reading and its overall goals than teacher-imposed requirements. If the goal of extensive reading is not merely reading improvement, but for students to become independent readers, students must experience taking responsibility for their own reading. As Dupuy, Tse, and Cook note, negotiated evaluation can be "liberating" for students as well as teachers (p. 14).

Should students read in class or for homework or both?

Once it is determined how much students could be expected to read and how they might be evaluated, a third curricular decision to be made is where students should read. Albert Harris and Edward Sipay state the issue this way for the first language reading teacher: "If we do not demonstrate that reading is a worthwhile activity by providing school time, how can we expect children to value reading?" (1990, p. 656). This is no less a consideration for second language students. When time is set aside for students to read in class, it shows students the value that is placed on reading and gives prestige to the activity.

At the same time, extensive reading requires students to read in quantity – more than it is possible to do in the classroom even in the best of circumstances. Much reading, therefore, will have to be done by the students for homework. But this is more than just a matter of expediency. As Keith Morrow and Marita Schocker point out in an article on how to involve students in reading, reading involves choice on many levels – and one important aspect of choice is "when and under what conditions the text is read" (1987, p. 254). Further, as John Klapper points out, "learners will more likely respond to reading books of their own choice at their own speed, rather than being compelled to conform to some uniform programme" (1992, p. 54).

Thus, out-of-class reading is a crucial component in building the habit of reading. Students have to find out when and where they like to read. In an informal survey by one of the authors of this book, one student said that she read foreign language library books in bed, in the school library, in the train, on breaks from work, and in a coffee shop. Another said that he read mainly at his desk at home, because that was the best place for him to concentrate. Where and when to read are matters of individual choice and preference, discovered by trial and error. Reading in one's own time and on one's own terms is the only way to begin to do this.

Interestingly, the two students just mentioned added that their native language reading habits were the same as those they had reported for foreign language reading. It seems that, because they were given the choice of where and when to read, foreign language reading had ceased to be something special and had become simply reading.

At what level of difficulty should students read?

For teachers who are lucky enough to have a large library with books of various levels, it is a good idea for all students to begin by reading very easy books. This will quickly build confidence and make it easier for them to begin to build both sight and general vocabularies. Reading in the second language directly without translation and without struggle will likely be a new experience. Reading very easy material, at the *i minus 1* level, builds confidence and makes it clear to students that this is a different kind of reading practice from what they are probably used to.

As students develop their language and reading competence, it is important that they *ladder up*. By this is meant that the level of materials the students read is in concert with their developing linguistic and reading competence. Material that was once beyond a student's capacity gradually becomes *i minus 1* as their *comfort zone* – the range of materials that can be read easily and with confidence – expands. Generally, laddering up occurs without the teacher's prompting because students are allowed to select their own material according to their interests. Students have an incentive to ladder up because, as a rule, the higher the level, the more interesting the books.

Students doing extensive reading do not always follow a straightforward, upward path, however. Marc Helgesen, teaching English in a women's junior college in Japan, noted that his students did not always move from lower- to higher-level books, but moved more randomly between levels. After reading a more challenging book, for example, a student might choose to read one or two easier books. This is natural, and switching back and forth between levels should not be discouraged. Some students will be eager to read on a topic that might present a slight challenge. Others will wish to read books recommended by classmates no matter how easy or difficult they are. And so students will read at different levels at different times – some material that is well within their comfort zone, and some that is slightly beyond it. Adult beginning students, for example, may be reading easy books and yet also be avidly consuming fashion and soccer magazines written for native speakers if such things are available in the library or the student lounge at break time. Because such students cannot understand much of the language in the magazines, they will ignore it. At the same time, they are reading a photo caption here, and an article on their favorite star there, and are thoroughly enjoying themselves.

There is a danger, however, that some students will try to read above their comfort level, not for enjoyment but because they think they ought to be reading more difficult material, or because they think it is the best way to make progress. Furthermore, students may struggle to continue reading difficult or uninteresting texts, believing that stopping and changing the material is an admission of defeat.

This is a symptom of what might be called the *macho maxim of second language reading instruction: no reading pain, no reading gain.* Students must understand through careful orientation that one of the primary goals of the program, building reading fluency, is achieved through much practice with *easy* texts. Struggling with difficult or uninteresting texts is not the way to build reading fluency. Students should realize that it is better to read more material that is easier than less material that is harder, and that it is better to enjoy what one reads than to be bored or uninterested. This points to the need for teachers to monitor their students' progress, making sure that students are engaging naturally with texts. Students could be advised to avoid material that has more than four or five unknown words per page – more unknown words than this means that the material is probably too difficult and something easier should be chosen.

Should students use dictionaries while reading?

This final curricular question might seem marginal compared to the previous four, but for students it may be of considerable importance. In addressing the question, the nature of fluent reading needs to be understood. Part of fluent and effective reading involves the reader ignoring unknown words and phrases or, if understanding them is essential, guessing their approximate meaning. Fluent reading is hindered by a reader stopping to use a dictionary. Stuart Luppescu and Richard Day (1993) found that the use of dictionaries by Japanese university EFL students doubled the time it took to read a short story.

Of course, to some extent, the problem of unknown language is not a major issue, for most of the vocabulary in the materials that students read should be familiar enough to be understood without recourse to a dictionary. But, inevitably, unknown or half-forgotten words will come up, and is it really so bad for students to be looking them up? If they do not look them up, aren't they missing an opportunity to develop their vocabulary? And wouldn't the draconian directive "no dictionaries" impinge on the students' freedom and choice – two important features of extensive reading?

It is true that dictionary use must depend on the students and their particular needs. There are strong reasons for considering a ban on dictionaries, however, at least initially. Extensive reading is probably very different from the way students have been trained to consider and deal with second language text. Dictionaries – or rather "no dictionaries" – can powerfully symbolize the differences between extensive and other approaches to reading in the minds of the students. Students must break the habit of looking up every unknown word.

Further, if students have the option of looking up words, then inevitably conscientious students will feel that they have to look up more and more words in order to understand the text "properly." Thus, when students are left to their own devices at home, a ban on dictionaries may be the only way for students to feel they can complete the assignment in good conscience. It may also be the only guarantee that the assignment is completed as the teacher intended – in other words, that the reading was indeed extensive in nature.

Students must, in Dupuy, Cook, and Tse's words, get "into the habit of reading daily and out of the habit of looking everything up in the dictionary" (1995, p. 2). An orientation for extensive reading novices will therefore probably include the instruction to never use dictionaries, and the reasons for such a directive.

Students who understand what extensive reading is can be given more freedom. When a word appears several times in a text and seems to hold important meaning, it is sensible to seek its meaning. If a word jumps out of the text as once learned, since forgotten, but naggingly familiar, students deserve the option of ignoring it in order to get on with the story or putting their minds at rest by looking it up. Having the freedom to use a dictionary allows students to get used to making decisions like this on a case-by-case basis. Students learn a flexible approach to unknown words depending on the way a word is used in the text and why one is reading the text.

Advanced students reading material written for native speakers may face real dilemmas. Should they read for a rather vague general understanding or try to understand more at the cost of laborious dictionary work? Perhaps such students would enjoy and get more out of reading easier books, saving the harder ones for later when they know more of the second language.

There is a useful technique for motivated students who are reading more difficult books for pleasure and are also aiming to build their vocabularies. They simply mark the words that they do not know as they encounter them (if in a library book, using a very light pencil, later erased) without interrupting their reading to check the meaning. At the end of a chapter, they go back and look up some of the words. For most students, three or four words per chapter is a reasonable number of words to check. Students then continue reading the next chapter in the same way. Reading is undisturbed and frustration is dealt with. Hindsight may also help the student better decide which words are more important to understand and which ones can be ignored.

Conclusion

Having considered the five curricular questions listed at the beginning of this chapter, teachers and administrators can begin to draw a mental blueprint for extensive reading in their own class or institution. The next step is to survey the spectrum of materials that might be used in extensive reading. This is a fundamental issue since, in order for students to read extensively, the right materials must be obtained and made readily available. The selection and provision of reading materials is the subject of the next two chapters.

Further reading

For details of Bernard Susser and Thomas Robb's weighted pages formula, see their 1989 article "Extensive Homework" in *The Language Teacher.* For convenience, we include their formula here for interested parties. It is based on standards. A standard page has 50 characters per line and 40 lines (= 2,000 characters). A standard book has 19 pages of text to 1 page of white space or illustration. The standard level of text readability is 7th grade level. These standards have no empirical base but were chosen so that books could be compared to each other. To calculate the weighting factor (WF) for a particular book, *(a)* count the characters on any full page of text, *(b)* choose a representative run of 20 continuous pages and count how many pages of white space and/or illustrations are included – adding together fractions of a page of white space as necessary, and *(c)* use a computerized readability level program or subjective estimation to assign a readability grade level. Put the results into the following formula:

$$\mathrm{WF} = \frac{\text{characters per page}}{2{,}000} \times \frac{\text{pages of print per 20 pages}}{19} \times (([\text{grade level} - 7] \times 0.1) + 1)$$

(Susser & Robb, 1989, p. 9)

9 *Materials: The lure and the ladder*

> The watchwords are quantity and variety, rather than quality, so that books are selected for their attractiveness and relevance to the pupils' lives rather than for literary merit.
>
> —Colin Davis (1995, p. 329)

> If the right books were available, the pupils lapped them up.
>
> —J. A. Bright and G. P. McGregor (1970, p. 72)

The purpose of this chapter is to:

- Introduce a variety of materials suitable for extensive reading.
- Suggest alternative reading materials for beginning and intermediate students when language learner literature is not available.

Ruth and Hallie Yopp made an interesting discovery when they asked fifty-six elementary-school teachers in the United States to name their best ideas for teaching children to read. Materials that motivate students was the number one overall best idea. Yopp and Yopp concluded that "providing students with motivating materials and involving them in a variety of interesting activities are critical to a successful reading program" (1991, p. 132).

The same can be said for second language reading programs. Without reading materials that are attractive, interesting, at a range of appropriate levels, and of an appropriate length, a program cannot exist, let alone succeed. More specifically, as Albert Harris and Edward Sipay explain, "The basic principles that underlie the successful development of an interest in reading have been admirably summarized as consisting of a 'lure and a ladder'" (1990, p. 674). In extensive reading, the lure is the interesting and attractive material designed to hook the students and reel them in. The ladder is the wide range of material, from very easy to challenging, that allows the students to progress upward in small steps as their reading fluency develops.

This chapter is an examination of major categories of material potentially useful for extensive reading. These are language learner literature, children's books, learners' own stories, newspapers, magazines, children's magazines, popular and simple literature, young adult literature, comics, and translations. We examine each category of reading material in turn. When making decisions about specific types of material for specific students, teachers can consider these questions:

- Will this material attract them?
- Do my students have enough language and background knowledge to be entertained or informed when reading it on their own?
- In terms of their self-images as readers, will reading it be an encouraging or a discouraging experience?

Language learner literature

Language learner literature is the very embodiment of the lure and the ladder: varied, attractive material at different levels of difficulty. It includes books of all kinds, as well as magazines and newspapers produced especially for second language learners. If it is available in the language you teach, language learner literature is the obvious first choice of reading material for all but advanced learners.

Literature adapted for language learners

One particular type of language learner literature requires additional comment here. This subcategory consists of classic works of literature adapted from the originals for second language students. Some people familiar with the originals have expressed disappointment and even horror at the adapted versions sold under the same name. This is an understandable reaction, but to dismiss adaptations in this way is to misunderstand their purpose and usefulness.

Movies based on works of literature provide a helpful analogy. When a movie shares the same title as a famous original, it professes to be a version of that original. But it is an adaptation for another medium and another audience. The movie version, for example, must be pruned of much detail, for only a certain number of characters and incidents can be included in the normal 2-hour running time. In other words, the makers of the movie tailor the content to suit the medium and the expectations of the intended audience.

It is rare for a movie version to catch the essence of the book on which it is based. But even when it does, the movie is still an independent experience that succeeds or fails on its own terms, regardless of its relationship to the original. And so it is with written adaptations of classics and other works of literature. Whether an adaptation is more or less successful at capturing the essence of its source is beside the point. Ultimately, an adaptation must be judged on its own terms: Is it a successful reading experience in and of itself? The questions to ask in considering whether an adaptation has a place in an extensive reading program, therefore, are the same as for any material: Does this book communicate to its audience of language learners? Is it likely to be enjoyed by my students?

Language learner literature does not exist in every language. If you teach a language that has no such literature, you have to look elsewhere for suitably easy reading material. One possibility is to look at language textbooks other than the ones your students are using to see if they include any interesting reading passages. You can also look at some of the other categories of material described below.

Children's books

If a language lacks language learner literature, teachers can turn to a sure source of easy reading material that exists in almost every language: books designed to teach children to read their first language. The books, many of a quality that appeals to children and adults alike, can add variety to any extensive reading library. This valuable resource should not be overlooked.

Books in this category range from picture books with no words (not suitable for reading practice) to simple storybooks with many illustrations. The major assets of these books are relatively easy language, attractive layout, big print, and appealing illustrations. Equally important is their length: They are usually short enough to be finished in 15 minutes or so. Although language can be colloquial, the illustrations help comprehension. Glossing (explanations or translations of difficult words) could be added to the books by the teacher as an aid to comprehension.

Adults do not necessarily feel insulted at being offered material for children. The appeal of these books to mature students is on several different fronts. Some books are enjoyed because they offer a delightful return to the world of children. Others may be appreciated as works of art and literature and windows on culture. Some deal with themes of interest to all ages, such as prejudice, the environment, and coming to terms with the death of a loved one. Teachers can decide which books are appropriate based on their knowledge of the students. If teachers lack confidence in making such decisions, Linda Thistlethwaite (1994), in an article discussing the use of children's books with adult readers, presents a scale for evaluating the appropriateness of individual books based on such factors as theme and illustrations.

The following account of adults learning a foreign language and using books written for children is informative. Francine Schumann relates her experiences of learning Persian with her husband while they were living in Iran.

> In Tehran they sold books for children in Persian that had fantastic art work. It was this art work which greatly attracted me, and I decided I wanted to learn to read using these children's books. John said I shouldn't waste money on them as they contained no vocabulary lists or transcriptions . . . and therefore, all my time would be spent looking up words in the dictionary and mispronouncing a good part of what I read. Finally at the end of the first month of our stay John agreed to try some.
>
> To my delight we had enormous success with them. The stories were so entertaining that they led to a much greater effort learning to read than did the [classroom] readers. In fact, studying now became that part of the day that we looked forward to as a special treat. The illustrations greatly aided our understanding of much of the action. . . . An added bonus was the insight these stories gave us to Iranian culture. (F. Schumann & J. Schumann, 1977, p. 245)

Although her experience may not be true for all adults who have used children's books to help them learn to read a second language, it does show how useful they might turn out to be.

Children's books are best chosen by recommendation, or by browsing in libraries and bookstores. Paperback editions are relatively cheap, so that it is possible gradually to build up a handsome library of books.

Learners' own stories

If you lack a published language learner literature, consider making your own. Ask your students to write a series of short compositions in the second language for reading by other students in their own class or lower-level classes. These compositions can be about topics that are familiar to them and likely to be of interest to others, such as:

- an interesting person I know
- a funny thing that happened to me
- a scary experience I once had
- a place I recommend visiting

- my hometown (or, in a multilingual class, my country)

Select the most interesting of these, if possible, using one from each student in the class. Type out each composition, rewriting, editing, and correcting as necessary so that the students' ideas appear in natural language. Add a title and the name of the author. Gloss any difficult language. Over a period of time, you will be able to build up a rather large collection of interesting and readable stories.

If students find writing difficult, or if the number of students in the class is small, and if there is an available computer with word-processing ability, students can individually dictate their stories to the teacher. The following procedure is adapted from one developed by Nancy Lee and Judith Neal (1992–1993) for helping a middle-school child with first language reading difficulties. A student dictates a story and the teacher types it. For students, watching the chosen words appear on the computer screen helps them gain familiarity with the written form of words. It is also an exciting experience. Lee and Neal talk of how their student "glowed with pleasure at choosing words and seeing them appear on the screen" (p. 281).

While the student dictates, the teacher makes oral suggestions for rephrasing or otherwise changing what the student said. If the student agrees with these oral revisions, they are typed as the student watches. At the end, a draft is printed out and given to the student to read over. If the student wishes to add or edit anything, this can be done before the final version of the story is printed out. Stories can be very short at first, but are likely to get longer as the student gets used to the procedure.

Newspapers

Cheap and widely available, newspapers can be a superb resource for intermediate and advanced students, particularly for reading outside the classroom. The layout, content categories (local news, world news, editorials, cartoons, advertisements, and so on), and rhetorical organization (headlines, summary paragraphs, detail paragraphs, ad copy, photo captions, and so on) are broadly similar across many cultures, which makes reading easier.

Newspaper articles tend to be short, which means that readers can quickly get a sense of accomplishment from finishing them. Brevity is also a benefit for less proficient second language readers who tire quickly of reading. In addition, because people typically read only those parts of a paper that interest them, newspapers can quickly be "finished." This is motivating: Second language readers can pick up a newspaper knowing they can successfully be done with it in as long or short a time as they wish.

There is something to interest almost everyone in a newspaper. The content is up to date. Crucially, it may already be familiar to learners if they have read or heard about the same news or topics in their own language. Learners may also be interested in, and thus possess background knowledge in, certain areas (for example, international politics, rock music, or American football). Such knowledge makes it possible for second language readers to make more sense of linguistically difficult material. Prior knowledge and interest in a topic are particularly necessary for lower-level learners.

Extensive reading ideally includes the reading of various materials for different purposes to practice appropriate choice of reading style. The variety of content in a newspaper provides some excellent reading practice of this kind, because different sections encourage reading in different ways. TV listings, sports results, horoscopes, and weather forecasts are an incitement to scanning. Browsing through a newspaper is also natural practice in skimming and scanning. Articles and captions, on the other hand, invite closer and more careful reading for as long as they hold the reader's interest.

Tabloid newspapers, with their shorter articles, may appear well suited to extensive reading. They are designed for first language readers who happen to share some of the same needs as second language readers: They do not want to invest a lot of time and effort in reading, and they want their interest aroused by headlines and images. Major drawbacks for second language readers, however, are unfamiliar colloquial language and pop-culture references.

Quality newspapers are useful for advanced-level students. Although initially less inviting with their acres of dense print, they provide solid pleasure to readers interested in particular topics.

The latest copies of newspapers can be made available for reading "on premises." Older papers could be borrowed by learners. Interested students could clip articles, and gradually assemble scrapbooks of appealing material, perhaps arranged by topics such as fashion and sport. Key vocabulary words can be glossed.

Because they are produced in such quantity, and become out of date the day after they are sold, old newspapers can be obtained virtually free. Foreign language newspapers may be produced or sold in the country where you teach. If not, with a little ingenuity it should be possible to find someone to collect, bundle up, and send you various old newspapers by surface mail from their country of origin.

Magazines

Weekly and monthly magazines are usually colorful and attractive, and their visual emphasis can help readers understand the content. Like newspapers, magazines are more appropriate for intermediate and advanced-level learners. Also like newspapers, magazines are browsed rather than read from cover to cover, and so can be quickly finished. Most magazines can usefully be kept in a library for about a year, after which they start both falling apart and going out of date. Magazines can be checked out by students for reading at home. Together with newspapers, high-interest, illustrated popular magazines can also be made available in lounge areas. This encourages spontaneous reading.

Magazine articles are often longer than those found in a newspaper. Unlike newspapers, which have a variety of content, magazines usually focus on one topic, for example, teen fashion and life, cars, tennis, current events, or heavy metal music. As a result, comparatively few people may be interested in a particular magazine. This means that a variety of magazines may be necessary to appeal to the different members of a second language reading class. The problem is that new magazines are not cheap. If there is no budget for new magazines, back issues can be a good substitute. It is harder to get hold of suitable used magazines, but with some organization it might be possible to get a supply from a local distributor or from contacts overseas.

Sample issues are a good approach to choosing which magazines to subscribe to. Buy a variety of different magazines, paste a sheet of paper on the back cover of each and instruct students to write any comments they might have, including whether they would like to read the magazine regularly and why.

Students can also be encouraged to buy second language magazines in their own area of interest and later make them available to their classmates. Usually, the only necessary encouragement for this is having a period of sustained silent reading during reading class. Students commonly bring second language magazines into this reading period; other classmates invariably notice these and ask to borrow them. With such sharing and cooperation, the class begins to take on the feeling of a reading community.

Children's magazines

Although the preceding category, magazines, is generally suitable for those with at least an intermediate fluency in the second language, there are magazines written for children of various ages, some of which are suitable for less proficient second language learners. They have many illustrations that help reading comprehension, and are attractively put together. Children's magazines also tend to include activities and games, including language games, which can be helpful for second language learners.

For adults, children's magazines may seem too childish to be of interest. Because the nature of an extensive reading approach calls for reader's choice, this is not really a problem. Those adults who are reluctant to read them do not have to.

In the United States, there are hundreds of interesting and informative English language magazines for children. These begin with magazines written for very young children, preschoolers aged 3 to 5, such as *Weekly Reader, Sesame Street Magazine,* and the conservation-oriented *Your Big Backyard.* They are written in language that is very easy to understand and have big, bright pictures, stories designed to be read aloud, and simple puzzles and games. Because they are intended for the very young child who has not yet – or has just – begun to read, the appeal of some of these preliterate magazines to older learners may be rather limited.

Magazines for older age groups have more potential to appeal to both young adults and adults. The style and layout of these magazines are more sophisticated than those for preschoolers. In the United States, for example, *Ranger Rick* (a monthly nature magazine) and the best-selling monthly *Highlights for Children* (motto: "fun with a purpose") are written for children aged approximately 6 to 12; *Cricket,* a world literature and art monthly, is aimed at children aged 7 to 14; *Surfer* ("about surfers, for surfers, by surfers") is aimed at a 10–50 age group (which is not to say that surfers over 50 would not enjoy it too).

In the United States, the Educational Press Association and the International Reading Association publish *Magazines for Kids and Teens,* an introduction and guide edited by Donald Stoll, with more than 200 magazines listed by target age (preschool, primary, middle school, junior high school, high school, and non-age-specific) and by subject (entertainment, ecology, sports, health, news, religion, and many more). Included are ordering addresses and details, and if and how a sample copy may be obtained.

Popular and simple literature

Carefully selected fiction and nonfiction books can be linguistically accessible to intermediate- and advanced-level learners if the books are short and straightforward in content and language. Again, browsing and recommendation are the best source of good titles. If no bibliography is available for the language you teach, you can ask for recommendations through your local teacher's magazine or newsletter.

Young adult literature

There is nothing quite like young adult literature for familiarizing teenage students with another culture. As Lilian Rönnqvist and Roger Sell point out, "A teenage novel can dramatize life in unfamiliar environments as experienced by characters of the learner's own age" (1994, p. 129). Fiction written for young adults can be particularly suitable for extensive reading, as the books are relatively short and have straightforward plots. The content is usually familiar, particularly in the common thriller and slice-of-teenage-life stories. The language, which tends toward the colloquial, can be a problem, but at the same time has its advantages. Rönnqvist and Sell repeatedly make the point that "teenage pupils positively like and want to understand these books, not least because they give access to the colloquial language used by native-speaker teenagers" (p. 125).

Teenage and young adult literature is a genre that produces addictive series and authors. English language series such as *Hardy Boys, Fear Street,* and the *Sweet Valley Twins* and *Sweet Valley High* books that Stephen Krashen has made famous in the ELT world sometimes run to more than a hundred different titles each. Thus, if a student gets hooked on a series, you – the teacher – may, as David Eskey (1995) once said, retire for a martini: Your job is done. Authors such as Judy Blume, Paula Danziger, and R. L. Stine attract a loyal following of English language learners, and some students will want to read everything their favorite author has ever written. Continually being asked to please get some more Judy Blume is the kind of pestering that fills a teacher's heart with joy.

Pages of small print – something even graded readers are sometimes guilty of – are off-putting to the novice reader. Publishers of adolescent literature rarely make that mistake. The books are more than 100 pages in length, but the print is large, the margins generous, and – very important – the chapters short. In sum, young adult literature can be a precious and well-loved resource in the upper reaches of an extensive reading library. It is one that may appeal to postteen adults as well.

Comics

Comic books written for native speakers would seem obvious choices for second language extensive reading because the stories are largely carried by illustrations. Their apparent simplicity may be deceptive, however. Comics are often drawn for readers familiar with the characters and their past adventures. Advanced learners will probably have little trouble with even the most stylized comics, but beginners should probably stick to comics drawn for younger readers.

William Grabe relates his own experiment reading American comic books translated into a second language:

> *Spiderman* was far above my head. It actually was boring . . . and it was impossible to understand. And what I decided was really motivating to me . . . was *Mickey Mouse* and *Donald Duck.* It really works. It's got an easy story line, it's not too hard to follow. It has some clever twists to it and I brought back a nice stack of *Mickey Mouse* and *Donald Duck* from Brazil. (1995)

Translations

A final, often overlooked, but excellent source of extensive reading material is literature that has been translated from the students' first language into the second language. A good example of this, for French speakers studying English as a second language, is *Le Petit Prince* translated into English as *The Little Prince.* The advantages of using such translated materials are several. Students have the necessary background and cultural knowledge to understand the story. An English-speaking colleague studying Japanese, for example, says that she reads Japanese translations of *Harlequin Romance* novels and Robert Parker detective stories because they are relatively easy for her to understand. Another advantage of translated books is that the characters, the plot, and much of the vocabulary will be familiar to the students if they have read the original.

Conclusion

Language learner literature is the first choice of reading material for students at the beginning and intermediate stages of their reading development because it is interesting and attractive and is designed to facilitate laddering up. Purists who complain about adaptations from literature for language learners probably should not. If the language you teach does not have language learner literature, children's first language books and magazines could be an acceptable substitute. Teachers can also help students write their own material for their classmates to read.

Intermediate students can read, in addition to language learner literature, such materials as newspapers, magazines, carefully selected popular and simple literature, young adult literature, comics, and translations of books from their first language.

Familiarity with the types and sources of materials for extensive reading makes possible the planning of a library, which is the next step in realizing an extensive reading program and the subject of the next chapter.

Further reading

A few bibliographies of English language popular and simple literature have been published with second language learners in mind. One of the most well known is Dorothy Brown's *A World of Books: An Annotated Reading List for ESL/EFL Students* (1988), which introduces about 120 worthwhile titles. Not all of these are suitable for out-of-class reading, but about forty of the books are described as particularly short and easy. Another useful list of books and authors can be found in Beatrice Mikulecky's *A Short Course in Teaching Reading Skills* (1990). This list of seventy titles is divided into books suitable for low-intermediate- and high-intermediate-level students. For younger learners, there is Dorothy Brown's *Books for a Small Planet* (1994).

For English as a second language teachers who wish to explore further afield for suitable books, the International Reading Association publishes *Teens' Favorite Books: Young Adults' Choices 1987–1992* and *More Teens' Favorite Books: Young Adults' Choices 1993–1995.* Both describe more than 100 titles chosen by teens themselves, and divided into subjects such as adventure, family life, fantasy and the supernatural, history, mystery and crime, nature, romance, science fiction, and sports. The second of the two publications also contains helpful articles on ways to promote reading. The lists on which these publications are based first appeared in the *Journal of Reading* (now renamed the *Journal of Adolescent and Adult Literacy*). In addition to the annual "best of" list chosen by teens and appearing in the November issue, the journal has monthly book reviews.

Good English language books for children aged 4–13 are similarly introduced in the International Reading Association's *Kids' Favorite Books: Children's Choices 1989–1991,* and the journal *The Reading Teacher,* which has been publishing such lists since 1975. The annual Children's Choice list is divided by age (beginning, 5–8, 8–10, 10–13) and appears in the October issue; and the monthly book reviews include a regular section titled "Books Too Good to Miss." The International Reading Association can be contacted at P.O. Box 8139, Newark, DE 19714–8139, USA.

10 *The extensive reading library*

> [Teachers] have first to ensure that attractive books are available and second to use every trick they know to persuade students to "get hooked on books".
>
> —Christine Nuttall (1996, p. 127)

The purpose of this chapter is to:

- Offer a range of suggestions and options for establishing a library of extensive reading materials.

Unlike other approaches to the teaching of second language reading, which usually involve selecting a textbook on which the lessons are based, an extensive reading program requires no less than a library of appropriate reading materials. Setting up such a library is a formidable undertaking. Major tasks include:

- deciding the size of the program
- making a budget
- determining the students' reading levels
- discovering student interests
- purchasing the reading materials
- cataloging and organizing the materials
- deciding where to place the materials
- setting up a checkout system
- displaying the materials

With so much to do before the first class meets, it is obvious that the planning for an extensive reading program should be done as far in advance of the beginning of the program as possible. A library normally cannot be set up in 1 or 2 months; it can take 6 months or more. We look now at the component tasks in turn.

Deciding the size of the program

As with any first-time endeavor, it is usually wise to start an extensive reading program small. How small to start depends on the number of students that the teacher(s) can easily manage; the amount of money available to cover the initial cost of a library of books; and the amount of time that can be devoted to making the materials ready. When a new program has been up and running a year, it can be expanded to include additional students. By then, teachers or administrators will have found out exactly what is involved, and can plan accordingly.

Making a budget

The school library and staff room may already have some suitable materials for extensive reading – books, newspapers, magazines – and perhaps arrangements can be made for them to be made available to students. It is unlikely, however, that the school library already has the type, range, and quantity of reading materials necessary to get an extensive reading program off the ground. Establishing a budget is therefore fundamental. How many books and other reading materials are necessary to begin the program? How much money is available to meet these needs?

More funds are needed during the first year of operation than subsequently, because most of the books purchased in the first year can be used again in the following years. After the first year, a smaller amount of money will be needed annually to replace books that are lost, worn out, unpopular, or out of date, to purchase new titles, and for any continuing subscriptions to newspapers or magazines. Expansion of a program will also, of course, require a larger initial budget.

If the school budget is insufficient, there are probably ways in which money can be raised outside the school system, including fund-raising events with the help of students and/or parents. Colin Davis relates from experience that "even in developing countries Parent/Teacher Associations have ways of collecting money if they are convinced of the educational benefit to their children of supporting such initiatives" (1995, p. 334).

Another possibility is to ask students to contribute the cost of one or two books in the form of a library fee. In return for this small individual outlay, the students are able to read a whole library of books. At the end of the year, the class can be asked to donate the books to the library. Whenever books are contributed by groups or individuals, the names of the donors can be placed inside the books.

The cost of books is a basic item of information in establishing a budget. Locally produced books may be cheaper than imported ones. The most suitable books should always be purchased, however, even if this means buying fewer books overall.

The minimum number of books to begin an extensive reading library is one book of suitable level per student, with perhaps ten extra books in addition to this. In order to allow plenty of choice, however, it is ideal to have two, three, or four different books for each student in a class. Beginning with double the number of books as there are students is realistic. With this solid beginning, the library can gradually grow as the years go by.

Determining the students' reading levels

Any group of students will display a range of levels of language ability and reading fluency, even though they may have all studied the second language for an equal amount of time. In an extensive reading program, it is easy to accommodate everyone because reading materials appropriate for a wide variety of levels can – and should – be ordered.

Unless students are advanced, obtain materials of all linguistic levels, beginning with the simplest language learner literature. But the bulk of the books should be a little below the level of the language the students are dealing with in class so that they may be read without the help of teacher or dictionary.

Experienced teachers will already have an intuitive feel for the language their students are able to handle. Those who do not can examine the texts that students use in class. This should give a fairly good feel for the vocabulary students have encountered and the structures they have studied.

Publishers usually mark their language learner literature as suitable for a particular level of learner – beginner or intermediate, for example – and this can help teachers locate books that are of approximately the right level for their students. Teachers can then give students samples of reading material – single reproduced pages from different books – and ask students to mark the words on the page they do not know. From this information it is possible to gauge accurately how appropriate particular books are for particular students. If several students read the same page and mark no unknown words, or just one or two, then that material is of approximately the right level for extensive reading. If there are many more unknown words, reading the book will probably be frustrating, demotivating, and less than useful for developing reading fluency.

Discovering student interests

Teachers are sometimes keen for students to read classical literature or other books of literary value rather than anything students would be likely to read on their own. Without wanting to dismiss such educational goals, second language extensive reading may not be the best context for such endeavors. The purpose, after all, is to get students to read as much, as often, and as willingly as possible. The easiest way to do this is to follow the example of popular culture and appeal to students on their own terms. For students to learn to read, they must, as far as possible, want to read. As John Klapper warns, "if we move too far from our learners' natural sphere of interest we run the risk of making extended reading a meaningless chore" (1992, p. 54).

Many teachers are well enough in tune with their students to know what those students will and will not find interesting to read. Teachers who are not sure can observe or ask what – if anything – their students read in their first language. They can also pay attention to what their students talk about and do in their free time.

If intuition, observation, and informal questioning are not enough to determine student interests, then more formal means can be used. Teachers can make a questionnaire to be answered by the students who are to be in the extensive reading program, or a similar group of students.

Interests questionnaire

The questionnaire can be either in the students' own language or in the second language. Questions should be not only about what students want to read in the second language, but also about the students' first language reading, and their hobbies, clubs, and free-time activities. This avoids any problem of students reporting about what they think they ought to read (or what they think the teacher wants to hear) rather than about what they actually do enjoy reading. One group of adult students in Japan unanimously chose "nonfiction" in a questionnaire asking them what they wished to read. When asked what they read in their own language, however, they answered comic books and general fiction. This relates perhaps to the notorious macho maxim of second language reading instruction: *no reading pain, no reading gain.* Students must realize that when it comes to learning to read, it is what is easy and enjoyable that is beneficial.

There are two broad types of questionnaire. A ranking questionnaire presents students with a series of choices and asks them to indicate their preferences. For example:

1. I enjoy movies which are about
   a. __ science fiction
   b. __ romance or love
   c. __ sports
   d. __ children
   e. __ animals

Students are told to put "1" beside their favorite choice, and so on until all items are ranked. Alternatively, they simply check those items that interest them. Ranking questionnaires are simple to analyze: It is just a matter of counting. Data are concrete and numerical, so trends and patterns can easily be seen. The disadvantage of this type of questionnaire, however, is that the teacher must already have some idea of what the students like in order to design questions that are comprehensive. Ranking questionnaires yield only relative rankings of the information they contain. One way to get around this problem is to involve the students themselves in designing the questionnaire.

An open-ended questionnaire asks students to list their favorite choices. For example:

1. What kind of movies do you enjoy?
2. What do you like to do in your spare time?
3. What do you and your friends talk about when you are having lunch?
4. What sorts of books do you read (in your own language)?

It is easier to prepare such a questionnaire as there is no danger of leaving out important answer choices. Answers, however, may be so diverse that it is hard to categorize and interpret them. A recommended option, therefore, is to combine the two types of questionnaire into a single instrument containing questions of both types.

The appeal of reading material has to do not only with the subjects being written about, however. Many books are popular simply because the stories are compelling and hard to put down. A bibliography of recommended titles, such as the Appendix to this book, can help you select books that your students will probably enjoy regardless of their particular interests. Local publishers' representatives may also be able to recommend books that are popular with the type of students you teach.

Purchasing the reading materials

After deciding what topics and kinds of books will probably interest the students, the next step is to select and buy the material. For schoolbooks, multiple copies of the same book (class sets) are usually ordered. An extensive reading library, on the other hand, requires as many different titles as possible in order to give students as much choice as possible. It is therefore a good idea to purchase only one copy of each book or magazine initially.

If the material is to be obtained from outside the country in which the program is located, advance planning is essential. It can take as long as 6 months for materials to arrive from abroad.

Cataloging and organizing the materials

As soon as they arrive, books and other materials must be listed in a master inventory. This allows you to check the collection regularly for loss or damage.

Next comes the task of organizing the collection by language level. Newspapers and magazines do not need to be so categorized, but it is essential that students have a way of knowing which books are linguistically suitable for them. Teachers may have to do a lot of reading in order to decide the levels to assign the books in the library. Again, teachers can copy a page from a book and ask students to underline the unknown words as an aid in determining difficulty level. Ordinary books for native speakers can be categorized as "easy," "average," and "hard" with an appropriate identifying mark.

If you are able to use language learner literature, the publishers have taken a lot of the burden out of organizing a library. Books will already be assigned a difficulty level. The problem is that each publisher has its own system of determining levels. If you use books from different publishers, you need to make your own master system of levels, for example, beginner, low-intermediate, high-intermediate, and advanced. Alternatively, adopt the level system of a major series and work out where books from other series fit into it.

Choose a number or color for each level in your library and attach a sticker on the cover of each book indicating its level. Books should be divided and shelved according to these levels.

The Appendix offers a master system of levels developed by the Edinburgh Project on Extensive Reading for language learner literature published in English. Books for native speakers can be fitted in at the top of this system, with "easy" books at level B, "average" at level A, and "hard" at level X.

Deciding where to place the materials

Where should the reading materials be located? How should they be monitored? The conflicting concerns here are security and access. Reading materials are expensive, and precious funds should not be wasted in replacing lost or stolen materials. On the other hand, overly restricting access to the materials makes it hard for students to browse and select reading matter that interests them – a key aspect of an extensive reading program.

A major aim of an extensive reading program is to create an environment where reading is encouraged. At the same time, you need to be realistic. Can newspapers and magazines be placed in a lounge area where students gather and relax? Can books be on open shelves or should they be locked up when a teacher is not present? Can students be trusted to check out books properly by themselves (by filling out a library card or notebook, for example), or do they need to be supervised by staff or student monitors? You must answer these questions as best you can before the program begins, or discover the answers by trial and (possibly expensive) error afterward.

One basic question is where to shelve the books. There are three alternatives within a school, each with advantages and disadvantages: the school library, a classroom library, and a delivery system.

The school library

The school library is the obvious place to keep most of the materials. One major advantage is that security and checkout become the responsibility of the library. Planning and organization become straightforward because the collection is subject to the same rules and regulations that apply to all library material. If your school has a library, you may consider asking for its cooperation. There is a severe limit to the extra work that already busy teachers can take on. And, believe us, running a library is a lot of extra work. The school library is an option, however, only if they agree to shelve the extensive reading materials in a separate section. If the materials are scattered all over the library by subject, the students will never find them.

One problem with using the school library is that the materials may be less accessible than the teacher wants them to be, especially during reading class. Another drawback is that students tend to use the library individually. This makes it difficult for them to suggest books to each other, and the excitement and stimulation of hands-on recommendation are lost. It also makes it harder for teachers to observe individual students engaged in the crucial activities of browsing and choosing books. When books disappear into a central library, so do important aspects of a reading program.

A classroom library

Some effective extensive reading programs place the materials in their classrooms. A classroom library allows students immediate access to the materials, especially during the time when the reading class is meeting.

Books can be freely obtained or changed during sustained silent reading periods. A classroom library also makes it easier for students to share reactions and recommendations, and for teachers to note any problems that students may have in selecting books.

The books in a classroom library can be locked up safely or be on open display in a library corner. If magazines, newspapers, or attractive scrapbooks of light reading material are available, they are likely to be picked up and browsed before and after class.

A delivery system

If more than one class use the same books, a delivery system should be considered. This involves placing the materials in a box or cart that can be moved easily from room to room. When not needed in a particular classroom, this movable feast of reading matter can be strategically located, for example, in a lounge or teachers' room, depending on security considerations.

These three options – school library, classroom library, and delivery system – are for school-based programs. Teachers who work on a more independent basis will probably deal with books in a different way.

A teacher's private library

Teachers who work on a freelance basis may decide to use extensive reading in one or more classes, perhaps in different schools. Such teachers may purchase and carry books to their classes, displaying them by spreading them out on a desk. Roberta Welch, teaching English in Tokyo, Japan, shares such an experience.

> I decided to start a library for my small classes of working adults. . . . I started with one class of company men and one women's class of government employees. Trying to consider my students' interests, I bought some of the most highly recommended books from [a bibliography of books for language learners]. . . . Because the books are small and light, it is not burdensome for me to carry them around to my various classes. . . . By now I have about 35 books which I am circulating in several classes, including a housewives' class and a small university class. Some students have really gotten the "reading bug" and even buy their own books, which they are willing to share with other class members. (October 1986, personal communication)

Welch's comments, incidentally, are an example of the principle of starting small when setting up a library or an extensive reading program.

Setting up a checkout system

Unless books are shelved in a central library, teachers need to make simple rules about the length of time a book can be checked out, the number of titles a student can check out at one time, and any penalties for late or lost books. Some programs successfully use students to assist in monitoring material. For example, one student or a group of students can be designated as librarians for a set period of time. With the teacher's assistance and prior training, they are responsible for making sure materials are checked out properly and returned on time. Student monitors can be very good at this. In a paper titled "How to Set Up a Class Reading Library," Sheila Cliffe notes that "students who would ignore their teacher's pleas to bring back the books tend to respond to peer pressure" (1990, p. 29). Similarly, Christine Nuttall advises teachers, "Students often know who has borrowed a 'missing' book and can recover it more easily than you" (1996, p. 139).

The standard system for checking out books is to paste a pocket in the inside back cover of each book. Inside the pocket, a library card is placed on which is written the title of the book. The card has spaces for students to write their names, school numbers, and the date the book was borrowed. When a book is checked out, the card is removed and kept in an index box. Sets of library cards and self-adhesive pockets can be purchased, or they can be fashioned from used envelopes and card stock. An alternative is a notebook in which each student has one or two blank pages for writing the titles of books borrowed, date borrowed, and date returned.

If magazines or newspapers can be borrowed overnight or for longer periods, the simplest method is a one-notebook checkout system. Students write their names, the name of the item, and the date borrowed on one line of the notebook. When they return the item, they check a column, or cross off their name.

Displaying the materials

It is an axiom of the retail business that attractively displayed goods draw customers. Think about an eye-catching display of fruit or vegetables. It is much more appealing than boxes of produce sitting on shelves. It is no different in a library. Students are drawn to materials that are well displayed and accessible.

The books are best displayed so that their front covers are visible. This is particularly important for language learner literature as the books are thin and may not even have a title printed on the spine. Christine Nuttall, in Chapter 8 of her *Teaching Reading Skills in a Foreign Language* (1996), offers several alternatives for displaying books – most involving hammer, nails, and wood. You do not have to go to those lengths, however, to create an attractive display. Books can be stood inside sturdy cardboard or plastic cartons of appropriate size, the front covers facing forward. The books may then be flipped through as one used to flip through albums in a record store.

In larger libraries, in addition to shelving the books by level, you may also want to divide books into other categories. Fiction and nonfiction are obvious choices. Another favorite is to keep popular books in a special section.

Conclusion

Good libraries are not made overnight, but you must start somewhere. In sum:

- Start small.
- Start preparations early.
- More money is needed in the first year than in later years because, once bought, most books can be used again.
- Buy materials at all levels of difficulty, but basically a little below the students' linguistic level.
- Buy one of each book, not multiple copies, so that the library is as varied as possible.
- If you do not know what your students would enjoy reading, ask them.
- To create an environment that encourages reading, newspapers, magazines, and books should be as accessible as possible while remaining secure from loss or theft.
- Mark all books by linguistic level.
- Decide whether the books will be placed in the school library (less work but less accessible) or in a classroom library (more work but more accessible).
- Display the materials as attractively as possible.

A library is an environment of possibilities that springs to life only when used. How to introduce students to reading material and reading in general is the subject of the next chapter.

Further reading

Colin Davis illustrates how a library can be established in even the most disadvantageous conditions in a 1995 article, "Extensive Reading: An Expensive Extravagance?" (He answers his own question with a resounding "No!") "In Cameroon, one book basket has to cater to a whole year, and so it is passed from class to class, with no opportunity for private reading at home" (p. 332).

Roger Cunningham details other constraints and how to work around them in his article "The Zanzibar English Reading Programme":

> Most classrooms are built with half-walls to allow light and ventilation, and have no doors or windows. This openness precludes shelves or display racks, making any permanent presence of books impossible. There are no secure cupboards to accommodate books, so "library corners" are not possible. CL [classroom library] boxes have to be brought from the store, staffroom or office to the classroom for each CL lesson, and displayed on tables. (1991, p. 672)

In the first edition of Christine Nuttall's book *Teaching Reading Skills in a Foreign Language* (1982), Chapter 12, "An Extensive Reading Programme" (pp. 167–191), is particularly strong on the details of setting up a library. That the chapter is almost unchanged in the 1996 edition of the book (now Chapter 8, pp. 127–148) may be initially disappointing, but it does show how the practical suggestions have stood the test of time. Nuttall enthusiasts will also be pleased to note that the frogs-in-the-library anecdote remains intact on page 134.

11 *Student orientation*

It is important to convince students of the value of extensive reading.

—Beatrice Dupuy, Lucy Tse, and Tom Cook (1996, p. 10)

The purpose of this chapter is to:

- Stress the importance of orienting students to an extensive reading approach.
- Offer suggestions for an orientation to an extensive reading program.

"Browsing newspapers, looking at soccer and fashion magazines, and reading mystery stories? Isn't this just goofing off? What has it got to do with school? I want to be taught!"

This would be a natural reaction from serious students who have not been told why they are doing what they are doing. Think about your students and how they have been previously taught second languages in general, and second language reading in particular. How are they likely to react to any changes you make in their reading classes and homework assignments? Innovations in teaching must be explained to students, and extensive reading is no exception.

An extensive reading program may be a challenge for students to understand for a number of reasons. Some of these relate to the students' beliefs about reading deriving from their first language culture, while others are linked to the students' previous experiences learning second language reading.

Mismatches between culturally derived attitudes toward reading and extensive reading can be serious, beginning with a basic unwillingness to read. Catherine Wallace points out that "the whole idea of reading silently and alone for pleasure may be a culturally alien one for many groups" (1992, p. 20). For example, "students who come from communities with limited literacy among the population may downplay the importance of literacy skills and do little extensive reading" (Grabe, 1991, p. 389). In addition, students from cultures in which written texts represent "truth" will find it hard to embrace a methodology that grants the reader as much authority as the text or teacher. Such students will likely be uncomfortable deciding which texts to read and their purposes for reading them. They will also resist the freedom to make of the texts what they will, including the option of stopping reading.

Even students from societies in which literacy includes extensive reading may not be able to extend such ideas to the reading of foreign language texts. Mary Lee Field, in a 1985 report, found that Chinese teachers of English when reading Chinese "use reading strategies and skills just like the ones used by native English speakers when reading in their own language" (p. 175). However, when Field asked them whether it was possible to transfer these first language skills to reading in English, they reported that "it was not possible, not even thinkable" (p. 175). For such students, incidentally, extensive reading can be just what is needed to help them see foreign language reading as "reading," that is, something that they do in their own language and not as an exotic pursuit or an academic exercise.

For other students, prior experience of learning second language reading may predispose them against extensive reading. Students who have been taught translation or reading skills will probably be conditioned to take as much time as necessary to understand every word of a text. Traditional methods of teaching reading also link progress and success with effort and hard work, with the result that students may not be able to accept the reading of a great deal of relatively easy material as a legitimate academic activity. Reading "with no slaving over a hot dictionary . . . may appear frivolous and a waste of time" (Bamford, 1984, p. 223). More specifically, students in a second language university preparation program may rebel against what seems to them to be a waste of valuable time. They may see no link between reading large quantities of easy material and equipping themselves with the skills to succeed academically. Finally, students used to traditional roles of both teachers and students may be confused and ill at ease in a program where teachers do not so much teach as guide, and students make many of their own decisions, such as what, when, and where to read.

All these reasons point to the necessity of a sensitive, careful orientation to the goals and methodology of extensive reading at the start of a program – what Beatrice Dupuy, Lucy Tse, and Tom Cook call "laying the groundwork" for extensive reading (1996, p. 10). Experience has also shown that this orientation process needs to be continued in various ways at appropriate intervals throughout the course until the students have truly made the principles and goals of extensive reading their own. At the same time, particularly in heterogeneous second language classrooms, certain students will have a harder time than others internalizing an extensive reading approach, and teachers may have to work harder to help these students get the most out of the program.

An orientation tells students what they will do and why they will be doing it. Topics covered should include the goals and procedures of the program and the principles that underlie them, as well as an introduction to the reading materials and their availability. Let us look at the topics of the orientation in more detail.

The goals of the program

It is a good idea to give the students an overview of the goals of the extensive reading program, as many of these are different from goals of other approaches to the teaching of second language reading. One of the primary goals of an extensive reading program is for students to become fluent readers through building their sight vocabulary. No matter what kind of reading students aspire to be able to do – technical or academic reading, for example – a large sight vocabulary is a necessary foundation for reading as native speakers do. This basic ability underpins all reading, but because it is an automatic process, it may be a somewhat abstract notion to try to explain to students. Instead, it can be said, in more concrete and exact terms, that the extensive reading program will provide practice in

- making meaning directly from a text without translation
- knowing the purpose for which one is reading, because different purposes require different ways of reading
- "going for meaning," that is, remaining focused on the overall meaning of what is being read without getting sidetracked by unfamiliar language or ideas
- guessing at or ignoring unfamiliar language or difficult ideas
- reading at an appropriate speed for one's purpose
- being satisfied, when appropriate, with less than total comprehension

Students can be told that they will practice all these things and, as a result, will grow to have increased confidence and ability to read in the second language. For some students, it will be enough to say that the goals of the program are for them to become fluent readers and to enjoy reading in the second language.

The procedures of the program

Students should be made familiar with another major difference between an extensive reading program and other second language reading approaches: its procedure of requiring students to read a large quantity of easy texts. It might be helpful to explain that the principle behind this is that you get better at what you practice, or "you learn to read by reading." Advise students that struggling through a second language text, mentally translating it into one's own language in order to understand it, is not true reading.

Tell students that, in order to practice reading, second language texts must be read in the same way as first language texts. Students need to know that this can only be accomplished by reading easy material because their second language ability is less than their first language ability. At this point, the macho maxim of second language reading instruction – *no reading pain, no reading gain* – might be explained and debunked and the motto of extensive reading substituted: *reading gain without reading pain.*

Self-selection of materials

Another procedure to be addressed is the matter of students selecting their own reading material. The responsibility this entails can be unsettling to students who have always been told by teachers what, when, where, and how to read. Other students may not have basic familiarity with second language reading materials and may have to be introduced to their features, for example, the back-cover blurb that summarizes a book, the list of chapter titles at the front that can give the reader a general idea of what to expect, and, in some books, the glossary at the back.

Students should be aware that they should choose material that can be read with ease and comfort. They might be told that you will be helping them in the beginning to select material that matches their reading abilities but that in the end they are the ones who determine what they read.

Part of this initial orientation to self-selection can be phrased in terms of vocabulary. Just as there are few words that the students do not know when they read in their own language, in order for them to be able to read naturally there should be no more than a few words that they do not know when they read in the second language. Students need a quick strategy to help them determine if a book is within their comfort zone for extensive reading. One way is to open the book at random and read a page, counting the words that are not known. The book can be read comfortably if there are no more than a certain number of unknown words on the page. For beginners, one unknown word per page is more than enough. Other students can use the *rule of hand*—no more than five unknown words on the sample page (one word for each digit).

No dictionaries

Directly related to the issue of unknown words is the role of the ubiquitous dictionary. As strange as it may seem to students, they should be aware that, in terms of reading, it is unnatural to be looking up words constantly in the dictionary.

But students think of dictionaries as a linguistic lifeline. They will wonder how they can survive without them. And why would they want to try? You can remind them that it is no fun to be looking up words constantly while reading and, besides, it breaks the reader's concentration. In addition, constant dictionary use means that students read less: You could mention that a study found that a group of students using dictionaries took almost twice as long to read a short story as did another group that did not use dictionaries (Luppescu & Day, 1993).

Of equal importance, students should understand that they must learn the techniques of fluent reading. This involves guessing the meaning of, or ignoring, the unknown words they inevitably encounter when reading in a second language. If they are ever to become fluent readers, they must train themselves to be comfortable with ambiguity. Remind students of what they do when they meet an unfamiliar word when reading in their own language. Most times, they are satisfied either to guess at or to ignore the word, and to look it up in a dictionary only as a rare last resort. Learning second language vocabulary is important, but it cannot be allowed to get in the way of learning to read. Students must realize that they are practicing reading, not learning vocabulary. When the two are incompatible in reading class, reading must take priority.

A simple and graphic way of explaining the differences between extensive reading and other approaches to the teaching of reading is to build up a chart on the chalkboard as in Figure 1 (based on Roberta Welch, 1997). The chart can be in the second language, or in the student's native language. Without devaluing intensive forms of teaching reading, the goals and features of extensive reading are introduced and compared with the kinds of reading instruction that the students may be used to.

Finally, the intensive column is erased and it is explained that extensive reading is what is going to be practiced. As Welch explains:

> With this brief introduction the students come to understand that the class will be conducted differently from their other reading classes. They should realize

Intensive	*Type of reading*	*Extensive*
Read accurately	Class goal	Read fluently
Translate Answer questions	Reading purpose	Get information Enjoy
Words and pronunciation	Focus	Meaning
Often difficult Teacher chooses	Material	Easy You choose
Not much	Amount	A lot
Slower	Speed	Faster
Must finish Use dictionary	Method	Stop if you don't like it No dictionary

Figure 1 Chart contrasting intensive and extensive reading.

that although extensive reading is not a method that they are used to, it is in-ended to help them develop into more fluent foreign language readers. (1997, p. 53)

Reading requirements

If there are any requirements, tell the students what they are: how many books or pages they must read and what reports they must write, and how fulfilling the requirements relates to grades. Remember, you will be asking them to read more than they have probably ever done before in the second language. A book a week may seem impossible for students whose only prior experience of reading the target language is translation, or the reading of short passages followed by answering comprehension questions and doing exercises.

Reassure mutinous students that the requirements you have set are indeed achievable. Make this clear by stating exactly how much time students should spend on homework every day or week. Add that they will not need to spend any more time than this on reading or writing. This, of course, will be an amount of homework that they are used to.

Explain what will be done in class. Make sure that students understand how any unusual class activities relate to the goals of the program. The reason for in-class sustained silent reading, for example, is the view – widely held by experts – that one learns to read by reading. Reading silently and individually in class is therefore one of the most appropriate activities that could be done in a reading class.

Reading materials

Introduce the newspapers, magazines, and books that are available for reading. Explain the system of difficulty levels in which the books are arranged, and how to identify the different levels. Clarify where the materials will be kept and which can be checked out, including how long they can be kept and any penalties for late return.

The orientation can conclude with some helpful hints:

- Reading easier material is better than reading harder material.
- Reading a lot is better than reading a little.
- Reading what you enjoy is better than reading what you think you ought to read.
- To stop reading a book you do not like is better than plowing on.

Conclusion

An orientation to an extensive reading program for students can include the following elements as appropriate:

- Principles and theory
  - We learn to read by reading
  - Research results
- Goals
  - To develop a large sight vocabulary
  - To increase general vocabulary knowledge
  - To enjoy reading
- Procedure
  - Reading large quantities of self-selected, easy texts
  - Reading fluently without a dictionary
  - Class activities (e.g., sustained silent reading, oral book reports)
- Requirements
  - Specific amount to be read
  - Records and reports to be written
- Materials
  - The system of levels (grades)
  - Availability and checkout procedures

Based on past experiences of second language reading, many students will not be expecting pleasure, ease, or success when doing extensive reading. They will have to take your word for it at first that what you are asking is not only possible but straightforward and even enjoyable. With proper initial orientation and ongoing guidance, however, students will – sooner rather than later, it is hoped – learn from experience. You will know they have done so when they say, as Rebecca Constantino's student did, "'You know, it's like you said, I know how to read, I just have to read in English like I normally read and I will be OK'" (1995, p. 69).

12 *Building a community of readers*

> Teachers must create within each classroom a positive atmosphere, a way of life conducive to promoting reading through positive affect.
> —Edward Dwyer and Evelyn Dwyer (1994, p. 72)

The purpose of this chapter is to:

- Offer suggestions for classroom activities in support of extensive reading.
- Explain how the teacher can begin to transform the reading classroom into a reading community.

This chapter focuses on the evolution of the extensive reading classroom into a reading community whose members value and engage in reading. The chapter opens with a discussion of the need for continuing guidance and counseling. Then a number of classroom activities that can be used to help create an environment supportive of reading are presented. The chapter closes with a discussion of the importance of the teacher serving as a role model.

Ongoing class guidance

The apparently relaxed atmosphere of an extensive reading program does not mean that learners are simply left to their own devices. Without encouragement of one sort or another to read in the second language, students may gradually lose interest. Apparent lack of concern on the part of the teacher about what and how much students are reading is a sure recipe for the demise of a program, and for good books to go to waste unread on library shelves.

Guidance, therefore, should not end with the initial orientation of students to extensive reading. Old habits die hard and old prejudices are hard to break. Pieter Nelson's experience, although not while teaching extensive reading, is indicative of what second language reading teachers can be up against. In spite of his best efforts, Nelson had to concede that

> very little progress has been made in encouraging the students to adopt a more casual attitude towards text. They remain very dissatisfied if a text is abandoned before they have understood every word, feeling that the teacher has cheated them in some way by not finishing the job. If the text is not analysed exhaustively in the classroom, the keener students take it home and subject it to the standard dictionary-translation approach. One semester seems too short a period to break them of this habit, firmly established during their school careers. (1984, p. 195)

The form of an extensive reading program – reading easier texts for general understanding in quantities too great to make translation an option – may help break such habits in behavioral terms. But as the example just cited makes clear, dedicated students may need reassurance that extensive reading is indeed the path for them to become fluent, effective readers. Teachers must keep a close eye on students' reading habits and emerging attitudes, particularly early in a program, and offer guidance as necessary. In Wayne Otto's view, "The essential point is that teachers need to give explicit, systematic, and persistent attention to helping novice readers – mainly by setting aside sufficient time and providing guidance in selection of appropriate materials – to attain fluency/automaticity" (1991, p. 97).

In more general terms, no matter how thoroughly a teacher has explained an extensive reading program to students, there are always things that need to be emphasized or added from time to time in the following weeks based on observing students read, and listening to and reading their reports. Such guidance can occasionally be offered to the whole class. Teachers should keep a record of what is said, in order to amend the initial orientation as necessary for next year's students.

Individual counseling

Students vary greatly in their reactions to extensive reading, and so benefit from individual attention. Counseling can be done informally through the teacher's written or spoken response to a student's book reports or reading logs, if these are used. It can also be done formally by setting aside time for the teacher to meet briefly with each student individually on a rotating basis.

Counseling is a chance for teachers to ask students about their reading experiences and to deal with any problems that students might be having. It may also be an opportunity to recommend specific books to students. Tricia Hedge sums up the role of the teacher-as-counselor: "to advise, assist, remedy, widen the student's interests and encourage him to analyse his own reading experience by talking about the books he has read" (1985, p. 95).

If formal and regular counseling is decided on, a checklist of questions might be useful. Questions that teachers can ask students include the following:

- Do you enjoy reading?
- What kind of books do you like?
- What books have you enjoyed recently?
- Do you have any problems with or worries about reading?
- About how long does it usually take you to finish reading a library book?

If notes are kept, it is interesting to compare the answers of a student at the beginning, during, and at the end of an extensive reading program. Such notes may also be useful when evaluating an extensive reading program.

In-class activities

Various classroom activities can further extensive reading and help students begin to see reading as a valuable, exciting, pleasurable, and worthwhile activity. All the following activities are suitable for any level of linguistic or reading ability.

Sustained silent reading (SSR)

Students and teacher silently read books or other material of their choice. Everyone in the room is reading something different. Giving students valuable class time in which to read is one of the things that teachers can do to demonstrate the value of reading and to establish a reading community. As Patricia Cunningham and James Cunningham express it:

> Sustained silent reading was a great idea because it made it possible to have real reading going on in real classrooms. Sustained silent reading has as its critical components the notions of reader choice of material, time to read, no reports or other "extrinsic" motivation for reading, and the need for any adults present to demonstrate the importance of reading by reading also. (1991, p. 46)

Richard Robinson and Joycelin Hulett view sustained silent reading as "highly motivational because it encourages reading that is meaningful to the individual as opposed to reading as an academic subject" (1991, p. 106).

The time set aside for sustained silent reading, also called DEAR (Drop Everything And Read) and USSR (Uninterrupted Sustained Silent Reading), can be anywhere from 15 or 20 minutes to the whole class period.

While students are engaged in silent reading, teachers have various options for how to spend this time. There is much to be gained if teachers can spend half or all of the silent reading period reading just as their students are. As Beatrice Dupuy, Tom Cook, and Lucy Tse explained in a TESOL 1995 workshop, "Turning ESL Students into Fluent Readers": "It is . . . important that students who are not accustomed to pleasure reading see other people enjoying it, especially an authority figure like the teacher" (1995, p. 3). Nonnative second language teachers can read the same kinds of books that their students are reading. Native-speaking teachers can also do this, or read in a foreign language they are learning or already know.

Silent reading in class can also give teachers a chance to observe individual students reading. Who seems to be concentrating? Who is sleepy? Who cannot settle down and keeps changing books? Who is a fast reader? A slow reader? Gathered over time, this kind of information is invaluable in helping teachers counsel and guide students in overcoming whatever barriers they face in order to get the most out of reading.

Teachers may want to be available to answer questions from individual students during part of the silent reading period. If students ask the meaning of a word, the teacher can either answer or suggest that the student guess or ignore the word. The questions a student asks can tell the teacher about that student's way of reading, and how well matched the student is with the reading material.

Some teachers use the silent reading period for individual student counseling. This is possible if the silent reading period is longer rather than shorter, and if the quiet teacher-student conversations do not disturb the other students who are reading.

What teachers should definitely *not* use the silent reading period for is office, with the possible exception of checking students' book reports or reading notebooks. As Dupuy, Cook, and Tse explain:

> The students need to know that the teacher takes this time seriously, and if we use the time to grade papers or prepare our lessons, the students will get the sense that SSR is busywork and are less likely to see its value. (1995, p. 3)

Conversely, what students should not do is use silent reading time to catch up with their homework from other classes that involves reading in the second language. The teacher can make this clear, at the same time encouraging students to bring to class other appropriate second language reading material they might wish to read.

Browsing and choosing

If books are shelved in the classroom, time can be set aside for students to browse and select books to check out. Again, this offers a chance for teachers to mingle and observe the modus operandi of individual students. On what basis do they seem to be choosing books? Is there healthy cooperation, with students recommending books to each other and helping each other choose? Who seems to be having trouble? Some students may not know how to go about choosing a book, and may need assistance from the teacher or other students.

Teachers read aloud to students

"Students," claim Nancy Lee and Judith Neal, "do not outgrow having teachers read aloud to them daily" (1992–1993, p. 281). Although Lee and Neal were referring to middle-school students, students of all ages – adults included – enjoy listening to stories. For beginners, especially those learning a language with a different script, being regularly read aloud to at the same time as silently reading the written text helps build sound/symbol correspondences and helps students feel comfortable in the alien print environment.

There are also more general benefits. Tiey Huay Yong and Saraswarthy Idamban (1997) report that reading aloud to their primary students in Singapore resulted in an increase in overall language proficiency, including listening comprehension. Catherine Pegolo found evidence to suggest that reading aloud to American university students learning French helped them acquire a "feel" for the rhythm of the target language (1985, p. 323). Pegolo believes that this can help the students learn how to read in chunks or meaningful sense groups, in contrast to the typical word-for-word strategy.

Reading aloud can be an initial strategy in promoting extensive reading, as Robin Smith reports in a fascinating article about a secondary school in Brunei (1997). In part because the students came from a nonreading culture, it was decided to use reading aloud as a way of introducing students to reading. Moreover, reading aloud fit in well with the oral tradition of the students' culture.

In any reading program, read-alouds can be a way of introducing students to genres, authors, and worthwhile books that they may not initially be attracted to. It can also allow students to appreciate more difficult prose and poetry.

The procedure is straightforward. Teachers read aloud to students while the students follow along, silently reading transparencies on an overhead projector or their own copies of the text. This latter requires a class set of books or photocopied text, at least one copy per two students. The length of time for reading aloud depends on the age of the students, their linguistic level, and the interest of the material. Teachers quickly learn to be sensitive to the attention span of their students. Never be afraid to abandon a reading that just is not working.

Read-aloud material should usually be at the same linguistic level at which most of the students are reading. Other criteria include the interests of students as well as of the teacher. The material can be as short as a poem or as long as a short story or brief chapter of a book. If a teacher copies only a small part of a book and hands out and reads this to the class, there may be a stampede afterward to borrow that book by students whose appetites have been whetted.

If a whole book is read in installments, a good choice of material is a fiction story with a dramatic or exciting progression of events – a thriller or romance, for example. Such books often have built-in suspense at the end of each chapter, which means that students will look forward to the continuation of the story in the next class. (Be sure to collect all copies of the book at the end of the reading so suspense is maintained!)

It is a good idea to prepare a very short, three- or four-sentence "the story so far" summary before each new part of a serial story is read aloud. This reviews the key topic vocabulary of the story, and those items can be listed on the chalkboard. The summary also ensures that students absent from the previous class are up to speed. Finally, the teacher's summary can act as a model for students who themselves have to summarize stories for written or oral reports. An option after listening to a segment of the story is for students to write answers to one or two comprehension questions.

Teachers who are not native speakers of the second language may be reluctant to read aloud to their students. In such situations, teachers can use professional audio recordings or ask colleagues who are native speakers of the second language to record some appropriate material, which can be played in class for students. Even native speakers may sometimes prefer to avail themselves of professional readers on audiocassette. The students read along silently as usual as they listen to the tape.

A less than perfect command of the second language or a less than skilled ability to read aloud should not deter teachers, however. Teachers – perhaps especially nonnative-speaking teachers – who get into the habit of reading aloud to their class act as role models for their students by sharing their love of reading. Whether the material read is a book, an article, a poem, or a paragraph, when read aloud the focus is on the material and the teacher's appreciation of it, not on the reader's shortcomings. The message being given to students is: Reading is important enough to do and share.

Repeated timed readings

For this exercise aimed at developing sight vocabulary, each student uses a book she or he is reading. If a student is between books, any book or material at an appropriate level will do.

Students make a light pencil mark at the point they want to begin reading. At the teacher's signal, students read silently at a comfortable pace until the teacher tells them to stop, after 2 or 3 minutes. The students mark their books, this time where they stopped reading. They then return to the beginning mark and the teacher announces the start of another identical time period. The students read the same part of the book for a second time until the teacher calls time. Students, who generally have read well beyond the point at which they first stopped, again mark their stopping place. The process is done a third time. Again, at the end of the time period, students will probably have read even further.

To be effective in building both automaticity and confidence, this exercise should be done on a regular basis. Students should be told not to skim but to read for meaning each of the three times they read. In contrast to most activities that have as their goal the development of sight vocabulary, this exercise is individualized and noncompetitive. Students read at their own pace, not against the rest of the class but only challenging themselves to become more fluent readers.

Repeated timed readings can be an ideal way of opening a period of sustained silent reading. At the end of the third timed period, students simply continue reading.

Rereading the same material

An activity similar to repeated timed reading is repeated nontimed reading, or, in more everyday terms, the rereading of books or other material. Not every book deserves a second or third read, of course, but if it does, the rereading is of great value to students, for it helps them in developing their sight vocabulary and therefore reading fluency (Samuels, 1979). Teachers should therefore promote rereading, and if any sort of reading requirements are employed, credit should be given for it.

Reading is always easier the second and third time around. Repeated reading of the same book is common in childhood, in part because children's literature encourages it through brevity, wit, and beauty. But adults reread books too, a phenomenon that partly accounts for the enduring popularity of books such as *The Little Prince* and *The Prophet.*

So useful and satisfying can rereading be that teachers should be on the lookout for books that invite it. Bibliographies that list books written or suitable for language learners should include a special section on titles that invite rereading.

Class reader

A class reader is a book that every student in the class reads simultaneously. Although class readers may be used for various purposes in second language education, they can also be used to support library reading. There are immediate drawbacks to their use, however. Each student needs a copy of the same book, and, for extensive reading purposes, the same book should not be used for too long. With a new set of books needed frequently (perhaps monthly), the financial cost of class reader sets may be greater than many programs or schools can afford. Class readers are also only suitable for classes with students of approximately the same levels of language and reading ability.

If a school must make a choice between buying a set or sets of class readers or an equal number of different books, there should be no discussion. A library of different books is a far more valuable and flexible resource. Class readers are a useful addition, but no extensive reading program should feel deprived if it does not have them.

When they support library reading, class readers are used during class for reading-related activities, with most actual reading being done for homework. Lessons using a class reader are a way for teachers to guide and stimulate reading, to teach culture, and to combine reading with other skills such as speaking and writing. Class readers thus take on more importance in programs where students are not used to reading, or when it is desirable to integrate reading with other aspects of the curriculum.

A class reader should be similar in level and content to the books the students are checking out of the library to read on their own. Some books are more suitable as class readers than others. A class reader should be a book of some substance, raising issues worth discussing and writing about.

David Hill, in *The EPER Guide to Organising Programmes of Extensive Reading,* outlines how to develop lesson plans for a class reader (1992, pp. 144–150). For language learner literature titles of up to 100 pages, he advises dividing the book into three parts, and using the book over four class sessions. The first lesson includes the teacher briefly introducing the background of the book to the students and perhaps reading a short extract out loud. Students then begin reading the first one third of the book and complete the reading for homework. In the second and third classes, the teacher checks the students' understanding of what they have read, and clarifies any points as necessary. The teacher then prepares the students for reading the next section of the book, which the students begin to read in class. In the final class, the whole book is discussed and the teacher helps the students prepare to write a report on the book.

Typical activities in a class reader lesson include asking students to predict what will come next, and discussion of cultural aspects of a story or the motivation of characters. Teachers can introduce useful reading skills such as predicting from chapter titles, ignoring unnecessary detail, and getting the main idea. Teachers can also deepen students' appreciation of writing by discussing conventions such as descriptive introductory paragraphs that set the mood, or counterpoint between the actions of two characters. In Hill's words, "After each Class Reader your students should feel encouraged to read more Library Readers and should be more skilled at reading them" (1992, p. 145).

For teachers of English, the Edinburgh Project on Extensive Reading has selected and written lesson plans for several suitable books at each difficulty level of language learner literature. See the Appendix for information on how to contact the EPER.

Reading laboratory

In some languages, boxes of reading cards called *reading laboratories* have been prepared for students learning to read their first language. In English, perhaps the best known are the Science Research Associates (SRA) Reading Labs. These and similar materials are sometimes marketed for and used in second language teaching, and they may be a useful addition to the second language extensive reading classroom.

Reading laboratories typically consist of short reading passages on cards, followed by comprehension questions. The cards are arranged in groups at ascending levels of difficulty. Students are free to select and read only those cards that interest them at a given level of difficulty. The comprehension questions are self-checking, and, having demonstrated a certain level of proficiency at a given level, students may move to the next level. Each card usually contains several exercises for vocabulary building and reading skill practice. Teachers can advise students to do only those exercises that seem useful, or none at all.

If class time is set aside for individualized, self-access work with reading lab cards, the teacher can observe students reading, and work with those students who may be having problems. Because lab cards are written for first language readers, even the easier reading passages are full of vocabulary items that second language readers find difficult. Many of these can be ignored; the meaning of others becomes clear from context. Students may need to be counseled in techniques for getting meaning when the number of unfamiliar words is higher than is comfortable for fluent reading. It is essential to keep reading speed up. Students must practice not getting bogged down or reverting to word-by-word deciphering.

Free time

This is exactly what it suggests – students and the teacher are free to do anything they want to do, with the sole proviso that the activity be connected to extensive reading. This type of unstructured activity is a powerful way of developing a sense of learner autonomy, as it gives students the authority and responsibility to do what they think they need to do in the process of learning to read.

Free time is the ultimate realization of the extensive reading classroom and community. How free the free time can be – indeed, whether it can be used at all – depends on how far students have internalized the goals and processes of extensive reading. It may not be suitable for students who do not particularly wish to be in the classroom. For students who need some guidance, the teacher might restrict the range of activities to such things as silent reading, browsing and choosing, record keeping, or writing reports.

For students, free time is the chance to engage in reading or reading-related activities within a community of other individuals doing the same thing. In multilevel classrooms, some students may take the role of teacher when helping students of lesser ability. For the teacher, free time offers the freedom to do anything to support students in their reading: role modeling, assisting, observing, counseling, checking homework, or reading logs. Just as the teacher, in offering the freedom, trusts the students to do what they need to do, the students trust that the teacher, whatever she or he might be doing, is doing the best for them.

Free time, by definition, has no set form, but the following description by Carlos Yorio of a classroom in an American university intensive English language program can give a flavor of the atmosphere free time can engender:

> Students appear to be having a great time. The classroom does not look like a class; in fact, there is a sign on the door that says: "Resource Centre/Activity Room." Two or three students are reading today's newspapers, others are reading magazines – *Sports Illustrated, Vogue, Newsweek, People.* The teacher is also reading a newspaper. Other students are writing letters, or playing Scrabble. After a while, about twenty minutes, the teacher moves around and asks the students "What are you reading?" She also makes comments about the topic and

occasionally answers questions about words students do not know. (1985, p. 153)

The teacher as role model

There is little question of the importance of the reading instructor's need to serve as a role model. As Barbara Taylor writes, a reading teacher has to "be a person who personally reads – for enjoyment and for learning" (1991, p. 123). As J. A. Bright and G. P. McGregor, in their book *Teaching English as a Second Language,* explain, "The teacher's own enjoyment of books, . . . pleasure in sharing it with pupils and daily interest are of the greatest importance. A teacher who does not read can hardly inspire others to do so" (1970, p. 69).

Being role models also means that teachers participate in the extensive reading program with their students. Bright and McGregor don't mince words:

> It is a general principle of . . . management that one should not ask anybody to do anything one is not prepared to do oneself. If we expect pupils to read the books in their library, we have an obligation to read them ourselves. (p. 70)

Teachers, native and nonnative alike, can read some of the books in the classroom library – books that seem of interest, of course, for it should not be more of a chore than it is for the students themselves. Teachers can then introduce and genuinely recommend the best of the books to their students. By sharing their enjoyment with students, and by answering as best they can their students' questions ("Did the bear die?" "Is it common for young girls to travel alone on the train in Britain?"), teachers are serving as powerful reader role models.

Teachers who tell their students how important and useful and enjoyable reading is, and yet are never seen reading, may be undermining themselves. As Christine Nuttall explains:

> Students follow the example of people they respect, and above all that of their teacher. If the teacher is seen to read with concentration, to enjoy reading and to make use of books, newspapers and so on, the students are more likely to take notice of her when she urges them to do the same. (1996, p. 229)

Keeping in mind that they are role models may change teachers' perceptions of the classroom and their role as teachers. Are there natural opportunities for the teacher to be seen as a reader? If not, how might such opportunities be made?

It may not be straightforward, of course. One teacher, an avid reader and conscious of his role, came to class early and read the newspaper before and while students arrived. He would sometimes subsequently read out or discuss an item of news with the students. Then one day as he ate lunch at his desk in the staff room while reading a novel, a student happened to come in. "I've never seen you reading a book," commented the student, adding, "What a surprise!"

Book talks by the teacher

Teachers can give 1-minute book reports to the whole class. They should consider holding the actual book and showing the cover to the class as they talk. The teacher may want to read the cover blurb, or a paragraph or two of the book, to whet the students' appetites.

Teacher book talks achieve at least four things. Over time, the teacher's talks can act as models to students for how to give their own oral book reports. Second, each talk introduces students to another book in the library – perhaps a new one. In addition, the talks allow the teacher to be seen by students as a reader. There is no better way for teachers to demonstrate to students how enjoyable reading can be than by communicating their own enjoyment of particular books. Finally, if teachers handle the books as they talk, they can show students how to browse a book to get a sense of its contents.

Help for struggling readers

Some students may be behind their classmates in second language reading fluency. There can be various reasons for this: inability to read in their first language, weak second language skills, a first language with no tradition of reading, or a first language with a different script from that of the second language (in a heterogeneous classroom). Because it is individualized, extensive reading allows such students to be reading books at a level that is lower than that of their classmates and more appropriate for them.

But even more assistance may be needed. It can help to pair a struggling student with a more fluent reading buddy who can spend time reading aloud to the student as the student follows along reading the same book silently. In addition or alternatively, publishers often sell audiotapes of books of language learner literature, and listening to these while reading silently can help students increase their reading fluency and motivation to read.

Teachers can also give struggling students the same kind of assistance. Out of class, or during an in-class free time period, teachers can read aloud several paragraphs from a book that the student is reading. Then the student can join in, as and when he or she feels comfortable doing so, reading aloud with the teacher. When the teacher believes the student is getting a good feel for the material, the student goes back and rereads silently from the point at which the teacher began reading aloud, and continues reading.

Conclusion

A successful and effective extensive reading program does not just happen; guidance, counseling, and the creation of activities to encourage and allow students to read as much as possible require careful thought and preparation. The extensive reading lesson is a chance to support and enhance the main activity of the program, reading, and to create a community of readers.

The stage is now set for an examination of the reading community in action. This is the subject of the next chapter.

Further reading

One of the few book-length treatments of extensive reading, *Successful Strategies for Extensive Reading,* edited by George Jacobs, Colin Davis, and Willy Renandya (1997), is chock full of fascinating accounts of practical activities in a wide variety of extensive reading programs. This is a volume that belongs on every second language reading teacher's bookshelf. Another book bursting with ideas for organizing an extensive reading program is Tricia Hedge's 1985 *Using Readers in Language Teaching.*

The idea of sustained silent reading in first language reading instruction can be traced back at least to Lyman Hunt. His seminal article on the subject, "The Effect of Self-selection, Interest, and Motivation upon Independent, Instructional, and Frustration Levels" (1970), is an inspiring introduction to this essential classroom practice. It was reprinted in *The Reading Teacher* in 1996–1997.

New Ways in Teaching Reading (1993, edited by Richard Day) has thirteen activities for the extensive reading classroom, including ideas for students' oral and written book reports. There is also an innovative section by Marc Helgesen with nine ideas for how students can read aloud in class in ways that are fun and valuable.

Teachers of high-intermediate and advanced learners of English will want to look at *Reading on Your Own: An Extensive Reading Course* (1992) by Mary Ellen Barrett and Maryanne Kearny Datesman. This is a textbook with readings and exercises, but designed to lead students into extensive reading: In essence, it is a class reader for students preparing to tackle ungraded material.

In Christine Nuttall's *Teaching Reading Skills in a Foreign Language* (1996), Chapter 14, "The Teacher as Reader" (pp. 229–231), stresses the importance of teachers being role models of reading for their students. This is followed by excellent suggestions on how teachers can become better readers themselves. One section, for example, is titled "If you don't read much in the target language."

In their 1991 book *Teaching Literature,* Ronald Carter and Michael Long give brief but valuable hints to teachers who wish to read aloud to their classes, but are perhaps hesitant to do so (pp. 81–83).

For a bookful of things to do with class readers, see Jean Greenwood's 1988 teacher's handbook *Class Readers.* Most of the activities are designed, as Alan Maley writes in the Foreword, "as a springboard to propel the learner into manifold language learning activities" (p. 3). More reading-oriented is Hedge's useful chapter on class readers in *Using Readers in Language Teaching* (pp. 109–119). For English teachers, the chapter includes lesson plans for Carol Christian's wonderful *Johnny Ring,* a book of language learner literature at low-intermediate level.

13 *The reading community in action*

> We should try to encourage learners to relate what they read to their own world of knowledge and experience.
>
> —Henry Widdowson (1979, p. 180)

The purpose of this chapter is to:

- Present some options for follow-up activities to reading.
- Discuss how the extensive reading classroom can function as a reading community.

This chapter examines how teachers can structure the extensive reading classroom in ways that are compatible with a community of readers. Specifically, the focus is what students do after reading. Because postreading activities are many and various, teachers have a lot of choice in what they might ask students to do.

When planning postreading activities, a basic consideration is why the students read what they did. The purpose of reading for information or enjoyment is just that: the insights derived from the information contained in the reading, the entertainment value of reading itself, or the thoughts provoked by the reading material. If readers are then required to do exercises to demonstrate comprehension, or to practice vocabulary or reading skills, it confuses or distracts from these reading purposes. Further, if students feel that they are required to remember things or that they will be tested, such expectations can even undermine the process of fluent reading itself.

Ideally, thereforc, no postreading work should be required, the act of reading being its own reward. Students read and that is all. Or they merely answer a simple question such as, "What did you think of it?" or "Would you recommend this book to others?" The best answer to the question "What should be done after reading?" is, therefore, "More reading."

There are reasons, however, for considering postreading activities. These include the need to monitor and evaluate students' reading. Teachers may have to determine if the reading was actually done, and they may also want to find out what the students got out of it. Another reason for considering postreading activities is that well-chosen ones can turn the individual solitary act of reading into a community event. By giving access to the private world of others, postreading activities allow students to support and motivate one another, and they allow teachers to guide and counsel students.

As reading usually tries to evoke a response in the reader, follow-up activities that tap into the learners' personal responses to the material are the most natural. Henry Widdowson suggests that teachers "encourage learners to relate what they read to their own world of knowledge and experience. . . . [thus] allowing them the same latitude of interpretation that we as practised readers permit ourselves" (1979, pp. 180–181). In short, the best follow-up gives students a chance to express their opinions, their feelings, and what the reading meant to them.

Four possible forms of student response to reading are:

- answering questions
- writing summaries
- writing reaction reports
- giving oral reports

These are not all equal in either naturalness or potential for deepening a sense of community. Neither are they mutually exclusive, and it is common for an extensive reading program to employ a combination of them. Let us look at each in turn.

Answering questions

Answering questions about a book is a standard follow-up option, and most books of language learner literature have a page of comprehension and other questions at the end. Correct answers to comprehension questions tell both the teacher and the student that the important points of a text were understood. Answering such questions may also be a useful examination skill for students to practice.

The worst comprehension questions are those that send students back to a text to search out irrelevant detail (e.g., "Forrest began to play the harmonica with Jenny's group. What was the name of the group?" asked at the end of the *Penguin Readers* version of *Forrest Gump* [Escott, 1996, p. 43]). But even questions that focus on important points of the story can set back students' progress toward becoming independent, self-motivated readers. In Henry Widdowson's words:

> Comprehension questions . . . commonly require the learner to rummage around in the text for information in a totally indiscriminate way, without regard to what purpose might be served in so doing. . . . Reading is thus represented as an end in itself, an activity that has no relevance to real knowledge and experience and therefore no real meaning. (1979, p. 180)

If questions are to be used, then, it is better for them to combine the check of comprehension with a probe of the students' responses to the story (e.g., "Which parts of the story do you find sad? Explain why in about 100 words" – also from Penguin's *Forrest Gump* [p. 44]).

A less routine, more personal, and more motivating alternative can be for students to write such questions for themselves or their classmates to answer. Such questions will also reveal what the book meant to the student.

Writing summaries

The most common form of follow-up is to ask students to write, in either the first or the target language, a short summary of the book – or part of the book – that they have read. It is important to say, however, that summaries are not necessary in order to find out if a student read a book. And summaries have serious drawbacks. Like answering comprehension questions, writing a summary of what you have read is a less than natural form of response to reading: As Beatrice Dupuy, Lucy Tse, and Tom Cook remind us, "In the real world, people do give their friends recommendations on books, but they do not generally do book summaries" (1996, p. 14). And, like comprehension questions, summaries can subtly communicate the message that reading, as Widdowson says, "has no relevance to real knowledge and experience and therefore no real meaning" (1979, p. 180).

Summaries are not particularly interesting for the student to write, and they are definitely not interesting for the teacher to read. They are of absolutely no help in developing a reading community: If a summary is all that students are required to write, a valuable opportunity for student-teacher communication will have been lost. In addition, there is the problem of students in large programs copying clandestinely circulated summaries instead of writing their own. Try as we may, we find it difficult to blame them. After all, as Dupuy, Tse, and Cook point out, "Students know that in the real world, people who read for pleasure do not do worksheets or write summaries of what they read" (1996, p. 14).

Writing reaction reports

Imagine that you have seen a movie or read a book and talk to someone about it afterward. It would be impossible to have much of a conversation if one of you had not read the whole book, or had fallen asleep midway through the movie. Similarly, it is almost always clear, particularly if the teacher has read the book in question, whether students have read the books they are writing a reaction report about. It is also clear how carefully they have read the book. A reaction report can therefore serve the basic purpose of checking whether reading was done. The usefulness of asking students to write reaction reports only begins here, however.

For students, reaction reports are a chance both to reflect on their reading and to engage in genuine communication with the teacher. For the teacher, it is fascinating to discover how students respond to what they read. Reaction reports allow teachers to move from outside observer to active participant in their students' reading experiences. Through this relationship with the student as a reader, the teacher may discuss ideas, answer questions, and recommend other books that the student might enjoy.

When students are first asked to write a reaction report, they may have no idea of how to go about it. First, they may need to be taught the basics of writing a short report. (In English, this would include paragraphing, and dividing the report into an introduction, the body, and a conclusion.) In addition, it is helpful to provide a fairly long list (perhaps in the student's own language) of possible subjects to write about, being careful to explain that, in any one report, students need choose just one or two items to address. A list of possible subjects for students to write about when reading fiction might include:

- characters they identify with
- points of the story or behavior that interest them
- points of the story or behavior that puzzle them
- personal experiences or thoughts related to the book
- favorite parts
- parts they dislike
- how they would change the story
- how they would act differently from the characters
- larger issues dealt with or raised by the story (e.g., war, sexism)
- experiences while reading (meeting familiar words, sleepiness, etc.)

Require that, whenever students talk of their personal experiences or thoughts, they mention the specific points in the book that inspired them.

Students can write their reaction reports as homework. Reports can be written on one side of a sheet of paper, and, in the case of beginners, can be as short as a paragraph. If a book takes more than a week to read, teachers can ask for a reaction to the pages read so far, or wait until the book is finished. When reading the reports, teachers can choose to correct mistakes of format (e.g., nonindented paragraphs) or form (grammar, vocabulary), or simply respond to the content of the reports.

From time to time, it may not be clear from the reaction report whether the student did in fact read the book. In these cases, when a student appears to be waffling or has written about things unrelated to the book, a personal interview with the student can quickly find the source of the problem.

Whatever written follow-up is required, it is highly recommended that students add how long it took them to both read the book (perhaps using the abbreviation *RT* for "reading time") and write the report (using the abbreviation *WT*). Teachers need to know that students are not spending too much time on either aspect of their homework.

Before handing the report back to the students, teachers can add a written reaction. A teacher's response can range from a simple "I'm glad you enjoyed it" to the teacher's reaction to the same book.

In what language should the reports be written? Keith Morrow and Marita Schocker make the point that

> a personal response to a text in . . . [a] foreign language is likely to be 'felt' in the native language. Attempting to mediate the response through the foreign language will merely lead to frustration (as it is realized that the foreign-language resources are not adequate to express the reactions) or to trivialization (if the response is brought down to the level that can be expressed). (1987, p. 255)

Here, much will depend on whether the teacher can understand the students' first language, and share their responses in it. Another factor is the overall second language program. Extensive reading can provide content for speaking and writing, and it may be desirable for students to practice these in the second language.

Figure 1 introduces some sample reaction reports from beginning-level students studying English as a foreign language. The first is for *Foul Play,* a darkly humorous story by Louis Alexander that concerns Maisie, a woman kept awake night after night by her neighbor Angus's rooster Henry. The others are written about Caroline Laidlaw's thriller *Countdown to Midnight,* Elizabeth Laird's *The House on the Hill,* Mike Esplen's *Marco,* and Betsy Pennink's nonfiction *This Is Washington.*

Brief as they are, these reports indicate first that the books were read, and second that they were read with comprehension and involvement. Note

FOUL
~~FOOL~~ PLAY

L G. Alexander / LONGMAN

I think Mrs. Maisie is good woman, but she can't bare Henry's crow, she could not help killing Henry. It's terrible. Mr, Angus didnt know Maisie's pain until she told ~~the~~ him. He should have been careful about Mrs, Maisie, if she was trouble with Henry's crow or not.
I think it's good They patch up a quarrel. they must thank Henry very much.
A. It's strange story.

COUNTDOWN TO MIDNIGHT

HEINEMANN NEW WAVE READERS

This is very ~~interested~~ interesting story. But I have two things I don't understand. At first why professor Cotter ~~fought~~ wrote down the computer codes. Yet he did so. It was no guarantee that his family were safe.

If I were him, I would written down the wrong codes. Second, ~~in spite of~~ despite they ~~to~~ broke the satellitedish, con and con's man didn't take vengeance on them. Joe's family were safe everyone, his mother said such as, "What an amazing story!"... It isn't said such a thing usually.

But this story is easy to read, and I am interested in this book.

(G) This is exciting story!

Figure 1 Sample reaction reports.

⌜THE HOUSE ON THE HILL⌟ ELIZABETH LAIRD / HEINEMANN

This story feels me sad. This is love story. But sad. In a sense, Paul find the fact that he loved Maria's beauty but not Maria, herself, at last, that is valuable for him and his heart's growth. I think, however, it's too sad story.

What's a money? It's important, maybe. But More Important Things there are in the world. Well, ofcourse, I don't know very rich people thinking. Anyway, at last Paul find that, I felt relieved to read that.

——— It's a terrible love story. <G> ———

⌜Marco⌟ MIKE ESPLEN / HEINEMANN

This story is flat one. Marco's Adventure end up in failure, only a day. He's a country boy. Nothing are around him. He is too pure to live in City. I was born in Tokyo and have lived in, so I don't know Marco's feeling that he want to go to a Big City so much, maybe. But, probably I think he find a country fit himself at last. Good.

By the way, I'm interested in the after that. His father is angry or...? Marco goes to city again? Maybe I think his father is not angry and he workes in a farm, it's always the same. I hope so,

——— Marco is too pure <A> ———

THIS IS WASHINGTON Betsy Pennink H.E.B.

I knew many things after I have finished reading this book. It was not until I finished reading it that I knew Lincoln had been killed. I was surprised at this incident.

I am interested in the Smithsonian Institution. I want to go to these museums because there are various kinds of things. For example, there is a piece of rock from the moon. If I can touch it, I'll think how fantastic.

I found Washington is a good place for tourist because there are wonderful buildings and monuments, and most of them are open to the public. That's why I want to take a trip to Washington some day.

Ⓖ It is useful

Figure 1 Sample reaction reports (continued).

Book Report: Fill this out even if you only read one page of the book.

Your name: ______________________________ Class: ______________________________

Title of book: ____

Author: ____

Publisher: ____

I read all/______ pages of the book. (Circle "all" or indicate the number of pages read)

How did you like the book? (circle one)

(a) Great! (I loved it)

(b) Good (I liked it)

(c) OK (I didn't mind reading it)

(d) Boring/Stupid (I wish I hadn't read it)

Write your feelings about the book below:

(continue on the back)

Figure 2 Book report form (based on Bamford, 1984, p. 220).

the variety of the responses, as the students set down thoughts and questions aroused by the reading, and what each book meant personally to them.

Finally, do not forget pictures. Younger readers and the artistically inclined can enjoy the opportunity to either copy their favorite illustration from a book or draw an original one in response to a story. Teachers can make clear that they welcome drawings instead of or in addition to reaction reports. Some of these can be used to decorate the classroom or library, and on occasion (if reduced in size on a copy machine and recolored by the artist) even pasted into the books themselves.

Book reports can be written in notebooks (as long as teachers read and hand back the notebooks in time for students to write their next report), on separate sheets of paper, or on special preprinted book report forms such as Figure 2 on page 147.

Mixed summary/reaction reports

It is not uncommon for teachers to combine a summary with a reaction report, requiring students to write a summary with personal responses added afterward.

Book reviews

Another variety of written report, one that can be enjoyable and motivating, is the book review. Book reviews – a form of writing a little different from a plain summary or a reaction report – can be written as a special assignment, or for the school newspaper. Teachers can encourage schools, school districts, or publishers to have annual book review competitions such as the one organized annually by a publisher of English language learner literature, Oxford University Press, in Japan. Oxford invites teachers to submit their students' work. The winners receive books, and the satisfaction of seeing their work published in a teacher's newsletter.

Because they are written for public consumption, book reviews move the written report from the realm of teacher-student interaction into the reading community itself. This is also true of the final major follow-up activities – student-student oral reports.

Giving oral reports

Unlike answering questions or writing reports, oral reports require some class time. Prior to class, individual students prepare their own 2-minute oral report on a book recently read. In class, the students, in groups of three or four, give their reports to their group, one at a time, in turn. Someone in the group can keep time, telling the student when the 2 minutes is up. All groups work simultaneously. The teacher may circulate among the groups, listening here and there. An option for ensuring that students really listen to the other reports is to require each listening student to ask the speaker one question after each report.

Depending on whether there are three or four students in the group (and all groups in the class do not need to be the same size) the whole process, including follow-up questions, will take anywhere from 10 to 15 minutes. Oral reports are best done in addition to some form of written homework, such as questions, summaries, or reaction reports.

Unlike reaction reports, which are written for the teacher, who may have read the book, oral reports are presented to classmates who may not have done so. A story summary of the plot in a sentence or two is therefore an essential part of the oral report, but the summary should not give away the story's conclusion. Students could use the blurb on the back cover of the book (if any) as this may already encapsulate the story in a tantalizing way. If students can pique the interest of their classmates and make them want to read the book, so much the better. "Selling the book" should indeed be the purpose of the oral reports, with students preparing them with just that aim.

Beginning students may need a skeleton report to help them, such as the following, adapted from Bamford (1984, p. 222). Students simply plug in the information about the particular book they have read.

- (Introduction) "Last week I read (title). It is a (type of book), and I (enjoyed/didn't enjoy) it."
- (Body) (Brief summary of the book or one of its short stories, preferably told with a cliff-hanging ending.) "If you want to find out what happens, you'll have to read the book!"
- (Conclusion) "I (recommend/don't recommend) this book."

Some students may begin by writing their oral reports out in full and reading them out loud. After a while, as they gain confidence, they can be encouraged to pay more attention to eye contact and interaction with their audience. At higher levels, of course, students will improvise freely as they relate what struck them about the book.

If possible, students should not return a book to the library until they have given their oral report. They can then have the actual book in their hands while giving the report. It is not very interesting to listen to a book report if you do not know the book that is being talked about. If the audience can see the actual book, however, the speech comes alive and is much more interesting to listen to. The cover and illustrations can be used to focus the attention of the audience while the speech is in progress. Classmates will also know exactly what the book looks like in case they themselves want to borrow it.

Book reviews and oral reports are only the beginning of the possibilities for students to access classmates' opinions of the books they read. There are other powerful activities and program features that have student-student interaction as their focus, and thus epitomize the reading community in action. Several of these are examined below: the popular books section; in-book opinion forms; rave reviews; a reading fair; and wall displays.

Popular books section

Whatever form of written follow-up is used, students can be asked to add a letter code or numerical score for the book they read. For example, 1 or 2 points would be a poor book, 3 an average book, 4 a good book, 5 an outstanding one. Alternatively, students could use the letters "P" (poor), "A" (average), "G" (good), and "O" (outstanding). Letter or number scores can then be averaged and used to find the most popular books in the library.

Teachers or student librarians can make a special section to display the top-scoring books at each level of language difficulty. If the front covers can be displayed, a photocopy of the book cover can be used to hold the space when the book is being borrowed. This also helps teachers to see immediately which popular books are seldom on the shelf. They may want to order more copies of these titles.

Popular books sections are exciting for a class because they are a visual embodiment of the collective opinion of its members. They encourage more reluctant readers with the promise of good reading experiences. And they tell students about their preferences as readers – by comparing what they like with what the class likes, students can see to what extent their views are shared by others. It is always interesting to note how others can have a different interpretation of or reaction to the same book.

In-book opinion forms

This next suggestion is useful in any library, but particularly so when a central library is used for keeping the books. When books are in a central library, the number of books may be large and several classes may use the same books. In situations like this, it may be hard for students to know what other students thought of a book. One way to solve this problem is to paste a preprinted form inside the front or back cover of each book (if the school library will allow it). Figures 3(a) and 3(b) show what such a form might look like. After students have read a book, they write a letter or number code of quality, and a brief comment on the form. Students browsing in the

Rating	Your Comment and Your Name

Figure 3(a) In-book opinion form. Copyright © Cambridge University Press.

Rating	Your Comment and Your Name
5	*I'm afraid earthquake happens to us.* *Shoko*
5	*Great!* *Gabriel is nice. He is cool.* *TOMOKO*
4	*"Who is really taking care of me," I think after reading this book.* *YOKO*
4	*I had a chance to think what's the most important thing by reading this book.* *Hisako*

Figure 3(b) In-book opinion form (filled out) for The Earthquake *by Elizabeth Laird.*

library on their own invariably turn to these comments and use them as a guide for which books to borrow. It might be appropriate in some programs to omit "Your Name" on the form and make the opinions anonymous, or to use "Your Initials."

Opinion forms indirectly serve to mark library books as the property of a community of readers. A student picking up a book is also picking up a record of how others reacted to the book. Reading the opinions of prior readers, regardless of whether the student chooses to read the book, is at once an acknowledgment of membership in the community and an interaction with its members.

Rave reviews

Students who enjoy a particular book can usually be persuaded to write a short ten- to thirty-word "come-on" for the book, explaining why others will probably enjoy it as much as they did. Standard-sized (a little smaller than the page size of a normal paperback) pieces of colored paper can be kept for these "rave reviews," which can then be attached to the books in question. Even more than opinion forms, these dazzling and direct expressions of opinion transform books into icons of a community.

A reading fair

Another activity that allows students to share themselves as readers is a reading fair. This is essentially a poster session. Students, individually or in pairs, prepare a poster of a book that they particularly enjoyed. What is put on a poster is limited only by the students' imaginations, and can include quotations, illustrations, or photocopies of a book's front and back covers. Posters should include some personal statements by the students. Students might view their posters the way they think about oral reports – as advertisements that attempt to convince their classmates to read their favorite books.

Given the amount of work involved in preparing a poster, a reading fair might be held only once a semester. The posters could be displayed in some prominent public place, such as the school library, to attract the attention of students outside the class. The fair could be held in conjunction with a school festival, if the school holds such an event. It could also be used as part of a library fund-raising event.

Like the best follow-up activities, posters connect reading with other aspects of students' lives. And in a similar way to a popular books section, posters symbolize a reading community in visual terms through the self-expression of its members.

Wall displays

Younger students often enjoy visible progress. A chart can be posted on the classroom wall, with each student's name, and spaces to write the names of the books that the students read. If the library of books is small, the chart can be a grid, with the names of the books on one axis, and the names of the students on the other. When a student finishes a particular book, the date it was completed and perhaps the student's personal rating of the book are written where the grids intersect.

Such incentives work as long as the whole class is making similar progress. If one or two students are lagging behind their classmates, however, such public displays can only humiliate. It may be preferable, therefore, to instead combine the students' reading into one publicly displayed class total. This could take the form of, for example, a large drawing of a thermometer, the temperature of which climbs as the class reads more books. In fact, classes of any age enjoy watching themselves gradually achieve – if a thermometer is used – boiling point.

Public displays such as these have the advantage of serving other purposes besides keeping the members of a class informed of their own achievements. This is well illustrated by Colin Davis, who reports on successful wall displays and interclass competition in secondary schools in Singapore:

> English teachers used a variety of motivational strategies to encourage the maximum amount of reading. The most successful of these was found to be the wall-display competition in which each class put up a cumulative pictorial display, to be judged at the end of the year. These displays showed, in some imaginative way, which books had been read by the class, and gave information about them. Immense enthusiasm and competitive spirit went into creating displays, which often showed true artistic flair, and engendered considerable class co-operation, as pupils who were avid readers encouraged others to keep up with them. Typical displays might show a reading aquarium, a reading graveyard, a reading train, and the traditional bookworm amid a garden of flowers, butterflies, and other creatures. (1995, pp. 331–332)

It is not clear from Davis's account if a book had to have been read by everyone in the class to be eligible for display. If the number of books in the library is small, it is feasible for a book to circulate around the class. Alternatively, if the library is larger, perhaps ten people reading the same book in a class could render that book eligible for inclusion in the display.

Kathleen Muzevich describes a first language reading program in an American elementary school in which competition among homerooms for prizes both symbolic (a flag) and actual (gift certificates) saw 1,000 students increase their yearly total of books read from 600 to 4,300. The homeroom whose students read the most books each month "captured the flag" which they could then keep in their classroom for a month. Muzevich describes the atmosphere the following year:

> As the year progressed, the competition between homerooms became fierce. Each month, the results for each homeroom were posted on a chart in the cafeteria. By the end of the third month, the book totals were off the chart, and we had to extend it. In some homerooms, students kept their own tally on the computer so that they could instantly compare their progress with neighboring homerooms. (1995–1996, p. 16)

That year, 8,713 books were read by the 1,000 students.

Interclass competition can be taken to such extremes, however, that enjoyment of reading takes a back seat to accumulating ever-increasing totals of books read. These and similar motivational strategies should therefore be employed with caution. Use them sparingly and do not allow them to become ends in themselves.

Conclusion

The activities described in this chapter are just a few of those that creative students and teachers might develop. In considering the effects of an activity or follow-up to reading, three questions may be useful:

- Does this relate reading to the student's own life and experiences?
- Does this support the student in becoming an independent reader?
- Does this allow the reader to support and be supported by other readers?

If the answers are positive, then that activity is almost certainly a healthy and natural outgrowth of the reading experience as expressed in a community of readers.

As attractive and motivating as these activities may be, however, it is appropriate to end with a note of caution. Richard Bamberger puts it this way: "*Forget the communication aspect.* Students should talk less about what they have read and instead use the time for reading more" (1991, p. 35). Point taken. Teachers must keep in mind that ultimately the most appropriate activity for the members of a reading community in action is reading.

14 *Program evaluation*

> The purpose of an evaluation study is to assess the quality, effectiveness, or general value of a program.
>
> —Donna Johnson (1992, p. 192)

> This is where you ask how well the programme is achieving [its] aims.
>
> —David Hill (1992, p. 118)

The purpose of this chapter is to:

- Suggest ways in which an extensive reading program can be evaluated.

Let us say that you have introduced some extensive reading in one of your classes. Because you have been observing your students' participation in the program, you have a good idea of how things are going. By reading the students' reaction reports to books and by talking to the students about their reading, you have a sense of their deepening engagement with texts. From the students' reading notebooks, you know the gains in how much students are reading, in how fast they are reading, and in the language levels at which they read. You see students returning to texts that they once found difficult to read, and now can read more fluently.

You also have a sense of the extent to which second language reading is becoming part of the students' lives – how they are growing into readers, as it were. As a teacher, you feel part of a classroom reading community, and you can see how that community is growing stronger as students cooperate, help each other, and are inspired by each other's and your example. You know which reading materials are popular, which are successful, and which are not. You know what materials should be added to the library. You also know to what extent the physical details of the program – availability of reading materials, checkout, and security – are working.

Such subjective, ongoing assessment of an extensive reading program, based on close participation, is sufficient for most teachers. As a direct result of such assessment, modification of the program is continual, in ways both large and small.

Sometimes, however, it is necessary to attempt to evaluate a program more formally. You may, for example, want to get a more complete picture of a program about which you know only a part. You may need to find out about an ongoing extensive reading class or course that you are taking over. You may need results that can be shown to others, for example, administrators or a funding source. Or you may simply wish to confirm your more informal observations.

There are three central issues in a formal evaluation: purpose, audience, and method. The last depends on the first two.

Purpose

Three common reasons for evaluating an extensive reading program are:

- to see whether a program has achieved its goals.
- to see what other results a program might have had, apart from the intended ones.
- to identify aspects of a program that might need change or improvement.

These are not mutually exclusive, and many evaluations include all three purposes.

Audience

The audience for an evaluation might be teachers, students, administrators, or funding agencies. The evaluation should match the intended audience: Distributing to school administrators the result of an evaluation done to discover weak points of a program might have a negative impact. Making school administrators aware of the program's achievements as well as its weaknesses might have a more desired result.

Method

The method of evaluation will normally be a test or a questionnaire or both, depending on the purpose of the evaluation. If you want to know the effect of the program on students' reading ability, for example, then the evaluation instrument could be a test that purports to measure reading ability (such as Beniko Mason and Tom Pendergast's cloze test introduced in Chapter 8 in the section Reading Tests). Such an instrument can be given as a pretest and posttest, with the results of all students averaged in order to reflect program-wide, not individual student, gains.

Many of the goals of an extensive reading program are concerned with attitude and behavior, however, and a questionnaire is a more appropriate instrument for attempting to measure growth in these areas. As with a test, a questionnaire should be administered to students at the beginning, and then again at the end, of a program, with the results of each administration averaged in order to compare them on a class or program-wide basis. Extra items can be added to the postprogram questionnaire to probe the students' reactions to the program itself.

Next we look in turn at the three purposes for evaluating a program mentioned above, and the questionnaire types and items appropriate to each.

Seeing if a program has achieved its goals

In Chapter 5, some common goals for an extensive reading program were listed. After completing the extensive reading program, the students will

1. Have a positive attitude toward reading in the second language.
2. Have confidence in their reading.
3. Have motivation to read in the second language.
4. Read without constantly stopping to look up unknown or difficult words in the dictionary.
5. Have increased their word recognition ability.
6. Know for what purpose they are reading when they read.
7. Read at an appropriate rate for their purpose in reading.
8. Know how to choose appropriate reading materials for their interests and language ability.

For evaluation purposes, these goals can be recast as statements to which the students can be invited to respond. A list of statements based on these goals might read, for example:

1. I like reading in the second language.
2. Being able to read in a second language is useful.
3. When I read, I expect that I will usually understand what I am reading.
4. I read in a second language because I want to.
5. When I read, I look up all or most of the words I don't know in a dictionary.
6. When I read, I always have a reason, for example, to find something out, or to enjoy myself.

7. Sometimes I read faster and sometimes I read slower, depending on why I am reading.
8. I know how to find reading material that suits me and that I want to read.

There is not necessarily a one-to-one relationship between the goals and the statements. In some cases, such as, statement 5, a goal is most easily stated in terms opposite from the actual goal of the program. A negative answer by the student, therefore, indicates positive achievement. Some goals, such as goal 5 ("Students will have increased their word recognition ability"), concern automatic processes that readers are usually not aware of when they read. Progress toward such goals must be evidenced indirectly, through higher scores on a reading test, or by using a questionnaire statement such as "I can read faster than before."

Three ways to frame a questionnaire item are as follows (see Figure 1).

- scale
- multiple-choice answers
- multiple-choice statements

When possible, a questionnaire should be in the students' first language. Since answering the questionnaire is not a test of students' reading ability, it should be easy to understand. Using the students' first language also means that the information you receive has more chance of being accurate and complete.

Once the questionnaire has been prepared, it is useful to pilot-test it on a smaller group of the students to see if the questions are clear and if they are providing useful information. Students can comment on which questions they found easy to answer and which hard to answer, and why. If piloting is not practical, give the instrument and revise it as necessary before giving it again the next year.

Seeing what other results a program might have had

To find out possible results of a program beyond those envisioned in the goals, open-ended questions are useful. Ask students to write what they think are the best points of the program, the worst points, and what they think they gained by participating in it. The vaguer and more general the questions, the better – for example, asking students if they think they have changed since entering the program, and if so, how. If you are interested in specific topics, by all means address these directly with questions such as:

- Do you think reading has helped your general second language ability?
- Has reading helped you know more about the second language culture?

Scale

Circle the number that best reflects your feelings (1 = strong no; 5 = strong yes).

I enjoy reading in a second language.

1 2 3 4 5

Multiple-choice answers

How much do you enjoy reading in a second language?

a. not at all

b. not very much

c. somewhat

d. quite a lot

e. very much

Multiple-choice statements

Choose the statement that best reflects your feelings.

a. When I read in the second language, I don't enjoy it at all.

b. When I read in the second language, I don't enjoy it very much.

c. When I read in the second language, I quite enjoy it

d. When I read in the second language, I enjoy it.

e. When I read in the second language, I enjoy it very much.

Figure 1 Three ways to frame a questionnaire item.

With open-ended questions, rather than alternatives from which to choose, space is provided for students to write in their responses.

Identifying aspects of a program needing improvement

To gather information for this kind of evaluation, ask students to comment on various aspects of the program. This can be done using a scale like the one suggested in Figure 2. Note that in this example, the optimum answer differs for different aspects of the program. The optimum answer for the Materials and checkout and the Class activities (opinion) scales is 5,

Materials and checkout (1 = poor; 3 = acceptable; 5 = excellent)					
The variety of books	1	2	3	4	5
The number of books	1	2	3	4	5
The quality of books	1	2	3	4	5
The condition of books	1	2	3	4	5
The checkout system	1	2	3	4	5
The number of newspapers	1	2	3	4	5
The number of magazines	1	2	3	4	5
The variety of magazines	1	2	3	4	5
The condition of magazines	1	2	3	4	5

Homework assignments (1 = not enough; 3 = about right; 5 = too much)					
The amount of reading	1	2	3	4	5
The amount of writing	1	2	3	4	5

Class activities (opinion) (1 = don't like; 3 = all right; 5 = really like)					
Sustained silent reading (SSR)	1	2	3	4	5
Teacher read-alouds	1	2	3	4	5
Oral reports in groups	1	2	3	4	5
Reading lab	1	2	3	4	5
Free time	1	2	3	4	5

Class activities (length) (1 = too short; 3 = just right; 5 = too long)					
Sustained silent reading	1	2	3	4	5
Teacher read-alouds	1	2	3	4	5
Oral reports in groups	1	2	3	4	5
Reading lab	1	2	3	4	5
Free time	1	2	3	4	5

Figure 2 Sample questionnaire to identify aspects of a program needing improvement.

whereas in the Homework assignments and Class activities (length) scales, 3 indicates optimum satisfaction.

Questionnaires can either have the students' names on them (useful if you want to clarify or pursue a response) or be anonymous, but you might get a better quality of response when inviting criticism if questionnaires are anonymous.

A simpler but more unpredictable way of identifying weaknesses in the program is to use open-ended questions rather than scales. Students are asked what they would change in the program if they could, and how they would change it. Answers will be less random and more thorough if specific categories to address are suggested: materials; homework; class activities (with subheadings such as "sustained silent reading," "read-aloud," "oral reports," "reading lab," as applicable); follow-up activities (written reports; oral reports); and so on.

Certain practical aspects of a program are properly evaluated based on record keeping and inspection of materials. How often do students return books late? How many books and other materials are missing or damaged? How long is it before a book needs to be replaced because it is worn out?

Results

Once the questionnaire has been administered, the answers from open questions must be assembled and organized. The volume of written responses may be large and random, and you may need to decide how to categorize the various types of answers in order to make better sense of them. Depending on who it is prepared for, a final report, while acknowledging all answers, will probably quote from a selection of the responses perceived to be most pertinent and useful.

Some information provided by an evaluation is likely to be positive, and some negative. Negative information may indicate that change is necessary, but it does not necessarily mean that a program should be modified or discontinued. Perhaps the instrument was faulty or did not measure what it was supposed to. Perhaps the wrong questions were asked, and you obtained information on areas that the program did not teach.

On the other hand, even positive results can be used to reexamine a program. Perhaps positive results can be built upon to achieve even greater results. Perhaps an aspect of a program that receives an overwhelmingly positive response can be expanded.

Conclusion

The method of evaluation – test, questionnaire, or other means – will depend on the purpose of the evaluation and the audience for whom it is intended. A formal evaluation can provide evidence of the state of an extensive reading program and the results it has achieved. Let us once more end on a note of caution, however. Lest enthusiasm for quantifiable data and a thirst to prove something with numbers and statistics carry one away, heed John McInness, who makes a point that applies as much to reading in the second language as it does to first language reading:

> It is impossible to describe numerically the child's appreciation of what [is read], the intensity of . . . interest in reading, the success [experienced] in using reading as a way of extending . . . real and imagined worlds, or . . . growing taste in literature. What can be reduced to statistical description has often been given precedence over these more elusive aspects of growth in reading. (1973, p. 103)

Tests and questionnaires cannot replace observing, sharing, talking with, questioning, listening . . . It is through such interaction that the sensitive teacher can come to know what might otherwise remain unnoticed: that a student is becoming a reader. Ultimately, an extensive reading program must be evaluated in terms of how successfully it provides the environment for this to happen.

Further reading

Charles Alderson provides a good general examination of program evaluation in the section "Guidelines for the Evaluation of Language Education" in his and Alan Beretta's edited volume *Evaluating Second Language Education* (1992).

Brief, clear guidelines for evaluating an extensive reading program can be found at the end of the program management section (pp. 118–120) of David Hill's 1992 volume *The EPER Guide to Organising Programmes of Extensive Reading.*

15 *Taking the approach less traveled*

> The primary consideration in all reading instruction should be for students to experience reading as pleasurable and useful. Only then will they be drawn to do the reading they must do to become fluent readers. And only then will they develop an eagerness to learn new skills to help them become better readers.
>
> —Julian Bamford & Richard Day (1997, p. 7)

The purpose of this chapter is to:

- Review the conditions necessary for extensive reading to flourish.
- Summarize the major themes of the book.

Through a landscape of academic reading skills, comprehension, translation, test-taking skills, and, as Mary Daane puts it, "vocabulary lists, prefixes, suffixes, root words, stated and implied main ideas, major and minor supporting details, transitional words, and inferential thinking" (1996, p. 235), there runs the relatively little-traveled byway that is extensive reading. Can that byway become the route of choice, a veritable superhighway that students travel to become effective, efficient, and independent second language readers? In order for that to happen, several conditions have to be met. There must be:

- *A broader focus for second language reading instruction.*

This requires widening the lens that tends to be so firmly focused on the immediate purposes of a reading course (e.g., passing examinations, translating, learning reading skills) to include the students as individuals. The goals of second language reading instruction may be, for example, for students to have the skills to deal efficiently with academic reading, or to pass the reading section of an examination. But there should also be the goal of students becoming fluent, independent, and confident readers.

In its zeal for efficiency, reading instruction has arguably strayed too far from the purposes and contexts of real-world reading. There are examinations to pass and skills to master, of course, but teachers must be clear about the difference between these and becoming a reader. They must also be clear about the value of being a reader. If they are not, "real reading does not stand a chance under the enormous pressure to teach students how to do well on 'reading' tests" (Henry, 1995, pp. 138–139).

Teachers must realize that being a reader gives students a context within which to experience the value of working toward the specific goals of a reading course. Thus, paradoxically, rather than diluting reading instruction or diverting attention away from immediate goals, time spent on real reading can make reading instruction more efficient and meaningful.

And so, as much as endeavoring to mold students into a tidy concept of what a good reader is – one who can find the main idea of a text, or who can correctly match a pronoun to its referent, for example – teachers should be involved in the less predictable business of encouraging students to discover how second language reading might fit into their lives. This broadening of the overall goal of reading instruction sees teachers aiming to produce not *skilled* readers, but skilled *readers*.

- *A more precise understanding of the cognitive needs of learners at all levels.*

A cognitive view of the reading process makes clear that reading depends on a large sight vocabulary and background knowledge, and that students acquire these through reading large amounts of easy and interesting material. The more precise an understanding teachers have of the reading process, the more apparent it is that students must read in quantity and with engagement. Such quantity and quality of reading will then become a priority in second language reading instruction.

- *A deeper understanding of the primary role of affect in the decision to read.*

Only when teachers know the primary role that affect plays in the decision to read can they take proper account of culture-based and past experience-based attitudes toward reading that students hold. Teachers will realize that students who do not value reading and do not expect to succeed at reading will only read with reluctance. Consequently, student affect will become an important consideration in second language reading instruction.

- *A realization of the need for custom-written second language reading materials.*

Teachers must broaden their understanding of authenticity to include materials written and adapted for language learners. They must also appreciate the essential role played in learning to read and becoming a reader by material that individual students find easy, interesting, and relevant.

For teachers to be able to provide students with the appropriate materials, language learner literature must develop as a genre in its own right. Reading material must advance in stages, parallel with the students' increasing knowledge of the second language and the second language culture. Books must contain appropriate support for comprehension and language learning. In this way, language learner literature can lead readers to a point where the full spectrum of second language written material is available to them.

- *A broader consideration of the effects of classroom activities and reading materials.*

Teachers must take into account the effect of a class activity and the reading material not just on students' ability to read, but on the students' self-images as readers, and on their feelings toward reading itself. The best conceived, most efficient, most effective reading activity may have a hidden, fatal undertow if it makes students less sure of themselves, and less interested in reading. Teachers must therefore broaden their consideration of classroom activities and materials to include their potential for creating engaged, avid, independent readers.

- *A broader view of the roles and responsibilities of students.*

Being a reader involves an element of autonomy. Teachers must therefore step back and allow individual students greater authority and independence. Students must learn to look as much to themselves as to the teacher, for developing skills in second language reading is an individual process. In metaphorical terms, students must gradually see themselves not as sponges or empty vessels waiting to be filled, but as explorers, perhaps, or as information-seekers and pleasure-seekers. In this way, they can eventually come to see themselves as readers.

- *A broader view of the roles and responsibilities of teachers.*

In order for students to become readers, teachers must be, for example, "advocates who promote attitudes" and "promoters who find time often to encourage literacy and celebrate the accomplishments of their students" (Heathington, 1994, p. 207). This requires teachers to see themselves in new ways. Instead of fountains of knowledge, trainers, or evaluators, teachers must consider themselves more in terms of being guides, advocates, and resource persons.

Always, and most of all, teachers must see themselves as readers in the target language. Teachers must understand that what they do as readers and who they are as readers is as important as what they say and teach about reading. Students can become readers only if they know what it means to be a reader and the meaning reading can have in a person's life – things that second language reading teachers may be alone in demonstrating to them.

- *A broader view of reading instruction on the part of administrators.*

Administrators (and parents of younger students) must share a view of second language reading instruction that includes students becoming readers. If so, they will do what they can to provide the necessary resources, and they will understand the different roles and responsibilities of teachers and students. They must appreciate, for example, why it is important for teachers to read with students, and why students are reading light, easy materials with few postreading activities and no examinations.

- *A broader research agenda.*

Research must continue on the impact of second language reading instruction on such variables as reading proficiency, vocabulary knowledge, language proficiency, and writing. In addition, greater attention must be paid to the influence of reading instruction on self-confidence, attitude toward reading, desire to read, and the habit of second language reading outside the classroom.

Perhaps most pressing of all is the need for longitudinal studies to strengthen the anecdotal evidence, such as the report by Mei Fung Elsa Shek at the beginning of Chapter 4. There must be qualitative and quantitative studies to discover what happens to graduates of reading programs, and why it happens. Do students read in the second language 3 or 5 or 10 years after the end of a reading program? What aspects of the reading program can be associated with a reading habit and a sense of the value of reading, or a lack of these?

Extensive reading and the teacher

But the most essential prerequisite for developing effective, efficient, and independent second language readers through extensive reading has always been the individual, committed teacher. In the process of writing this book, we have read reports of second language extensive reading programs, and corresponded with schools around the world. Cutting across all of the differences the programs had – in resources, student age, cultural background, purpose of study, and program organization – there was one inevitable similarity. In schools where large numbers of books were read, one or more teachers were always behind the difference. There is no doubt, therefore, that the essential conditions for extensive reading are a teacher's enthusiasm for reading and encouragement of students to read.

Our intention in writing this volume has been to kindle enthusiasm for extensive reading among teachers, teachers-to-be, and others concerned with second language reading. We have also aimed to support that enthusiasm with theory and with practical suggestions, as well as (if one teaches English as a second language) access to resources in the Appendix.

The teacher – one teacher – makes the difference. If you have enthusiasm for extensive reading, do not wait for others. The time to begin is now.

Appendix
A bibliography of language learner literature in English

> I was born in the year 1632, in the city of York, of a good family. At a very early age I wanted to go to sea.
>
> —Opening lines of Michael West's 1931 adaptation of Daniel Defoe's 1719 novel *Robinson Crusoe,* still in print in a revised edition. (West & Swan 1976, p. 1)

The purpose of this Appendix is to:

- View language learner literature in a way that encourages its future development.
- Present an EPER (Edinburgh Project on Extensive Reading) bibliography of high-quality language learner literature in English.
- Introduce EPER as a resource for teachers organizing extensive reading programs.

This Appendix aims both to provide a practical resource and to consider language learner literature in a way that will forward its development as a genre. It consists of a bibliography of high-quality language learner literature in English. The books are arranged in order of difficulty, progressing from easier to more difficult, for grading is the most salient feature of language learner literature. Books are then listed by name and author, to focus attention on the individual works rather than the series in which they are published.

Unlike their first language counterparts, teachers' magazines and journals concerned with second language reading do not include regular reviews of new language learner literature titles. By including only the best of books in this bibliography, we wish to encourage such a review process, in which opinion is given as to which individual titles are more or less successful.

The research presented here is the work of David Hill and the Edinburgh Project on Extensive Reading (EPER). EPER is a non-profit-making unit within the Institute for Applied Language Studies of the University of Edinburgh. Its purpose is to promote extensive reading as a major element in the teaching of foreign languages, with a special focus on the teaching of English as a foreign or second language. Apart from maintaining the database from which the present bibliography is drawn, EPER develops and publishes support materials for teachers of extensive reading, and trains teachers in writing fiction for language learners. Further information about EPER and contact details can be found at the end of this Appendix.

In this bibliography, when a book retells an existing work, the name of the author of the original work has been moved into parentheses after the title, and the name of the adapter is credited as the author. In some cases, regrettably, the adapter's name is not given in the book.

In contrast to their first language counterparts, authors who rewrite, retell, or adapt an existing work as language learner literature are largely unsung. Publishers place on the cover of the adaptation only the name of the author of the original work on which the adaptation was based, and hide the adapter's name inside.

It is true that, as books are adapted for more advanced language learners, retelling shades into abridgment, and the work of the original author takes on more importance in relation to that of the adapter. In these cases, the original author's name should more properly share the author's space in the bibliography. The point we are making is only that books should properly recognize the respective contributions of the author of the original work and the author of the adapted version, with credit given accordingly.

Giving authors who adapt books the recognition they deserve invites pride and accountability. These are not faceless hacks providing a product, but *authors* telling a story – their own or someone else's – to language learners. The authors listed in this bibliography have written books that EPER considers above average. When names appear again and again, therefore, it is not the result of mere industry, but represents extraordinary achievement. These are the names of the best writers of language learner literature in English.

As this bibliography reveals, language learner literature in English is published almost exclusively in the United Kingdom. The reasons for this are in part historical. Michael West's original supplementary readers for India began to be published in the late 1920s by Longmans, Green and Company in London, and British publishers have continued the tradition ever since. The other reason for U.K. domination is in part economic. David Hill notes that graded readers are "greatly prized by foreign teachers and learners of English" and less so by applied linguists and native-speaking teachers (1997, p. 57). The British ELT publishing business's sphere of

2. These two gentlemen are Mr. Longman and Mr. Green. They have just paid their printer's bill. What are they now waiting for the printer to produce? His account? His bill? His receipt?

Michael West's sketch of his publishers (from West's New Method Reader IV Revision Exercises) (1936, p. 109).

influence in Europe and the former colonies has ensured the necessary marketplace for the genre to blossom.

As the bibliography also makes clear, books by African authors published for an African market have blossomed in their own right. Hill suggests that these books, "outstanding for their combination of realism and humour . . . be used widely outside Africa to underpin multi-cultural studies" (1997, p. 62). They also deserve a place in any library both on their own merit and as a healthy balance to Eurocentric cultural dominance.

In addition to the region (to indicate cultural background) and genre, the bibliography indicates the gender of the main character of each book. Male protagonists dominate, although Hill (1997, pp. 61–62) notes that this is changing. Prior to 1980, 80 percent of the books were mainly about men, versus 10 percent featuring female lead characters (the other 10 percent of the books being about both sexes equally, animals, etc.). In books published since 1990, however, the ratio is 55 percent to 22 percent (Hill, 1997, p. 62). This is an improvement, but obviously note still needs to be taken of the gender of the main characters both to allow informed choice and to encourage the correction of this imbalance.

Finally, the bibliography recognizes outstanding individual books. Once more in contrast to first language equivalents – children's and young adult literature – there are no awards for outstanding language learner literature. And so, in a list which already includes only high-quality titles – the nominees, so to speak – the very best books are indicated by printing the title and author's name in bold. In a sense, these can represent the first awards for English language learner literature. The outstanding books indicated here can be considered to have received the (entirely unofficial, unsanctioned, but nevertheless de facto) "EPER Award for Excellence in Language Learner Literature."

We hope that this special selection will encourage further recognition of excellence in language learner literature. Awards should be established to honor the best books – both fiction and nonfiction – published in a given language in a given year. These awards could be international or regional, sponsored by learned societies, teachers' organizations, professional journals, publishers' groups – anyone, in fact, with a vested interest in raising the standards of second language reading education. Once won, an award would be an achievement that publishers would obviously display on the book itself. Such recognition of individual titles and authors would in turn raise standards and expectations for other works.

By recognizing authors and by celebrating outstanding works, we hope this presentation of EPER's research will stimulate the continuing development of language learner literature and be a model for similar bibliographies in other languages.

An EPER bibliography of high-quality language learner literature

Criteria for inclusion

The EPER database of English graded readers holds records of 3,500 titles, of which 1,650 are in print. The bibliography given here (starting on page 174) contains the approximately 600 titles that EPER considers the best in print, that is, those that scored 4 or 5 out of 5 on a quality rating based on global assessment of the features that contribute to making a book a good read. These features include the clarity of the plot, the support of the illustrations, the appearance of the printed page, and, most important, the interest of the story or book itself.

Levels of difficulty

The list of titles is divided into eight levels of difficulty, which have been developed by EPER to provide a common scale on which to place books from various series and various publishers, and to permit the learner to make easy progress from level to level. The EPER levels reflect use in the classroom rather than strict analysis of the linguistic properties of the text.

Indeed, nontextual factors such as the number of illustrations and size of print are often decisive factors in fixing the level for a particular title. Teachers should be ready to alter levels if their students find some titles much more difficult or much easier than the level given initially.

The following table sets out the EPER levels and the corresponding levels within the Cambridge, TOEFL, and TOEIC systems. It also indicates the age and level at which primary and secondary students can make the transition to ungraded books written for their age group.

EPER levels for language learner literature in English

EPER level	*Average vocabulary*	*Student level*	*Cambridge*	*TOEFL*	*TOEIC*	*Transition to L1 books*
G	300	Starter	—	—	—	
F	500	Beginner	—	—	—	
E	800	Elementary	—	350	150	
D	1,200	Low Intermediate	—	400	300	Ages 10–12
C	1,600	Intermediate	—	450	450	
B	1,900	High Intermediate	FCE*	480	530	Ages 13–15
A	2,200	Advanced	CAE*	520	650	
X	3,000	Bridge	CPE*	550	730	

*FCE = First Certificate in English; CAE = Certificate in Advanced English; CPE = Certificate of Proficiency in English.

Age

Within each level of the bibliography, the books are grouped for particular age groups: primary; primary and secondary; secondary; secondary and adult. These apply directly to European learners and may need modification for learners in other cultures.

GENRE, REGIONAL SETTING, AND MAIN CHARACTER

The genre, regional setting, and gender of the predominant character(s) of each book are usually indicated. When the genre is of a general nature, the setting mixed or imaginary, or the protagonists both male and female, or nonhuman, this is indicated by a dash (–).

PUBLISHER AND SERIES

A code for the name of the publisher and the series in which the book appears follows each entry. A list of codes, series, and publishers follows the bibliography (starting on page 213).

A bibliography of high-quality language learner literature in English*

EPER LEVEL G					
Title	*Author*	*Genre*	*Region*	*Gender*	*Publisher/ Series*
Books most suitable for primary-aged students (8–11 years old)					
Jasper	**C. J. Moore**	—	Europe	Male	HCR1
A Present for Ann	C. J. Moore	—	Europe	—	HCR1
Tim's Magic Paintbrush	Kate Melliss	Family	Europe	—	HCR1
Where's Rose?	Judy West	Family	Europe	—	HCR1
The Crazy Sandwich Bar	C. J. Moore	—	Europe	—	HCR2
Jack and His Computer	**C. J. Moore**	—	Europe	Male	HCR2
Meet the Spookies	Amanda Cant	Humor	Europe	—	HCR2
Speedy the Flying Camel	F. H. Cornish	Fantasy	Europe	—	HCR2
Ayo and His Pencil	**Ifeoma Okoye**	School	Africa	Male	HJAWS-A
The Bighead	**Rod Ellis & Susan Murray**	Adventure	Africa	Male	HJAWS-A
Chika's House	**Ifeoma Okoye**	Family	Africa	Male	HJAWS-A
Kofi Loses His Way	**Amu Djoleto**	Adventure	Africa	Male	HJAWS-A
Monday Morning	**Vic & Wendy Rodseth**	Family	Africa	—	HJAWS-A
The Old Man and His Hat	**Rod Ellis & Susan Murray**	Fable	Africa	Male	HJAWS-A
The Red Flag	Cyprian Ekwensi	Adventure	Africa	Male	HJAWS-A

*Reproduced by permission of © IALS (EPER), University of Edinburgh.

Title	*Author*	*Genre*	*Region*	*Gender*	*Publisher/ Series*
Emmanuel's Father	**Susan Woodward**	Family	Africa	Male	HJAWS-B
The Girl Who Knows about Cars	**Amu Djoleto**	—	Africa	Female	HJAWS-B
The Honeyguide Bird	**Patricia Sealey**	—	Africa	—	HJAWS-B
Neka Goes to Market	**Ifeoma Okoye**	Family	Africa	Female	HJAWS-B
Thabo's Takkies	Nola Turkington	—	Africa	—	HJAWS-B
Winter Caps	**Wendy Young**	—	Africa	Male	HJAWS-B
Femi and His Dog	**Olajiri Olanlokun**	—	Africa	Male	HJAWS-C
Mzwakhe's Bike	**Rod Ellis & Susan Murray**	Family	Africa	Male	HJAWS-C
Nomathemba's Fire	Ray Leitch	Adventure	Africa	Female	HJAWS-C
One Tuesday Down by the River	**Renata**	Environment	Africa	—	HJAWS-C
Sharleen the Speed Freak	**Judy Norton**	Family	Africa	Female	HJAWS-C
The Talking Lizard	**Patricia Sealey**	School	Africa	Male	HJAWS-C
Too Many Carrots	**Ian & Barbara Herbert**	—	Africa	Male	HJAWS-C
Tumelo and the Blue Birds	**Gaele Sobott-Mogwe**	Fantasy	Africa	Male	HJAWS-C
Look at Bill	S. Rance	Humor	Europe	—	MCR1
Jack and the Beanstalk	L. M. Arnold & Alice E. Varty	Fable	Europe	Male	MCR2
The Little Red Hen	L. M. Arnold & Alice E. Varty	Fable	Europe	—	MCR2
The Car and the Donkey Cart	**L. M. Arnold & Alice E. Varty**	Fable	Europe	Male	MCR3
The Two Lions	L. M. Arnold & Alice E. Varty	Fable	Europe	—	MCR3
No Problem!	Rosina Umelo	Humor	Africa	Female	MHSJ1

Title	*Author*	*Genre*	*Region*	*Gender*	*Publisher/ Series*
Striped Paint	Rosina Umelo	Humor	Africa	Female	MHSJ1
Ten Ripe Mangoes	David Cobb	—	Africa	Female	MHSJ1
Under the Cotton Tree	David Cobb	—	Africa	Male	MHSJ1
Little Red Riding Hood	Sue Arengo	Fable	Europe	Female	OCLT1
Cinderella	Sue Arengo	Fable	Europe	Female	OCLT2
The Lion and the Mouse	Carol Barnett	Fable	Europe	Male	OSIE1
The Rabbit and the Tortoise	Carol Barnett	Fable	Europe	Male	OSIE1
The Town Mouse and the Country Mouse	Carol Barnett	Fable	Europe	Female	OSIE1
The Boy and the Wolf	Carol Barnett	Fable	Europe	Male	OSIE2
Goldilocks and the Three Bears	Carol Barnett	Fable	Europe	Female	OSIE2
The Little Red Hen	Carol Barnett	Fable	Europe	—	OSIE2
The Boy and the Donkey	Carol Barnett	Fable	Europe	Male	OSIE3
The Mice and the Cat	Carol Barnett	Fable	Europe	—	OSIE3
The Milkmaid and Her Milk	Carol Barnett	Fable	Europe	Female	OSIE3
All about Us & How I Met My Friend, Boris	**Shelagh Rixon**	Fable	—	—	PHR1
Boris's Quiet Walk & Count Horror's Car	**Shelagh Rixon**	Fable	—	—	PHR1
Stone Soup & The Enormous Onion	**Shelagh Rixon**	Fable	—	—	PHR1
The Story of Chicken Licken & The Three Billy Goats Gruff	**Shelagh Rixon**	Fable	—	—	PHR1

Title	*Author*	*Genre*	*Region*	*Gender*	*Publisher/ Series*
The Tortoise and the Hare: Two Stories	**Shelagh Rixon**	Fable	—	—	PHR1
The Tug of War & The Terrible "Plop"	**Shelagh Rixon**	Fable	—	—	PHR1
Books most suitable for secondary-aged students (11–16 years old)					
Alissa	**C. J. Moore**	—	Middle East	Female	HGR1
The Arcade	Stephen Colbourn	Horror/ghost	UK	Male	HGR1
Blue Fins	Sarah Axten	—	Pacific	Female	HGR1
The Briefcase	Stephen Colbourn	—	Europe	Male	HGR1
L.A. Detective	Philip Prowse	Thriller/crime	N America	Male	HGR1
The Lost Ship	Stephen Colbourn	Thriller/crime	Caribbean	Male	HGR1
Lucky Number	John Milne	—	S America	Male	HGR1
The Magic Barber	**John Milne**	Humor	N America	—	HGR1
Paradise Island	Norman Whitney	—	Caribbean	Female	HGR1
Photo Finish	**Polly Sweetnam**	Thriller/crime	UK	Female	HGR1
Sara Says No!	Norman Whitney	—	N America	Female	HGR1
Sugar and Candy	Elizabeth Laird	—	N America	Female	HGR1
Bookshop Trick	John Escott	Thriller/crime	UK	Female	HNW1
Brilliant!	Alan C. McLean	Sport	UK	Male	HNW1
Fire!	Karen E. Spiller	—	Europe	Male	HNW1
Star Picture	John Escott	—	UK	Female	HNW1

Title	*Author*	*Genre*	*Region*	*Gender*	*Publisher/ Series*
Billy and the Queen	Stephen Rabley	Adventure	UK	Male	LES
Dino's Day in London	Stephen Rabley	—	UK	Male	LES
The Fireboy	Stephen Rabley	—	Middle East	Male	LES
Flying Home	Stephen Rabley	Animal	N America	—	LES
Hannah and the Hurricane	John Escott	Adventure	N America	Female	LES
The Last Photo	Bernard Smith	—	UK	—	LES
Maisie and the Dolphin	Stephen Rabley	Animal	Caribbean	Female	LES
Marcel and the Mona Lisa	Stephen Rabley	Thriller/crime	Europe	Male	LES
Marcel and the White Star	Stephen Rabley	Thriller/crime	Europe	Male	LES
Simon and the Spy	Elizabeth Laird	Thriller/crime	UK	Male	LES
The Troy Stone	Stephen Rabley	History	Europe	Male	LES
Books suitable for secondary-aged students and adults (11 and older)					
April in Moscow	Stephen Rabley	Romance	Europe	Female	LES
Between Two Worlds	Stephen Rabley	—	Australasia	Female	LES
Blue Moon Valley	Stephen Rabley	Romance	Asia	Female	LES
Dead Man's River	Elizabeth Laird	History	N America	Male	LES
The Leopard and the Lighthouse	Anne Collins	Animal	Africa	—	LES
Tinkers Farm	Stephen Rabley	History	N America	—	LES
Tinkers Island	Stephen Rabley	Adventure	Asia	Female	LES

EPER LEVEL F

Title	*Author*	*Genre*	*Region*	*Gender*	*Publisher/ Series*
Books most suitable for primary-aged students (8–11 years old)					
Hatman's Holiday	C. J. Moore	—	Europe	Male	HCR3
The Magnificent Mango	Judy West	—	Indian Subcont	—	HCR3
Miss Electra's Friends	Caroline Hearns	—	Europe	Female	HCR3
The Unhappy Ghost	**C. J. Moore**	—	Europe	Female	HCR3
The Fastest Trolley in the World	C. J. Moore	—	UK	Male	HCR4
First to Fly	Kieran McGovern	Biography	N America	Male	HCR4
Salty to the Rescue	Caroline Laidlaw	Fantasy	N America	—	HCR4
Accidents	Hugh Hawes	Health	Africa	Male	LCCR1
Good Food	Colette Hawes	Health	Africa	Male	LCCR1
The Emperor's New Clothes (Hans Christian Andersen)	**D. K. Swan**	Fable	Europe	Male	LFFT
The Four Musicians	**D. K. Swan**	Fable	Europe	—	LFFT
Goldilocks and the Three Bears	D. K. Swan	Fable	Europe	Female	LFFT
Little Red Riding Hood	D. K. Swan	Fable	Europe	Female	LFFT
The Princess and the Pea (Hans Christian Andersen)	**D. K. Swan**	Fable	Europe	Female	LFFT
Puss in Boots	**D. K. Swan**	Fable	Europe	Male	LFFT
Rapunzel	**D. K. Swan**	Fable	Europe	Female	LFFT

Title	*Author*	*Genre*	*Region*	*Gender*	*Publisher/ Series*
Rumpelstiltskin	D. K. Swan	Fable	Europe	Female	LFFT
Sleeping Beauty	D. K. Swan	Fable	Europe	Female	LFFT
The Ugly Duckling (Hans Christian Andersen)	**D. K. Swan**	Fable	Europe	—	LFFT
Lolo's Kittens	Jenny Robson	Animal	Africa	Female	LGEMS1
The Wolf and the Seven Little Kids	L. M. Arnold & Alice E. Varty	Fable	Europe	—	MCR4
The Best Bed in the World	Charlotte Mbali	—	Africa	Female	MHSJ1
Raindrops in Africa	Margaret House	Humor	Africa	—	MHSJ1
The All-Day Dreamer	Karen W. Mbugua & Geoff Baier	School	Africa	Male	MHSJ2
The Bug Collector	Gillian Leggat	—	Africa	—	MHSJ2
Choose Me!	Lynn Kramer	Adventure	Africa	Male	MHSJ2
The Grasshopper War	Thokozile Chaane	Fable	—	—	MHSJ2
Henry the Last	Michael Palmer	Sport	Africa	Male	MHSJ2
Lissa's Rainbow Dress	Joyce Ama Addo	—	Africa	Female	MHSJ2
Nondo the Cow	Diane Rasteiro	Animal	Africa	Male	MHSJ2
Beauty and the Beast	Sue Arengo	Fable	Europe	Female	OCLT3
Snow White and the Seven Dwarfs	Sue Arengo	Fable	Europe	Female	OCLT3
Books suitable for primary- and secondary-aged students (8–16 years old)					
The Girl Who Laughed	Carol Christian	Fable	Africa	Female	EER3

Title	*Author*	*Genre*	*Region*	*Gender*	*Publisher/ Series*
Night Ride	Sandra M. Simons	Adventure	N America	Female	HBNR
Train Wreck	**Sandra M. Simons**	Adventure	N America	Male	HBNR
The Bright Lights	Jenny Robson	—	Africa	Female	HJAWS1
Caught in the Act	Patricia Sealey	—	Africa	Female	HJAWS1
The Paper Chase	Dianne Stewart	—	Africa	Male	HJAWS1
Taxi to Johannesburg	M. Bopape et al.	Adventure	Africa	Male	HJAWS1
Trolley Trouble	**H. A. Whyle**	—	Africa	Male	HJAWS1
Twins in Trouble	Amu Djoleto	—	Africa	Male	HJAWS1
Weird Wambo	Gaele Mogwe	—	Africa	Female	HJAWS1
Winner's Magic	**Jenny Robson**	Sport	Africa	Male	HJAWS1
Adam and Eve	Carol Christian	Religious	Middle East	—	MBIB1
The Good Samaritan & The Wise and Foolish Bridesmaids	Carol Christian	Religious	Middle East	—	MBIB1
Jesus Is Born	Carol Christian	Religious	Middle East	Female	MBIB1
Jonah	Carol Christian	Religious	Middle East	Male	MBIB1
Moses in Egypt	Carol Christian	Religious	Middle East	—	MBIB1
Noah	Carol Christian	Religious	Middle East	Male	MBIB1
Books most suitable for secondary-aged students (11–16 years old)					
Double Danger	Tony Hopwood	Thriller/crime	Asia	Female	HNW2
Escape from Castle Czarka	Alan C. McLean	Adventure	Europe	—	HNW2

Title	*Author*	*Genre*	*Region*	*Gender*	*Publisher/ Series*
The House on the Moors	Paul Shipton	Horror/ghost	UK	—	HNW2
Karateka	Sue Leather & Marje Brash	—	UK	Female	HNW2
Kate's Revenge	Philip Prowse	Western	N America	Female	HNW2
Zargon Zoo	**Paul Shipton**	Humor	—	Male	HNW2
Dancing Shoes	Colin Granger	—	UK	Female	HNW3
One Pair of Eyes	Caroline Laidlaw	—	UK	—	HNW3
Sheela and the Robbers	John Escott	—	UK	Female	HNW3
The Smiling Buddha	Michael Palmer	Thriller/crime	Asia	—	HNW3
The Singer Not the Song	Liz Driscoll	Romance	UK	Female	HNW4
Juan's Eyes	Carol Christian	—	S America	Male	MR1
Great Hollywood Stunts	Rosemary Border	Culture	N America	Male	MR2
The Locked Room	**Peter Viney**	Thriller/crime	UK	Male	OSL1
The Watchers	Jennifer Bassett	Horror/ghost	Europe	—	OSL1
Books suitable for secondary-aged students and adults (11 and older)					
Dangerous Journey	Alwyn Cox	Adventure	S America	Male	HGR2
Dear Jan – Love Ruth	Nick McIver	Romance	UK	—	HGR2
Death of a Soldier	Philip Prowse	Thriller/crime	UK	Male	HGR2
The Garden	**Elizabeth Laird**	Romance	UK	Female	HGR2
The House on the Hill	Elizabeth Laird	Romance	UK	Male	HGR2

Title	*Author*	*Genre*	*Region*	*Gender*	*Publisher/ Series*
L.A. Raid	Philip Prowse	Thriller/crime	N America	Male	HGR2
The Long Tunnel	John Milne	Thriller/crime	UK	Male	HGR2
Marco	Mike Esplen	—	Europe	Male	HGR2
The Night Visitor	**Richard MacAndrew & Cathy Lawday**	Horror/ghost	UK	—	HGR2
Rich Man, Poor Man	T. C. Jupp	—	Middle East	Male	HGR2
The Sky's the Limit	Norman Whitney	—	UK	Male	HGR2
The Wall	Stephen Colbourn	Sci-fi	—	Male	HGR2
Winning and Losing	T. C. Jupp	—	Middle East	Male	HGR2
Ali and His Camera	**Raymond Pizante**	—	Middle East	Male	LO1
The Amazon Rally	Eduardo Amos & Elisabeth Prescher	Thriller/crime	S America	Male	LO1
Ask Me Again	**Elizabeth Laird**	Romance	UK	Female	LO1
The Barcelona Game	**Stephen Rabley**	—	Europe	Female	LO1
Island for Sale	Anne Collins	Humor	UK	Male	LO1
Marcel Goes to Hollywood	**Stephen Rabley**	Thriller/crime	N America	Male	LO1
Mike's Lucky Day	Leslie Dunkling	Romance	UK	Male	LO1
The Missing Coins	John Escott	Thriller/crime	UK	—	LO1
A Job for Pedro	John Escott	—	UK	Male	PR1
Surfer!	**Paul Harvey**	Sport	UK	Male	PR1

EPER LEVEL E

Title	*Author*	*Genre*	*Region*	*Gender*	*Publisher/ Series*
Books most suitable for primary-aged students (8–11 years old)					
Axle Tom	Caroline Laidlaw	—	Europe	Male	HCR5
Button Soup	C. J. Moore	—	Europe	—	HCR5
Summer in the City	Maureen Barnett	Family	UK	—	HCR5
The Adventures of Ali Baba	L. M. Arnold & Alice E. Varty	Fable	Middle East	Male	MCR5
Honeybrown and the Bees	Jill Inyundo	—	Africa	Female	MHSJ2
Lissa's Rainbow Dress	Joyce Ama Addo	Family	Africa	Female	MHSJ2
The Calabash and the Box	Bobson Sesay	Adventure	Africa	Male	MHSJ3
Check, Come Here!	Edison Yongai	Animal	Africa	Male	MHSJ3
Chimpanzee Rescue	Margaret House	Animal	Africa	—	MHSJ3
Fair Shares	Lynn Kramer	—	Africa	Female	MHSJ3
Knife Boy	Michael Montgomery	—	Africa	Male	MHSJ3
Paa Bena and the New Canoe	Phyllis Addy	—	Africa	Male	MHSJ3
Tickets for the Zed Band	Lynn Kramer	—	Africa	Male	MHSJ3
Books suitable for primary- and secondary-aged students (8–16 years old)					
The Angel Who Wore Shoes	**Dan Fulani**	Thriller/crime	Africa	Male	HJAWS2
Bottletop Michael	Robert Dickson	Fantasy	Africa	Male	HJAWS2
The Boy Who Rode a Lion	**James Ngumy**	Adventure	Africa	Male	HJAWS2

Title	*Author*	*Genre*	*Region*	*Gender*	*Publisher/ Series*
The Buried Treasure	A. Adimora-Ezeigbo	—	Africa	Female	HJAWS2
The Empty Water Tank	**Michael L. Brown**	—	Africa	Male	HJAWS2
The Ghost of Ratemo	James Ngumy	Thriller/crime	Africa	Male	HJAWS2
Kagiso's Mad Uncle	Keith Whiteley	—	Africa	Male	HJAWS2
Masquerade Time	Cyprian Ekwensi	—	Africa	Male	HJAWS2
The Midnight Caller	Rosina Umelo	Thriller/crime	Africa	Male	HJAWS2
Mr Kalogo's Factory	Paulinos V. Magombe	—	Africa	Male	HJAWS2
Mr Pobee's Poda Poda	Omojowo V. Lawson	—	Africa	—	HJAWS2
The Prize	A. Adimora-Eziegbo	—	Africa	Female	HJAWS2
The Secret of Nkwe Hill	M. K. Haar	—	Africa	Male	HJAWS2
The Strange Piece of Paper	**Patricia Sealey**	Thriller/crime	Africa	Female	HJAWS2
Down with Fever	Pauletta Edwards	Health	Africa	Male	LCCR2
I Can Do It Too	Anise Waljee	Health	Africa	—	LCCR2
A Simple Cure	Colette Hawes	Health	Africa	Male	LCCR2
Teaching Thomas	Keith Lowe	Health	Africa	Male	LCCR2
Tshoganetso's Grandmother	Amanda Brown	—	Africa	Female	LGEMS2
The Market Children	Richard Mabala	—	Africa	—	LRE1
Tree Thieves	T. Ba	Geography	Africa	Female	LRE1
Jesus Begins God's Work	Carol Christian	Religious	Middle East	—	MBIB2
Jesus Dies and Lives Again	Carol Christian	Religious	Middle East	Male	MBIB2

Title	*Author*	*Genre*	*Region*	*Gender*	*Publisher/ Series*
Joseph	Carol Christian	Religious	Middle East	Male	MBIB2
Lost but Found	Carol Christian	Religious	Middle East	—	MBIB2
Ruth	Carol Christian	Religious	Middle East	Female	MBIB2
When Jesus Was a Boy	Carol Christian	Religious	Middle East	Male	MBIB2
Water Girl	Michael Montgomery	—	Africa	Female	MHSJ3
Karabo's Accident	**Frances Cross**	Family	Africa	Male	MMT1
The Little Apprentice Tailor	**Marcus Kamara**	Adventure	Africa	Male	MMT1
Martha's Big News	**Lorna Evans**	Family	Africa	Female	MMT1
Tanzai and Bube	John Haynes	Adventure	Africa	Male	MMT1
We're Still Moving!	**Richard Musman**	—	Africa	Female	MMT1
Incredible Rescues – Amazing Escapes	Hazel Imbert	Adventure	—	—	PHR2
Robert's Computer Mystery	Jane Moates	Family	UK	Male	PHR2
Books most suitable for secondary-aged students (11–16 years old)					
Clara	**Elizabeth Laird**	—	UK	Female	HNW4
Poor Little Rich Girl	Elaine O'Reilly	Thriller/crime	Europe	Female	HNW4
The Call of the Wild (Jack London)	D. K. Swan	Animal	N America	—	LPC
Far from the Madding Crowd (Thomas Hardy)	D. K. Swan	Romance	UK	—	LPC
Gulliver's Travels (Jonathan Swift)	D. K. Swan	Fantasy	—	Male	LPC
Moonfleet (John Meade Falkner)	D. K. Swan	Adventure	UK	Male	LPC

Title	*Author*	*Genre*	*Region*	*Gender*	*Publisher/ Series*
The Prince and the Pauper (Mark Twain)	D. K. Swan	Adventure	UK	Male	LPC
Robinson Crusoe (Daniel Defoe)	D. K. Swan	Adventure	Pacific	Male	LPC
Round the World in Eighty Days (Jules Verne)	D. K. Swan	Adventure	—	Male	LPC
Silas Marner (George Eliot)	D. K. Swan	—	UK	Male	LPC
The Bus	Richard Hughes	Adventure	Middle East	Male	MBS1
Where Is Paula?	Diana Mitchener	Thriller/crime	UK	Male	MBS1
The Empress	Mike Poulton	Environment	Africa	Female	MLE1
The Brownes Go on Holiday	**Terry Jennings**	Environment	Africa	—	MLE2
Leela and the Frogs	**Terry Jennings**	Environment	Africa	Female	MLE2
Manu's Beetles	David Hunt	Environment	Africa	Male	MLE2
The Ranger Book of Monsters	Cathy Tuttle	Fable	—	Male	MR3
Books suitable for secondary-aged students and adults (11 and older)					
Another World	**Elaine O'Reilly**	Sci-fi	—	—	LO2
The Earthquake	Elizabeth Laird	Romance	Europe	Male	LO2
The Face on the Screen & Other Short Stories	Paul Victor	Horror/ghost	UK	Male	LO2
Girl against the Jungle	**Monica Vincent**	Adventure	S America	Female	LO2

Title	*Author*	*Genre*	*Region*	*Gender*	*Publisher/ Series*
Project Omega	Elaine O'Reilly	Thriller/crime	N America	Female	LO2
The Lost Love & Other Stories	Jan Carew	Horror/ghost	UK	Male	LO2
Wanted: Anna Marker	Kris Anderson	Thriller/crime	Asia	Female	LO2
Scotland	D. R. Hill	Travel	UK	—	LSRB
The Coldest Place on Earth	**Tim Vicary**	History	Antarctic	Male	OBW1
The Elephant Man	Tim Vicary	Biography	UK	Male	OBW1
Love or Money?	Rowena Akinyemi	Thriller/crime	UK	—	OBW1
Mary Queen of Scots	**Tim Vicary**	Biography	UK	Female	OBW1
The Monkey's Paw (W. W. Jacobs)	Diane Mowat	Horror/ghost	UK	—	OBW1
One-Way Ticket	Jennifer Bassett	—	UK	—	OBW1
The Phantom of the Opera	**Jennifer Bassett**	Horror/ghost	Europe	—	OBW1
The President's Murderer	Jennifer Bassett	Thriller/crime	Europe	Male	OBW1
The Witches of Pendle	Rowena Akinyemi	History	UK	Female	OBW1
Girl Meets Boy	**Derek Strange**	Romance	Europe	—	PR1

EPER LEVEL D					
Title	*Author*	*Genre*	*Region*	*Gender*	*Publisher/ Series*
Books most suitable for primary-aged students (8–11 years old)					
Chichi's Nature Diary	Wendy Ijioma	Science	Africa	Female	MHSJ3
Books suitable for primary- and secondary-aged students (8–16 years old)					
Adventures of Sinbad the Sailor	**D. K. Swan**	Fable	Middle East	Male	LC1
Black Beauty (Anna Sewell)	D. K. Swan	Animal	UK	—	LC1
Five Famous Fairy Tales	D. K. Swan	Fable	Europe	—	LC1
Heidi (Johanna Spyri)	**Celia Turvey**	—	Europe	Female	LC1
The Jungle Book (Rudyard Kipling)	D. K. Swan	Animal	Indian Subcont	Male	LC1
The Cholera Crisis	Hugh Hawes	Health	Africa	—	LCCR3
Deadly Habits	Hugh Hawes	Health	Africa	Male	LCCR3
Freda Doesn't Get Pregnant	**Hugh Hawes**	Health	Africa	—	LCCR3
Who Killed Danny?	Anise Walji	Thriller/crime	Africa	Male	LCCR3
Amos and the Leopard	M. L. Brown	Animal	Africa	Male	LRE2
Fear in the Forest	Maurice Sotabinda	Environment	Africa	Male	MLE3
The Poachers	**Mike Poulton**	Environment	Africa	Male	MLE3
Just a Bit of Wood	Wendy Ijioma	Environment	Africa	Male	MLE4
Well Done, David!	**Mike Poulton**	Environment	Africa	Male	MLE4
Danger in the Palace	Grace Nkansa	Adventure	Africa	Male	MMT2

Title	*Author*	*Genre*	*Region*	*Gender*	*Publisher/ Series*
Dark Blue Is for Dreams	**Rosina Umelo**	—	Africa	Female	MMT2
Map on the Wall	**Colin Swatridge**	Adventure	Africa	Male	MMT2
One in a Million	Emma Johnson	Adventure	Africa	Male	MMT2
Chinese Myths 1	Penny Cameron	Fable	Asia	—	WER1
Inspector Fung, Detective	Penny Cameron	Thriller/crime	Asia	—	WER1
Books most suitable for secondary-aged students (11–16 years old)					
The Boy Who Was Afraid (Armstrong Sperry)	Stephen Colbourn	—	Pacific	Male	HGR3
The Runaways (Victor Canning)	F. Peers	—	UK	Male	HGR3
Treasure Island (R. L. Stevenson)	Stephen Colbourn	Adventure	UK	Male	HGR3
Hamadi and the Stolen Cattle	**Chris Burchell**	Adventure	Africa	Male	HJAWS3
The Haunted Taxi Driver	Kofi Sekyi	Horror/ghost	Africa	Male	HJAWS3
Kodua's Ark	Y. A. Boateng	—	Africa	Male	HJAWS3
Lindiwi Finds a Way	Eileen Molver	—	Africa	Female	HJAWS3
Miss John	Y. A. Boateng	—	Africa	Female	HJAWS3
The Old Man and the Rabbit	**Tracey Lloyd**	—	Africa	Male	HJAWS3
The Old Warrior	**Dawn Smargiassi**	—	Africa	Male	HJAWS3
Regina's Dream	Gillian Leggat	—	Africa	Female	HJAWS3
Tikrit	Chris Burchell	—	Africa	Male	HJAWS3
The Young Builder	**Gillian Leggat**	—	Africa	Male	HJAWS3

Title	*Author*	*Genre*	*Region*	*Gender*	*Publisher/ Series*
Away Match	**Susan Axbey**	Romance	Europe	Female	HNW5
Lost in London	**Colin Granger**	—	UK	Female	HNW5
Mystery on Mallorca	**Alan C. McLean**	Thriller/crime	Europe	Female	HNW5
Wish at Corroboree Rock	Stella Martin	—	Australasia	Male	HNW5
Zulu Spear	Olive Langa	History	Africa	Male	MMT1
Johnny Ring	Carol Christian	History	N America	Male	MR4
The Children of the New Forest (Captain Marryat)	Rowena Akinyemi	Adventure	UK	—	OBWG2
Robinson Crusoe (Daniel Defoe)	Diane Mowat	Adventure	Pacific	Male	OBWG2
A Stranger at Green Knowe (Lucy M. Boston)	Diane Mowat	Animal	UK	Male	OBWG2
Just So Stories (Rudyard Kipling)	Rosemary Border	Fable	—	—	OPER1
The Lost Umbrella of Kim Chu (Eleanor Estes)		Adventure	N America	Female	OPER1
The Secret Garden (Frances H. Burnett)	**Kieran McGovern**	—	UK	Female	OPER1
The Wizard of Oz (L. Frank Baum)	David Foulds	Fantasy	—	Female	OPER1
John's Story	Carol Mathews	—	UK	—	PHBS1
Grandad's Eleven	Jeremy Taylor	Sport	UK	Male	PR2
Money to Burn	John Escott	Thriller/crime	UK	Female	PR2
Chocky (John Wyndham)	**Robin Waterfield**	Sci-fi	UK	Male	PR2

Title	*Author*	*Genre*	*Region*	*Gender*	*Publisher/ Series*
Books suitable for secondary-aged students and adults (11 and older)					
The Canterville Ghost & Other Stories (Oscar Wilde)	**Stephen Colbourn**	Humor	UK	Male	HGR3
A Christmas Carol (Charles Dickens)	**F. H. Cornish**	—	UK	Male	HGR3
Dr Jekyll and Mr Hyde (R. L. Stevenson)	**Stephen Colbourn**	Horror/ghost	UK	Male	HGR3
The Flower Seller	Richard Prescott	Thriller/crime	UK	Male	HGR3
The Goalkeeper's Revenge (Bill Naughton)	Peter Hodson	—	UK	Male	HGR3
The Hound of the Baskervilles (Sir A. Conan Doyle)	Stephen Colbourn	Thriller/crime	UK	Male	HGR3
Lady Portia's Revenge & Other Stories	**David Evans**	—	UK	—	HGR3
The Lost World (Sir A. Conan Doyle)	Anne Collins	Adventure	S America	Male	HGR3
The Narrow Path (Francis Selormey)	John Milne	Biography	Africa	Male	HGR3
The Picture of Dorian Gray (Oscar Wilde)	F. H. Cornish	Horror/ghost	UK	Male	HGR3
The Promise	R. Scott-Buccleuch	—	S America	Male	HGR3
A River Ran Out of Eden (James Vance Marshall)	**Peter Hodson**	—	N America	Male	HGR3
Road to Nowhere	John Milne	—	Middle East	Male	HGR3

Title	*Author*	*Genre*	*Region*	*Gender*	*Publisher/ Series*
Room 13 & Other Ghost Stories (M. R. James)	Stephen Colbourn	Horror/ghost	UK	Male	HGR3
Silver Blaze & Other Stories (Sir A. Conan Doyle)	Anne Collins	Thriller/crime	UK	Male	HGR3
The Stranger	Norman Whitney	—	UK	Female	HGR3
Tales of Horror (Bram Stoker)	John Davey	Horror/ghost	Europe	Male	HGR3
Tales of Ten Worlds (Arthur C. Clarke)	Helen Reid Thomas	Sci-fi	—	Male	HGR3
The Verger & Other Stories (W. Somerset Maugham)	John Milne	—	UK	Male	HGR3
The Woman in Black (Susan Hill)	**Margaret Tarner**	Horror/ghost	UK	Male	HGR3
Inspector Holt: The Bridge	John Tully	Thriller/crime	Middle East	Male	LEL2
Lord Arthur Savile's Crime (Oscar Wilde)	Anon	Humor	UK	Male	LEL2
The Magic Garden	**K. R. Cripwell**	—	Africa	Male	LEL2
Three Sherlock Holmes Adventures (Sir A. Conan Doyle)	Lewis Jones	Thriller/crime	UK	Male	LEL2
The Gold Lasso	**Stephen Rabley**	Thriller/crime	N America	Male	LO2
K's First Case	L. G. Alexander	Thriller/crime	UK	Female	LO2
The Climb	John Escott	Adventure	Europe	Female	LO3
The Lost Twin	Raymond Pizante	Thriller/crime	UK	Male	LO3
Photo of the Tall Man	Stephen Rabley	Thriller/crime	UK	Female	LO3
Ireland	Patrick Tolfree	Travel	Europe	—	LSRB

Title	*Author*	*Genre*	*Region*	*Gender*	*Publisher/ Series*
The Death of Karen Silkwood	Joyce Hannam	Biography	N America	Female	OBW2
Ear-rings from Frankfurt	Reg Wright	Thriller/crime	Europe	Female	OBW2
Grace Darling	**Tim Vicary**	History	UK	Female	OBW2
Henry VIII and His Six Wives	**Janet Hardy-Gould**	Biography	UK	—	OBW2
New Yorkers (O. Henry)	Diane Mowat	—	N America	—	OBW2
The Piano	Rosemary Border	—	UK	Male	OBW2
Return to Earth (John Christopher)	Susan Binder	Sci-fi	UK	—	OBW2
Voodoo Island	Michael Duckworth	Horror/ghost	Caribbean	—	OBW2
William Shakespeare	**Jennifer Bassett**	Biography	UK	Male	OBW2
Life Lines	Peter Viney	—	UK	Female	OSL3
Sunnyvista City	**Peter Viney**	Sci-fi	—	Male	OSL3
The Hitch-Hiker	Tim Vicary	Horror/ghost	UK	Female	OSL4
A Tidy Ghost	**Peter Viney**	—	UK	—	OSL4
The Diary	**Paul Stewart**	Thriller/crime	UK	Male	PR2
Don't Look behind You (Lois Duncan)	Chris Grant-Bear	Adventure	N America	Female	PR2
The Fox (D. H. Lawrence)	Philip Prowse	Romance	UK	—	PR2
The Room in the Tower & Other Ghost Stories (Rudyard Kipling et al.)	Carolyn Jones & Derek Strange	Horror/ghost	UK	—	PR2
Simply Suspense (Frank Stockton et al.)	J. Y. K. Kerr	Horror/ghost	UK	—	PR2

EPER LEVEL C

Title	*Author*	*Genre*	*Region*	*Gender*	*Publisher/ Series*
Books suitable for primary- and secondary-aged students (8–16 years old)					
The Runner	Amanda Brown	History	Africa	Female	LGEMS4
Books most suitable for secondary-aged students (11–16 years old)					
Follow the Crow	**Hugh Lewin**	Spy	Africa	Male	HJAWS4
The Lonely Stranger	**Mike Sadler**	Thriller/crime	Africa	Male	HJAWS4
Paulo's Strange Adventure	**Barbara Kimenye**	Thriller/crime	Africa	Male	HJAWS4
The Secret Valley	Mike Sadler	Adventure	Africa	—	HJAWS4
Street Gang Kid	**Shirley Boje**	Adventure	Africa	Male	HJAWS4
A Christmas Carol (Charles Dickens)	D. K. Swan & Michael West	—	UK	Male	LC2
Gulliver's Travels (Jonathan Swift)	D. K. Swan & Michael West	Fantasy	Europe	Male	LC2
Kidnapped (R. L. Stevenson)	D. K. Swan	Adventure	UK	Male	LC2
The Prince and the Pauper (Mark Twain)	D. K. Swan & Michael West	Adventure	UK	Male	LC2
Round the World in Eighty Days (Jules Verne)	D. K. Swan	Adventure	—	Male	LC2
The Secret Garden (Frances Hodgson Burnett)	**Sue Ullstein**	—	UK	Female	LC2
Tales from the Arabian Nights	John Turvey	Fable	Middle East	—	LC2

Title	*Author*	*Genre*	*Region*	*Gender*	*Publisher/ Series*
The Wind in the Willows (Kenneth Grahame)	Sue Ullstein	Animal	UK	Male	LC2
The Adventures of Tom Sawyer (Mark Twain)	**D. K. Swan**	Adventure	N America	Male	LC3
The Count of Monte Cristo (Alexandre Dumas)	D. K. Swan & Michael West	—	Europe	Male	LC3
Dracula (Bram Stoker)	**John Turvey**	Horror/ghost	Europe	Male	LC3
Dr Jekyll and Mr Hyde (R. L. Stevenson)	D. K. Swan	Horror/ghost	UK	Male	LC3
Emil and the Detectives (Erich Kastner)	**E. M. Attwood & D. K. Swan**	Thriller/crime	Europe	—	LC3
The Return of Sherlock Holmes (Sir A. Conan Doyle)	Alan Pugh	Thriller/crime	UK	Male	LC3
Robinson Crusoe (Daniel Defoe)	D. K. Swan & Michael West	Adventure	Pacific	Male	LC3
The Snow Goose & Other Stories (Paul Gallico)	Christine Rose	—	UK	—	LC3
The Swiss Family Robinson (Johann Wyss)	D. K. Swan & Michael West	—	Pacific	—	LC3
Vanity Fair (William Thackeray)	D. K. Swan	Romance	UK	Female	LC3
The Young King & Other Stories (Oscar Wilde)	D. K. Swan & Michael West	Fable	Europe	—	LC3
The White Mountains (John Christopher)	A. G. Eyre	Sci-Fi	Europe	Male	LF1
The Chain of Evening	**Amanda Brown**	Thriller/crime	Africa	—	LRE3
The Winner	**Clara Izokun-Etiobhio**	Science	Africa	Male	LRE3

Title	*Author*	*Genre*	*Region*	*Gender*	*Publisher/ Series*
Days of Silence	Rosina Umelo	Adventure	Africa	—	MMT3
Fineboy	Maurice Sotabinda	School	Africa	Male	MMT3
Front Page Story	John Byrne	Thriller/crime	Africa	Male	MMT3
Juwon's Battle	**Victor Thorpe**	—	Africa	Female	MMT3
Never Leave Me	**Hope Dube**	Romance	Africa	Female	MMT3
The Call of the Wild (Jack London)	Nick Bullard	Animal	N America	—	OBWG3
A Christmas Carol (Charles Dickens)	**Clare West**	—	UK	Male	OBWG3
Kidnapped (R. L. Stevenson)	Clare West	Adventure	UK	Male	OBWG3
On the Edge (Gillian Cross)	Clare West	Thriller/crime	UK	—	OBWG3
The Railway Children (Edith Nesbit)	**John Escott**	Adventure	UK	—	OBWG3
The Secret Garden (Frances Hodgson Burnett)	**Clare West**	—	UK	Female	OBWG3
Who, Sir? Me, Sir? (K. M. Peyton)	**Diane Mowat**	School	UK	Male	OBWG3
The Wind in the Willows (Kenneth Grahame)	Jennifer Bassett	Animal	UK	Male	OBWG3
The Dagger and Wings & Other Father Brown Stories (G. K. Chesterton)		Thriller/crime	UK	Male	OPER2
The Flying Heads & Other Strange Stories		Horror/ghost	Asia	—	OPER2
Gulliver's Travels – a Voyage to Lilliput (Jonathan Swift)		Fantasy	—	Male	OPER2

Title	*Author*	*Genre*	*Region*	*Gender*	*Publisher/ Series*
The Jungle Book (Rudyard Kipling)		Animal	Indian Subcont	Male	OPER2
Life without Katy & Other Stories (O. Henry)		—	N America	—	OPER2
The Prince and the Pauper (Mark Twain)	Rosemary Border	Adventure	UK	Male	OPER2
The Stone Junk & Other Stories	D. H. Howe	Fable	Asia	—	OPER2
The Adventures of the Monkey King	Helen Kirkpatrick	Fable	Asia	Male	PETAP3
The Big Match	**Kieran McGovern**	Adventure	UK	—	PHBS2
Happy Endings	Harry Gilbert	—	UK	—	PHBS2
Channel Runner	**Jeremy Taylor**	Sport	UK	Female	PR3
Madame Doubtfire (Anne Fine)	J. Y. K. Kerr	Humor	N America	Male	PR3
Escape	V. C. Vickers	History	Asia	—	WER2
Books suitable for secondary-aged students and adults (11 and older)					
Banker (Dick Francis)	Stephen Colbourn	Thriller/crime	UK	Male	HGR4
The Bonetti Inheritance	**Richard Prescott**	Thriller/crime	Europe	—	HGR4
Bristol Murder	Philip Prowse	Thriller/crime	UK	Male	HGR4
Dracula (Bram Stoker)	Margaret Tarner	Horror/ghost	Europe	Male	HGR4
The Franchise Affair (Josephine Tey)	Margaret Tarner	Thriller/crime	UK	Male	HGR4
The Good Earth (Pearl Buck)	**Stephen Colbourn**	—	Asia	—	HGR4

Title	*Author*	*Genre*	*Region*	*Gender*	*Publisher/ Series*
The Hairless Mexican & The Traitor (W. Somerset Maugham)	Philip King	Thriller/crime	Europe	Male	HGR4
A Marriage of Convenience & Other Stories (W. Somerset Maugham)	D. R. Hill	—	Europe	—	HGR4
The Moon Is Down (John Steinbeck)	Michael J. Paine	—	Europe	Male	HGR4
Old Mali and the Boy (D. R. Sherman)	John Milne	—	Indian Subcont	Male	HGR4
Oliver Twist (Charles Dickens)	**Margaret Tarner**	—	UK	Male	HGR4
The Pearl (John Steinbeck)	**Michael J. Paine**	—	S America	—	HGR4
The Queen of Spades & Other Stories (Aleksandr Pushkin)	Stephen Colbourn	—	Europe	—	HGR4
Shane (Jack Schaefer)	**John Milne**	Western	N America	Male	HGR4
The Sign of Four (Sir A. Conan Doyle)	Anne Collins	Thriller/crime	UK	Male	HGR4
Silas Marner (George Eliot)	**Margaret Tarner**	—	UK	Male	HGR4
The Smuggler	Piers Plowright	Thriller/crime	Europe	Male	HGR4
The Speckled Band & Other Stories (Sir A. Conan Doyle)	Anne Collins	Thriller/crime	UK	Male	HGR4
Tales of Goha	Leslie Caplan	Humor	Middle East	Male	HGR4
Things Fall Apart (Chinua Achebe)	**John Davey**	—	Africa	Male	HGR4
The Three Strangers & Other Stories (Thomas Hardy)	Margaret Tarner	Horror/ghost	UK	—	HGR4
A Town Like Alice (Nevil Shute)	D. R. Hill	—	Asia	Female	HGR4

Title	*Author*	*Genre*	*Region*	*Gender*	*Publisher/ Series*
Walkabout (James Vance Marshall)	Jim Alderson	—	Australasia	—	HGR4
When Rain Clouds Gather (Bessie Head)	Margaret Tarner	—	Africa	—	HGR4
The Woman Who Disappeared	Philip Prowse	Thriller/crime	N America	Male	HGR4
The Innocent Prisoner	Kwasi Koranteng	Thriller/crime	Africa	Male	HJAWS4
King Forever	Cyprian Ekwensi	—	Africa	Male	HJAWS4
Love Is a Challenge	Hope Dube	—	Africa	Female	HJAWS4
Oscar Wilde Short Stories (Oscar Wilde)	Jen Macdonell	Fable	Europe	—	LEL3
Island of the Blue Dolphins (Scott O'Dell)	Roland John	Adventure	N America	Female	LF1
A Scandal in Bohemia & Other Stories (Sir A. Conan Doyle)	Ronald Holt	Thriller/crime	UK	Male	LF1
Silas Marner (George Eliot)	A. J. Brayley	—	UK	Male	LF1
The Thirty-Nine Steps (John Buchan)	Roland John	Thriller/crime	UK	Male	LF1
Chance of a Lifetime	Margaret Iggulden	—	Europe	Female	LO3
Dangerous Game	William Harris & L. G. Alexander	Horror/ghost	UK	Male	LO3
The Ring	**Bernard Smith**	Romance	S America	Male	LO3
Goodbye Summer Blues	Philip Prowse	Thriller/crime	N America	Male	LO4
Gandhi: His Life Was the Message	Donn Byrne	Biography	Indian Subcont	Male	LSRB
As the Inspector Said . . . (Cyril Hare et al.)	John Escott	Thriller/crime	UK	—	OBW3
The Brontë Story	**Tim Vicary**	Biography	UK	—	OBW3

Title	*Author*	*Genre*	*Region*	*Gender*	*Publisher/ Series*
Chemical Secret	Tim Vicary	Thriller/crime	UK	Male	OBW3
Frankenstein (Mary Shelley)	Patrick Nobes	Horror/ghost	Europe	Male	OBW3
Go, Lovely Rose (H. E. Bates)	**Rosemary Border**	—	UK	—	OBW3
Justice	**Tim Vicary**	Thriller/crime	UK	Female	OBW3
Love Story (Erich Segal)	Rosemary Border	Romance	N America	Male	OBW3
The Picture of Dorian Gray (Oscar Wilde)	Jill Nevile	Horror/ghost	UK	Male	OBW3
Skyjack!	Tim Vicary	Thriller/crime	Europe	—	OBW3
Tales of Mystery and Imagination (Edgar Allan Poe)	**Margaret Naudi**	Horror/ghost	N America	—	OBW3
Tooth and Claw (Saki)	**Rosemary Border**	Humor	UK	—	OBW3
Wyatt's Hurricane (Desmond Bagley)	Jennifer Bassett	Thriller/crime	Caribbean	Male	OBW3
The Black Cat & Other Stories (Edgar Allan Poe)	David Wharry	Horror/ghost	N America	Male	PR3
The Darling Buds of May (H. E. Bates)	David Wharry	—	UK	—	PR3
Forrest Gump (Winston Groom)	John Escott	—	N America	Male	PR3
Summer of My German Soldier (Bette Greene)	Karen Holmes	Romance	N America	Female	PR3
The Thirty-Nine Steps (John Buchan)	J. Y. K. Kerr	Thriller/crime	UK	Male	PR3

EPER LEVEL B

Title	*Author*	*Genre*	*Region*	*Gender*	*Publisher/ Series*
Books most suitable for secondary-aged students (11–16 years old)					
The Adventures of Huckleberry Finn (Mark Twain)	D. K. Swan	Adventure	N America	Male	LC4
The Call of the Wild (Jack London)	Brian Heaton & D. K. Swan	Animal	N America	Male	LC4
The Canterville Ghost & Other Stories (Oscar Wilde)	D. K. Swan	Humor	UK	—	LC4
David Copperfield (Charles Dickens)	D. K. Swan & Michael West	—	UK	Male	LC4
Little Women (Louisa May Alcott)	D. K. Swan & Michael West	Family	N America	Female	LC4
Oliver Twist (Charles Dickens)	Margaret Maison, D. K. Swan, & Michael West	—	UK	Male	LC4
Tales of Mystery and Imagination (Edgar Allan Poe)	Roland John & Michael West	Horror/ghost	N America	Male	LC4
Three Adventures of Sherlock Holmes (Sir A. Conan Doyle)	Frances Johnston	Thriller/crime	UK	Male	LC4
Treasure Island (R. L. Stevenson)	Roland John & Michael West	Adventure	Caribbean	Male	LC4
Wuthering Heights (Emily Brontë)	Celia Turvey	Romance	UK	—	LC4
Something to Play For	Michael Titlestad	Adventure	Africa	Male	LGEMS5
Tuesday the Tenth	Andy Hopkins & Joc Potter	—	UK	—	MBS3
The Past Tells a Story	**Lorna Evans**	Science	Africa	—	MMT2

Title	*Author*	*Genre*	*Region*	*Gender*	*Publisher/ Series*
Jojo in New York	**Kofi Quaye**	Thriller/crime	N America	Male	MMT4
Kayo's House	Barbara Kimenye	Romance	Africa	Female	MMT4
Presents from Mr Bakare	Mary Harrison	Thriller/crime	Africa	Male	MMT4
Sara's Friends	**Rosina Umelo**	—	Africa	Female	MMT4
Sunbird's Paradise	**James Ngumy**	—	Africa	Male	MMT4
Trouble in the City	Hope Dube	Thriller/crime	Africa	Male	MMT4
Great Disasters	Michael Evans	History	—	—	MR5
A Journey through Japan	Alan Booth	Travel	Asia	Male	MR5
Alice's Adventures in Wonderland (Lewis Carroll)	Jennifer Bassett	Fantasy	UK	Female	OBWG2
Through the Looking Glass (Lewis Carroll)	Jennifer Bassett	Fantasy	UK	Female	OBWG3
The Eagle of the Ninth (Rosemary Sutcliff)	**John Escott**	History	UK	Male	OBWG4
Gulliver's Travels (Jonathan Swift)	**Clare West**	Fantasy	Europe	Male	OBWG4
Little Women (Louisa May Alcott)	**John Escott**	Family	N America	Female	OBWG4
The Silver Sword (Ian Serraillier)	**John Escott**	Adventure	Europe	—	OBWG4
Treasure Island (R. L. Stevenson)	John Escott	Adventure	UK	Male	OBWG4
We Didn't Mean to Go to Sea (Arthur Ransome)	**Ralph Mowat**	Adventure	UK	—	OBWG4
The Whispering Knights (Penelope Lively)	Clare West	Horror/ghost	UK	Female	OBWG4

Title	*Author*	*Genre*	*Region*	*Gender*	*Publisher/ Series*
Around the World in Eighty Days (Jules Verne)		Adventure	—	Male	OPER3
The Hound of the Baskervilles (Sir A. Conan Doyle)		Thriller/crime	UK	Male	OPER3
A Tale of Two Cities (Charles Dickens)		History	Europe	Male	OPER3
Tales of Crime and Detection (Dorothy Sayers et al.)		Thriller/crime	UK	Male	OPER3
The Water Margin	Rosemary Border	Fable	Asia	Male	PETAP4
Thetha & Other Stories	Jack Nolan	Sci-fi	—	Male	WER4
Books suitable for secondary-aged students and adults (11 and older)					
Jurassic Park (Michael Crichton)	F. H. Cornish	Sci-fi	Caribbean	—	HGR4
Pride and Prejudice (Jane Austen)	Margaret Tarner	Romance	UK	—	HGR4
Wuthering Heights (Emily Brontë)	F. H. Cornish	Romance	UK	—	HGR4
Great Expectations (Charles Dickens)	**Florence Bell**	—	UK	Male	HGR5
The Great Ponds (Elechi Amadi)	John Davey	—	Africa	Male	HGR5
The Man of Property (John Galsworthy)	**Margaret Tarner**	—	UK	—	HGR5
Mine Boy (Peter Abrahams)	**Rod Nesbitt**	—	Africa	Male	HGR5
Of Mice and Men (John Steinbeck)	Martin Winks	—	N America	Male	HGR5
Weep Not, Child (James Ngugi)	Margaret Tarner	—	Africa	Male	HGR5
The Cruel War	**Kwasi Koranteng**	Thriller/crime	Africa	Male	HJAWS5

Title	*Author*	*Genre*	*Region*	*Gender*	*Publisher/ Series*
Cry Softly, Thule Nene	Shirley Boje	—	Africa	Female	HJAWS5
The Ivory Poachers	Linda Pfotenhauer	Thriller/crime	Africa	Female	HJAWS5
Ma'ami	**Okinba Launko**	—	Africa	Female	HJAWS5
Taxi!	Barbara Kimenye	Thriller/crime	Africa	Male	HJAWS5
Travellers	**Keith Whitely**	—	Africa	—	HJAWS5
A Christmas Carol (Charles Dickens)	Viola Huggins	—	UK	Male	LEL4
Rear Window (Cornell Woolrich)	**Lewis Jones**	Thriller/crime	N America	Male	LEL4
The Forger	Robert O'Neill	Thriller/crime	Europe	Male	LO4
The Great Discovery	Mandy Loader	Thriller/crime	Middle East	Male	LO4
The Book of British Humour	Judith King, Ronald Ridout, & D. K. Swan	Humor	UK	Male	LSRB
Desert, Mountain, Sea	Sue Leather	Adventure	—	Female	OBW4
Dr Jekyll and Mr Hyde (R. L. Stevenson)	**Rosemary Border**	Horror/ghost	UK	Male	OBW4
The Hound of the Baskervilles (Sir A. Conan Doyle)	Patrick Nobes	Thriller/crime	UK	Male	OBW4
Mr Midshipman Hornblower (C. S. Forester)	**Rosemary Border**	History	Europe	Male	OBW4
Reflex (Dick Francis)	Rowena Akinyemi	Thriller/crime	UK	Male	OBW4
Silas Marner (George Eliot)	Clare West	—	UK	Male	OBW4

Title	*Author*	*Genre*	*Region*	*Gender*	*Publisher/ Series*
The Songs of Distant Earth (Arthur C. Clarke)	**Jennifer Bassett**	Sci-fi	—	—	OBW4
The Thirty-Nine Steps (John Buchan)	**Nick Bullard**	Thriller/crime	UK	Male	OBW4
The Unquiet Grave (M. R. James)	**Peter Hawkins**	Horror/ghost	UK	Male	OBW4
The Boys from Brazil (Ira Levin)	Cherry Gilchist	Thriller/crime	N America	Male	PR4
The Client (John Grisham)	Jane McAlpin	Thriller/crime	N America	Male	PR4
White Fang (Jack London)	Robin Waterfield	Animal	N America	—	PR4

EPER LEVEL A					
Title	*Author*	*Genre*	*Region*	*Gender*	*Publisher/ Series*
Books most suitable for secondary-aged students (11–16 years old)					
Unoma at College	Teresa Meniru	Adventure	Africa	Female	EAL
Adventure in Thailand	John Dent	Thriller/crime	Asia	Male	GJUP5
You Never Know	John Dent	Thriller/crime	Asia	Male	GSTR3
The Adventures of Tom Sawyer (Mark Twain)	W. J. Hoggett	Adventure	N America	Male	LF3
Halima	Meshack Asare	—	Africa	Female	MMT4
Sport in Africa	Ossie Stuart	Sport	Africa	—	MMT4
Just So Stories (Rudyard Kipling)	Susan Swatridge	Fable	—	—	MSR1
Moonfleet (John Meade Falkner)	Richard Sellwood	Adventure	UK	Male	MSR1
Dr Jekyll and Mr Hyde & Other Stories (R. L. Stevenson)		Horror/ghost	UK	Male	OPER4
The Gifts & Other Stories (O. Henry et al.)		—	N America	Male	OPER4
King Solomon's Mines (Sir H. Rider Haggard)		Adventure	Africa	Male	OPER4
A Night of Terror & Other Strange Tales (G. de Maupassant)		Horror/ghost	Europe	Male	OPER4
Seven Stories (H. G. Wells)		Horror/ghost	UK	Male	OPER4

Title	*Author*	*Genre*	*Region*	*Gender*	*Publisher/ Series*
Tales of Mystery and Imagination (Edgar Allan Poe)		Horror/ghost	N America	Male	OPER4
Tess of the d'Urbervilles (Thomas Hardy)	Katherine Mattock	Romance	UK	Female	OPER4
The Thirty-Nine Steps (John Buchan)	**David Foulds**	Thriller/crime	UK	Male	OPER4
You Only Live Twice (Ian Fleming)		Thriller/crime	Asia	Male	OPER4
Let's Talk about Art	Richard Williams	Culture	UK	—	PHBS4
Books suitable for secondary-aged students and adults (11 and older)					
The Grapes of Wrath (John Steinbeck)	Margaret Tarner	—	N America	Male	HGR5
Rebecca (Daphne du Maurier)	Margaret Tarner	Thriller/crime	UK	Female	HGR5
The Money Game	**Barbara Kimenye**	Humor	Africa	Male	HJAWS5
Wuthering Heights (Emily Brontë)	Sally Lowe	Romance	UK	—	LEL5
Jamaica Inn (Daphne du Maurier)	A. S. M. Ronaldson	Romance	UK	Female	LF3
Outstanding Short Stories (H. G. Wells et al.)	G. C. Thornley	—	—	—	LF3
The Prisoner of Zenda (Anthony Hope)	G. F. Wear	Adventure	Europe	Male	LF3
Rebecca (Daphne du Maurier)	A. S. M. Ronaldson	Thriller/crime	UK	Female	LF3
Round the World in Eighty Days (Jules Verne)	H. E. Palmer	Adventure	—	Male	LF3
Sherlock Holmes Short Stories (Sir A. Conan Doyle)	Anthony Laude	Thriller/crime	UK	Male	LF3

Title	*Author*	*Genre*	*Region*	*Gender*	*Publisher/ Series*
Stories of Detection and Mystery (G. K. Chesterton et al.)	Margery Morris	Thriller/crime	UK	Male	LF3
Taste & Other Tales (Roald Dahl)	Richard Caldon	—	UK	Male	LF3
The Call of the Wild (Jack London)	Margery Green	Animal	N America	Male	MSR1
Captain Blood (Rafael Sabatini)	E. F. Dodd	Thriller/crime	UK	Male	MSR1
Little Women (Louisa May Alcott)	Susan Swatridge	Family	N America	Female	MSR1
Nicholas Nickleby (Charles Dickens)	Margery Green	—	UK	Male	MSR1
Brat Farrar (Josephine Tey)	**Ralph Mowat**	Thriller/crime	UK	Male	OBW5
The Bride Price (Buchi Emecheta)	**Rosemary Border**	Romance	Africa	—	OBW5
David Copperfield (Charles Dickens)	**Clare West**	—	UK	Male	OBW5
Far from the Madding Crowd (Thomas Hardy)	**Clare West**	Romance	UK	—	OBW5
Great Expectations (Charles Dickens)	**Clare West**	—	UK	Male	OBW5
Heat and Dust (Ruth Prawer Jhabvala)	Clare West	Romance	Indian Subcont	Female	OBW5
I, Robot (Isaac Asimov)	Rowena Akinyemi	Sci-fi	N America	Female	OBW5
King's Ransom (Ed McBain)	Rosalie Kerr	Thriller/crime	N America	Male	OBW5
The Warden (Anthony Trollope)	J. Y. K. Kerr	—	UK	Male	PR5
Web (John Wyndham)	Joc Potter & Andy Hopkins	Fantasy	Pacific	Male	PR5

EPER LEVEL X

Title	*Author*	*Genre*	*Region*	*Gender*	*Publisher/ Series*
Books most suitable for secondary-aged students (11–16 years old)					
Odenigbo	Thomas Chigbo	—	Africa	Male	EAL
The Torn Veil & Other Stories	Mabel Donve Danquah & Phebean Itayemi	—	Africa	Female	EAL
Frankenstein (Mary Shelley)		Horror/ghost	Europe	Male	OPER5
Kidnapped (R. L. Stevenson)		Adventure	UK	Male	OPER5
The Mayor of Casterbridge (Thomas Hardy)		—	UK	—	OPER5
The Old Wives' Tale (Arnold Bennett)	L. A. Hill	—	UK	Female	OPER5
Pride and Prejudice (Jane Austen)		Romance	UK	Female	OPER5
Three Men in a Boat (Jerome K. Jerome)	David Foulds	Humor	UK	Male	OPER5
Wuthering Heights (Emily Brontë)		Romance	UK	—	OPER5
Books suitable for secondary-aged students and adults (11 and older)					
Alexander the Great	Hugh Gethin	Biography	Middle East	Male	GR
The Seven Wonders of the Ancient World	Hugh Gethin & Judith Brown	History	Middle East	—	GR
The Citadel (A. J. Cronin)	**Norman Wymer**	—	UK	Male	LF3
Cry the Beloved Country (Alan Paton)	**G. F. Wear**	—	Africa	Male	LF4

Title	*Author*	*Genre*	*Region*	*Gender*	*Publisher/ Series*
Flowers for Mrs Harris (Paul Gallico)	R. H. Durham	—	UK	Female	LF4
Moby Dick (Herman Melville)	Colin Swatridge	—	N America	Male	MSR1
The Adventures of Huckleberry Finn (Mark Twain)	Kerry Edwards	Adventure	N America	Male	MSR2
All Quiet on the Western Front (Erich Maria Remarque)	Colin Swatridge	—	Europe	Male	MSR2
Anna of the Five Towns (Arnold Bennett)	Susan Swatridge	Romance	UK	Female	MSR2
Emma (Jane Austen)	Mary Calvert	Romance	UK	Female	MSR2
Far from the Madding Crowd (Thomas Hardy)	Susan Swatridge	Romance	UK	—	MSR2
The Greatest Tales of Sherlock Holmes (Sir A. Conan Doyle)	Kerry Edwards	Thriller/crime	UK	Male	MSR2
The Greengage Summer (Rumer Godden)	**Susan Swatridge**	Romance	Europe	Female	MSR2
A Passage to India (E. M. Forster)	Colin Swatridge	—	Indian Subcont	—	MSR2
The Rocking-Horse Winner & Other Stories (D. H. Lawrence)	Colin Swatridge	—	UK	—	MSR2
The Scarlet Pimpernel (Baroness Orczy)	E. F. Dodd	Thriller/crime	Europe	Male	MSR2
Twenty Thousand Leagues under the Sea (Jules Verne)	Mary Tomalin	Sci-fi	—	Male	MSR2
Cry Freedom (John Briley)	**Rowena Akinyemi**	Biography	Africa	Male	OBW6
Deadheads (Reginald Hill)	Rosalie Kerr	Thriller/crime	UK	Male	OBW6

Title	*Author*	*Genre*	*Region*	*Gender*	*Publisher/ Series*
Dublin People (Maeve Binchy)	Jennifer Bassett	—	Europe	—	OBW6
The Enemy (Desmond Bagley)	Ralph Mowat	Thriller/crime	UK	Male	OBW6
Jane Eyre (Charlotte Brontë)	**Clare West**	Romance	UK	Female	OBW6
Meteor (John Wyndham)	**Patrick Nobes**	Sci-fi	—	—	OBW6
Night without End (Alistair Maclean)	**Margaret Naudi**	Thriller/crime	Arctic	Male	OBW6
Oliver Twist (Charles Dickens)	Richard Rogers	—	UK	Male	OBW6
Pride and Prejudice (Jane Austen)	**Clare West**	Romance	UK	—	OBW6
Tess of the d'Urbervilles (Thomas Hardy)	Clare West	Romance	UK	Female	OBW6
The Edge (Dick Francis)	Robin Waterfield	Thriller/crime	N America	Male	PR6
Misery (Stephen King)	**Robin Waterfield**	Horror/ghost	N America	—	PR6
Mrs Packletide's Tiger & Other Stories (Saki)	**J. Y. K. Kerr**	—	UK	—	PR6

Description of the series

The series from which the titles in this bibliography are drawn are listed below. In parentheses after each entry are the ages for which the books in the series are suitable, the EPER difficulty levels that the series spans, and the number of in-print titles in the series contained in the EPER database. The name of the publishing company is also given. Contact addresses for these publishing companies follow the list.

A brief characterization of each series is also given, in most cases based on David Hill's reviews of these series (1997). This is mainly to assist those who might wish to order books beyond those listed in the bibliography, and who wish to identify the stronger series.

EAL *Evans African Library,* published for African schools, look brighter and are more substantial than Evans English Readers but vary in quality (secondary; EPER levels B–X; 21 titles). (Evans Brothers Ltd.)

EER *Evans English Readers* are an uneven, dated-looking series for African schools (primary; EPER levels G–C; 35 titles). (Evans Brothers Ltd.)

GJUP *Jupiter Readers* are original stories in a textbook-oriented format for Hong Kong schools (secondary; EPER levels E–X; 16 titles). (Galaxy Publishers)

GR *Georgian Readers* are high-quality nonfiction dealing with ancient Greece (secondary-adult; EPER level X; 2 titles). (Georgian Press)

GSTR *Sing Tao Readers* are original stories in textbook-oriented format for Hong Kong schools (secondary; EPER levels E–X; 15 titles). (Galaxy Publishers)

HBNR *HBJ New Readers* are generally mediocre original stories (secondary-adult; EPER level F; 15 titles). (Harcourt Brace Jovanovich)

HCR *Heinemann Children's Readers.* "The strengths of these books lie in the illustrated glossaries and the variety of genres" (Hill, 1997, p. 68) (primary; EPER levels G–E; 20 titles). (Heinemann)

HGR *Heinemann Guided Readers* are superb books of outstanding quality and appeal (secondary-adult; EPER levels G–A; 118 titles). (Heinemann)

HJAWS *Heinemann Junior African Writer Series* "[draws] on many established authors, who have written stories that are well crafted" (Hill, 1997, p. 68) (primary-secondary; EPER levels G–A; 59 titles). (Heinemann) (This series is listed in the publisher's International Catalogue.)

HNW *Heinemann New Wave Readers* are original stories of varying quality – some excellent – aimed at European teenagers (secondary; EPER levels G–D; 30 titles). (Heinemann)

LC *Longman Classics.* These classy-looking books are the language learner literature equivalents of BBC/PBS classic dramas (primary-adult; EPER levels D–B; 47 titles). Addison Wesley Longman)

LCCR *Longman Child to Child Readers* present issues related to health education. The stories "should not be as weak as they are" (Hill, 1997, p. 70) (primary; EPER levels F–D; 14 titles). (Addison Wesley Longman) (This series is listed in the publisher's International Catalogue.)

LEL *Longman English Library* are new issues of the better titles in the old uneven *Collins English Library/Nelson Readers* series (secondary-adult; EPER levels E–X; 50 titles). (Addison Wesley Longman)

LES *Easystarts* are pleasant, easy stories for all ages (secondary-adult; EPER level G; 20 titles). (Addison Wesley Longman)

LF *Longman Fiction* are slightly revised editions of *Longman Structural Readers, Simplified English Series* and *Bridge Series,* forming a solid but slightly disappointing new series (secondary-adult; EPER levels C–ungraded; 50 titles). (Addison Wesley Longman)

LFFT *Favourite Fairy Tales* attractively retell well-known stories from Europe (primary; EPER level F; 10 titles). (Addison Wesley Longman)

LGEMS *Longman Gems* are original stories published in Botswana in textbook-oriented format for schools (primary-secondary; EPER levels F–B; 21 titles). (Addison Wesley Longman) (This series is listed in the publisher's International Catalogue.)

LO *Longman Originals* are original stories of varying quality, some excellent (secondary-adult; EPER levels F–B; 50 titles). (Addison Wesley Longman)

LPC *Longman Picture Classics* "are remarkably successful in their own terms" (Hill, 1997, p. 69) (secondary; EPER level E; 20 titles). (Addison Wesley Longman)

LRE *Longman Reading for the Environment* presents issues related to conservation. "The stories are stronger [than Longman Child to Child Readers]" (Hill, 1997, p. 70) (primary-secondary; EPER levels E–C; 6 titles). (Addison Wesley Longman) (This series is listed in the publisher's International Catalogue.)

LSRB *Longman Structural Readers Background* are excellent nonfiction books (secondary-adult; EPER levels E–B; 8 titles). (Addison Wesley Longman)

MBIB *Macmillan Bible Stories* re-create stories from the Old and New Testaments with "fine artwork and sympathetic text" (Hill, 1997, p. 71) (primary-secondary; EPER levels E–D; 12 titles). (Macmillan Education Ltd)

MBS *Macmillan Bookshelf* are original stories varying from adequate to poor (secondary-adult; EPER levels E–B; 26 titles). (Prentice Hall)

MCR *Carnival Readers* are fables and fairy tales (primary; EPER levels G–E; 10 titles). (Macmillan Education Ltd)

MHSJ *Hop Step and Jump* are excellent fiction and nonfiction aimed at African students, with "neat and humourous" stories as well as ones that "carry a message on such subjects as bullying and gender roles" (Hill, 1997, p. 71) (primary; EPER levels G–D; 34 titles). (Macmillan Education Ltd)

MLE *Macmillan Living Earth* series, which Hill rates excellent in content and presentation (1997, p. 71), addresses environmental themes (primary-secondary; EPER levels E–D; 9 titles). (Macmillan Education Ltd)

MMT *Mactracks,* for African students, allow well-known African authors to discuss social and economic issues through fiction. "Nearly all the titles are well worth reading" (Hill, 1997, p. 71) (secondary; EPER levels F–A; 33 titles). (Macmillan Education Ltd)

MR *Rangers* are mainly original stories of uneven quality (primary-adult; EPER levels F–X; 55 titles). (Prentice Hall)

MSR *Stories to Remember* are "generally readable" abridged classics (Hill, 1997, p. 70) (secondary-adult; EPER levels A–X; 58 titles). (Macmillan Education Ltd)

OBW *Oxford Bookworms* are an excellent series of adult-oriented stories that are "consistently well written . . . flowing and readable" (Hill, 1997, p. 71) (secondary-adult; EPER levels E–X; 75 titles). (Oxford University Press)

OBWG *Oxford Bookworms: Green Series* are an excellent series of classics and modern fiction for children. These are "consistently good" (Hill, 1997, p. 71) (primary-secondary; EPER levels E–B; 23 titles). (Oxford University Press)

OCLT *Classic Tales* present well-known fairy tales in an attractive large format (primary; EPER levels G–F; 6 titles). (Oxford University Press)

OPER *Oxford Progressive English Readers* are classic stories published in Hong Kong. "The quality of simplification is generally quite high" (Hill, 1997, p. 72) (secondary; EPER levels D–X; 76 titles). (Oxford University Press [China])

OSIE *Stepping into English* are bright versions of fables (primary; EPER level G; 9 titles). (Oxford University Press)

OSL *Storylines* are "short and pithy" (Hill, 1997, p. 71) original stories, originally published as *Streamline Readers* and given an attractive reissue (secondary-adult; EPER levels F–D; 12 titles). (Oxford University Press)

PETAP *Tapir English Readers* are original stories and classics published in Malaysia in textbook format (secondary; EPER levels E–A; 35 titles). (Penerbit Fajar Bakti)

PHBS *Phoenix Bookshelf* are original stories of differing quality (secondary-adult; EPER levels E–X; 18 titles). (Prentice Hall)

PHR *Phoenix Readers* Stage 1 "re-tell traditional fables in a racy style" (Hill, 1997, p. 75) (primary; EPER level G; 6 titles). (Prentice Hall)

PR *Penguin Readers* are a large and shockingly uneven series (primary-adult; EPER levels E–X; 85 titles). (Penguin)

RR *Richmond Readers* (not included in the list) are stories adapted in a way linguistically suitable for Spanish and Italian learners of English (secondary-adult; EPER levels E–A; 40 titles). (Richmond Publishing)

WER *Witman English Readers* are original stories for Hong Kong secondary students in a textbook-oriented format (primary-secondary; EPER levels D–A; 50 titles). (Witman Publishing Co. (H.K.) Ltd.)

The publishers

Evans Brothers Ltd., 2a Portman Mansions, Chiltern Street, London W1M 1LE, UK.

Galaxy Publishers, A306 & B308 3/F, 420–424 Kwun Tong Road, Kowloon, Hong Kong, PRC.

Georgian Press, 56 Sandy Lane, Leyland, Preston PR5 1ED, UK.

Harcourt Brace Jovanovich, Holt, Rinehart & Winston, 1120 South Capital of Texas Highway, Austin, Texas 78746–6487, USA.

Heinemann, Halley Court, Jordan Hill, Oxford OX2 8EJ, UK.

Addison Wesley Longman Ltd, Edinburgh Gate, Harlow, Essex CM20 2JE, UK.

Macmillan Education Ltd, Houndmills, Basingstoke, Hampshire RG21 6XS, UK.

Oxford University Press, Walton Street, Oxford OX2 6DP, UK.

Oxford University Press (China) Ltd., 18th Floor Warwick House, Taikoo Place, 979 King's Road, Quarry Bay, Hong Kong, PRC.

Penerbit Fajar Bakti Sdn Bhd, 4 Jalan Pemaju U1/15, Seksyen U1, Hicom Glenmarie Industrial Park, 40150 Shah Alam, Selangor Darul Ehsan, Malaysia.

Penguin, 27 Wrights Lane, London W8 5TZ, UK.

Prentice Hall, Simon & Schuster, Campus 400, Maylands Avenue, Hemel Hempstead, HP2 7EZ, UK.

Richmond Publishing, 19 Berghem Mews, Blythe Road, London W14 0HN, UK.

Witman Publishing Co. (H.K.) Ltd., 9–11 Tsat Tse Mui Road, G/F., North Point, Hong Kong, PRC.

Further information about EPER

The EPER database of graded readers can help teachers and librarians select the best titles for their students. General or customized lists are available, giving the EPER level and quality rating for each title.

EPER publishes a variety of aids designed to assist teachers in setting up extensive reading programs. These include placement/progress tests, extensive reading tests, comprehension questions for library readers, teachers' notes and lesson plans for class readers, and reading cards for beginners (in effect, reading material a level below the lowest level "G" on the EPER scale). Samples of some of these materials are available in a Resource Pack for Organizing Extensive Reading Programs.

EPER has built up expertise in designing, implementing, monitoring, and evaluating reading programs in many countries, and makes this expertise available through consultancies. It also trains teachers in writing fiction for language learners with a view to producing local series in different parts of the world.

The Edinburgh Project on Extensive Reading welcomes contact from anyone interested in extensive reading. Write to EPER, Institute for Applied Language Studies, University of Edinburgh, 21 Hill Place, Edinburgh EH8 9DP, UK.

References

Page numbers appearing in brackets at the end of an entry indicate the pages on which the author and work are mentioned.

Adams, M. J. (1990). *Beginning to read: Thinking and learning about print.* Cambridge, MA: MIT Press. [12]

Adams, M. J. (1994). Modeling the connections between word recognition and reading. In R. B. Ruddell, M. R. Ruddell, & H. Singer (Eds.), *Theoretical models and processes of reading* (4th ed.) (pp. 838–863). Newark, DE: International Reading Association. [12, 13, 14]

Aebersold, J. A., & Field, M. L. (1997). *From reader to reading teacher: Issues and strategies for second language classrooms.* New York: Cambridge University Press. [xiii, 25]

Ajzen, I. (1988). *Attitudes, personality, and behavior.* Milton Keyes: Open University Press. [22]

Alderson, J. C. (1992). Guidelines for the evaluation of language education. In J. C. Alderson & A. Beretta (Eds.), *Evaluating second language education* (pp. 274–304). Cambridge: Cambridge University Press. [163]

Alderson, J. C., & Urquhart, A. H. (Eds.). (1984). *Reading in a foreign language.* Harlow, Essex: Longman. [15–16, 59, 61, 65–66]

Alexander, L. G. (1983). *Foul play.* Harlow, Essex: Longman. [144, 145]

Anderson, R. C., & Freebody, P. (1981). Vocabulary knowledge. In J. T. Guthrie (Ed.), *Comprehension and teaching: Research reviews* (pp. 77–117). Newark, DE: International Reading Association. [14]

Athey, I. (1985). Reading research in the affective domain. In H. Singer & R. B. Ruddell (Eds.), *Theoretical models and processes of reading* (3rd ed.) (pp. 527–557). Newark, DE: International Reading Association. [21]

Bamberger, R. (1991). Ten best ideas for reading teachers. In E. Fry (Ed.), *Ten best ideas for reading teachers* (pp. 35–36). Reading, MA: Addison-Wesley. [155]

Bamford, J. (1984). Extensive reading by means of graded readers. *Reading in a Foreign Language, 2*(2), 218–260. [119, 147, 149]

Bamford, J., & Day, R. R. (1997). Extensive reading: What is it? Why bother? *The Language Teacher, 21*(5), 6–8, 12. [164]

Barnett, M. A. (1989). *More than meets the eye. Foreign language reading: Theory and practice.* Englewood Cliffs, NJ: Prentice Hall Regents. [10]

Barrett, M. E., & Kearny Datesman, M. (1992). *Reading on your own: An extensive reading course.* Boston: Heinle & Heinle. [138–139]

Beck, I. L. (1981). Reading problems and instructional practices. In G. E. MacKinnon & T. G. Waller (Eds.), *Reading research: Advances in theory and practice* (Vol. 2, pp. 53–95). New York: Academic Press. [5]

Berman, R. A. (1984). Syntactic components of the foreign language reading process. In J. C. Alderson & A. H. Urquhart (Eds.), *Reading in a foreign language* (pp. 139–156). Harlow, Essex: Longman. [59]

Bierce, A. (1911). *The devil's dictionary.* New York: Dover. [55]

Bondy, E. (1990). Seeing it their way: What children's definitions of reading tell us about improving teacher education. *Journal of Teacher Education, 41*(5), 33–45. [7]

Breen, M. P. (1985). Authenticity in the language classroom. *Applied Linguistics, 6*(1), 60–70. (Original work published in 1982.) [61]

Bright, J. A., & McGregor, G. P. (1970). *Teaching English as a second language.* London: Longman. [85, 96, 136]

Brown, D. S. (1988). *A world of books: An annotated reading list for ESL/EFL students* (2nd ed.). Washington, DC: TESOL. [106]

Brown, D. S. (1994). *Books for a small planet: A multicultural-intercultural bibliography for young English language learners.* Alexandria, VA: TESOL. [106]

Brumfit, C. J. (1985). Graded material and the use of the lexicon. In C. J. Brumfit & R. A. Carter (Eds.), *Language and literature teaching* (pp. 96–99). Oxford: Pergamon. (Original work published in 1981.) [66, 67, 75–76]

Brumfit, C. (1993). Simplification in pedagogy. In M. L. Tickoo (Ed.), *Simplification: Theory and application* (pp. 1–6). Singapore: SEAMEO Regional Language Centre. [61]

Burnett, F. H. (1911). *The secret garden.* New York: HarperCollins. [31]

Carrell, P. L., Devine, J., & Eskey, D. E. (Eds.). (1988). *Interactive approaches to second language reading.* Cambridge: Cambridge University Press. [19–20]

Carter, R., & Long, M. N. (1991). *Teaching literature.* Harlow, Essex: Longman. [56, 74, 79, 139]

Chall, J. S. (1987). Two vocabularies for reading: Recognition and meaning. In M. G. McKeown & M. E. Curtis (Eds.), *The nature of vocabulary acquisition* (pp. 7–17). Hillsdale, NJ: Lawrence Erlbaum. [17]

Cho, K.-S., & Krashen, S. D. (1994). Acquisition of vocabulary from the Sweet Valley Kids series: Adult ESL acquisition. *Journal of Reading, 37*(8), 662–667. [34, 35–36, 37]

Clarke, D. F. (1989). Communicative theory and its influence on materials production. *Language Teaching, 22*(2), 73–86. [55]

Cliffe, S. (1990). How to set up a class reading library. *The Language Teacher, 14*(12), 29–30. [115]

Christian, C. (1975). *Johnny Ring.* London: Macmillan. [139]

Coady, J. (1993). Research on ESL/EFL vocabulary acquisition: Putting it in context. In T. Huckin, M. Haynes, & J. Coady (Eds.), *Second language reading and vocabulary learning* (pp. 3–23). Norwood, NJ: Ablex. [17]

Comfort, A. (1972). *The joy of sex.* New York: Crown. [67]

Constantino, R. (1995). Learning to read in a second language doesn't have to hurt: The effect of pleasure reading. *Journal of Adolescent & Adult Literacy, 39*(1), 68–69. [125]

Cramer, E. H., & Castle, M. (Eds.). (1994). *Fostering the love of reading: The affective domain in reading education.* Newark, DE: International Reading Association. [31]

Csikszentmihalyi, M. (1990a). *Flow: The psychology of optimal experience.* New York: Harper & Row. [30]

Csikszentmihalyi, M. (1990b). Literacy and intrinsic motivation. *DAEDALUS, Journal of the American Academy of Arts and Sciences, 119*(2), 115–140. [21]

Cunningham, P., & Cunningham, J. (1991). Ten best ideas for elementary reading teachers. In E. Fry (Ed.), *Ten best ideas for reading teachers* (pp. 42–50). Reading, MA: Addison-Wesley. [128]

Cunningham, R. (1991). The Zanzibar reading programme. *Reading in a Foreign Language, 8*(1), 663–675. [117]

Daane, M. (1996). [Review of *If not now: Developmental readers in the college classroom*]. *Journal of Adolescent & Adult Literacy, 40*(3), 235–237. [164]

Davies, A. (1984). Simple, simplified and simplification: What is authentic? In J. C. Alderson & A. H. Urquhart (Eds.), *Reading in a foreign language* (pp. 181–195). Harlow, Essex: Longman. [53, 61]

Davies, A., & Widdowson, H. G. (1974). Reading and writing. In J. P. B. Allen & S. P. Corder (Eds.), *The Edinburgh course in applied linguistics,* Vol. 3, *Techniques in applied linguistics* (pp. 155–201). Oxford: Oxford University Press. [60, 79]

Davis, C. (1995). Extensive reading: An expensive extravagance? *ELT Journal, 49*(4), 329–336. [47–48, 96, 108, 116–117, 154]

Davis, J. N., Gorell, L. C., Kline, R. R., & Hsieh, G. (1992). Readers and second languages: A survey of undergraduate attitudes toward the study of literature. *The Modern Language Journal, 76*(3), 320–332. [47]

Day, R. R. (Ed.). (1993). *New ways in teaching reading.* Alexandria, VA: TESOL. [47, 138]

Day, R. R., & Swan, J. (1998). Incidental learning of foreign language spelling through targeted reading. *TESL Reporter, 31*(1), 1–9.

Devine, J. (1984). ESL readers' internalized models of the reading process. In J. Handscombe, R. A. Orem, & B. P. Taylor (Eds.), *On TESOL '83. The question of control* (pp. 95–108). Washington, DC: TESOL. [7]

Dickinson, L. (1995). Autonomy and motivation: A literature review. *System, 23*(2), 165–174. [27]

Dupuy, B., Cook, T., & Tse, L. (1995). Turning ESL students into fluent readers: A workshop. Paper presented at the TESOL Conference, Long Beach, CA. [94, 129]

Dupuy, B., Tse, L., & Cook, T. (1996). Bringing books into the classroom: First steps in turning college-level ESL students into readers. *TESOL Journal, 5*(4), 10–15. [90, 118, 119, 142]

Dwyer, E. J., & Dwyer, E. E. (1994). How teacher attitudes influence reading achievement. In E. H. Cramer & M. Castle (Eds.), *Fostering the love of reading: The affective domain in reading education* (pp. 66–73). Newark, DE: International Reading Association. [126]

Eagly, A. H., & Chaiken, S. (1993). *The psychology of attitudes.* Fort Worth, TX: Harcourt Brace Jovanovich. [22]

Elley, W. B. (1991). Acquiring literacy in a second language: The effect of book-based programs. *Language Learning, 41*(3), 375–411. [34, 35, 38]

Elley, W. B. (1992). *How in the world do students read? IEA study of reading literacy.* New York: International Association for the Evaluation of Educational Achievement. [7]

Elley, W. B., & Mangubhai, F. (1981). *The impact of a book flood in Fiji primary schools.* Wellington: New Zealand Council for Educational Research. [33, 34, 35, 37]

Escott, J. (1996). *Forrest Gump.* London: Penguin. (Adapted from the original book by Winston Groom.) [141, 142]

Eskey, D. E. (1986). Theoretical foundations. In F. Dubin, D. E. Eskey, & W. Grabe (Eds.), *Teaching second language reading for academic purposes* (pp. 3–23). Reading, MA: Addison-Wesley. [4]

Eskey, D. E. (1995). Remarks made at Colloquium on Research in Reading in a Second Language, TESOL Conference, Long Beach, CA. [47, 104]

Esplen, M. (1976). *Marco.* London: Heinemann. [144, 146]

Feather, N. T. (1982). Introduction and overview. In N. T. Feather (Ed.), *Expectations and actions: Expectancy-value models in psychology* (pp. 1–14). Hillsdale, NJ: Lawrence Erlbaum. [27, 31]

Field, M. L. (1985). A psycholinguistic model of the Chinese ESL reader. In P. Larson, E. L. Judd, & D. S. Messerschmitt (Eds.), *On TESOL '84. A brave new world for TESOL* (pp. 171–183). Washington, DC: TESOL. [119]

Franken, R. E. (1988). *Human motivation* (2nd ed.). Pacific Grove, CA: Brooks/Cole. [27]

Gardner, R. C., & Lambert, W. E. (1959). Motivational variables in second language acquisition. *Canadian Journal of Psychology, 13,* 266–272. [21]

Gilbran, K. (1966). *The prophet.* New York: Knopf. [132]

Gill, M. (1992). Reading, culture and cognition. *Edinburgh Working Papers in Applied Linguistics, 3,* 49–66. [11]

Grabe, W. (1986). The transition from theory to practice in teaching reading. In F. Dubin, D. E. Eskey, & W. Grabe (Eds.), *Teaching second language reading for academic purposes* (pp. 25–48). Reading, MA: Addison-Wesley. [19, 40, 45, 84]

Grabe, W. (1988). Reassessing the term "interactive." In P. L. Carrell, J. Devine, & D. E. Eskey (Eds.), *Interactive approaches to second language reading* (pp. 56–70). Cambridge: Cambridge University Press. [17]

Grabe, W. (1991). Current developments in second language reading research. *TESOL Quarterly, 25*(3), 375–406. [6, 118]

Grabe, W. (1995). Remarks made at Colloquium on Research in Reading in a Second Language, TESOL Conference, Long Beach, CA. [7, 41, 47, 105]

Greenwood, J. (1988). *Class readers.* Oxford: Oxford University Press. [139]

Grellet, F. (1981). *Developing reading skills: A practical guide to reading comprehension exercises.* Cambridge: Cambridge University Press. [53, 55]

Hafiz, F. M., & Tudor, I. (1989). Extensive reading and the development of language skills. *ELT Journal, 43*(1), 4–13. [34, 35, 36, 37]

Hafiz, F. M., & Tudor, I. (1990). Graded readers as an input medium in L2 learning. *System, 18*(1), 31–42. [34, 35, 36]

Harris, A. J., & Sipay, E. R. (1990). *How to increase reading ability: A guide to developmental and remedial methods* (9th ed.). White Plains, NY: Longman. [xiii, 14, 16, 18, 24, 90, 96]

Harrison, C. (1992). The reading process and learning to read. In C. Harrison & M. Coles (Eds.), *The reading for real handbook* (pp. 3–28). London: Routledge. [13, 20, 30–31]

Heathington, B. S. (1994). Affect versus skills: Choices for teachers. In E. H. Cramer & M. Castle (Eds.), *Fostering the love of reading: The affective domain in reading education* (pp. 199–208). Newark, DE: International Reading Association. [24, 166]

Hedge, T. (1985). *Using readers in language teaching.* London: Macmillan. [79, 138, 139]

Hedge, T. (1988). *Oxford bookworms: Guidelines for authors.* Oxford: Oxford University Press. [66, 67]

Hedge, T., & Bassett, J. (forthcoming). *Oxford bookworms: Guidelines for authors* (rev. ed.). Oxford: Oxford University Press. [67–74]

Henry, J. (1995). *If not now: Developmental readers in the college classroom.* Portsmouth, NH: Boynton/Cook. [165]

Hill, D. R. (1992). *The EPER guide to organising programmes of extensive reading.* Edinburgh: Institute for Applied Language Studies, University of Edinburgh. [42–43, 48–49, 133–134, 156, 163]

Hill, D. R. (1995, June). Mixed bag of nuggets as Penguin mine for gold. *EL Gazette,* 17. [58]

Hill, D. R. (1997). Survey review: Graded readers. *ELT Journal, 51*(1), 57–81. [76, 77–78, 79, 170–171, 213–216]

Hill, D. R., & Reid Thomas, H. (1988). Survey review: Graded readers (Part I). *ELT Journal, 42*(1), 44–52. [57, 85]

Hindmarsh, R. (1980). *Cambridge English lexicon.* Cambridge: Cambridge University Press. [66]

Honeyfield, J. (1977). Simplification. *TESOL Quarterly, 11*(4), 431–440. [62]

Howatt, A. P. R. (1984). *A history of English language teaching.* Oxford: Oxford University Press. [9]

Huckin, T., & Haynes, M. (1993). Summary and future directions. In T. Huckin, M. Haynes, & J. Coady (Eds.), *Second language reading and vocabulary learning* (pp. 289–298). Norwood, NJ: Ablex. [18]

Huckin, T., Haynes, M., & Coady, J. (Eds.). (1993). *Second language reading and vocabulary learning.* Norwood, NJ: Ablex. [20]

Hunt, L. C., Jr. (1970). The effect of self-selection, interest, and motivation upon independent, instructional, and frustrational levels. *The Reading Teacher, 24*(2), 146–151, 158. (Reprinted in *The Reading Teacher, 50*(4), 278–282 [1996–1997]). [138]

Jacobs, G. M., Davis, C., & Renandya, W. A. (Eds.). (1997). *Successful strategies for extensive reading.* Singapore: SEAMEO Regional Language Centre. [138]

Janopoulos, M. (1986). The relationship of pleasure reading and second language writing proficiency. *TESOL Quarterly, 20*(4), 763–768. [34, 37]

Jensen, L. (1986). Advanced reading skills in a comprehensive course. In F. Dubin, D. E. Eskey, & W. Grabe (Eds.), *Teaching second language reading for academic purposes* (pp. 103–124). Reading, MA: Addison-Wesley. [40]

Johnson, D. M. (1992). *Approaches to research in second language learning.* New York: Longman. [156]

Johnson, P. (1981). Effects on reading comprehension of language complexity and cultural background of a text. *TESOL Quarterly, 15*(2), 169–181. [59, 65]

Johnston, P., & Allington, R. (1991). Remediation. In R. Barr, M. L. Kamil, P. B. Mosenthal, & P. D. Pearson (Eds.), *Handbook of reading research* (Vol. 2, pp. 984–1012). White Plains, NY: Longman. [30]

Just, M. A., & Carpenter, P. A. (1987). *The psychology of reading and language comprehension.* Boston: Allyn & Bacon. [13, 20]

Kelly, L. G. (1969). *25 centuries of language teaching.* Rowley, MA: Newbury House. [5, 63]

Kids' favorite books: Children's choices 1989–1991. (1991). Newark, DE: International Reading Association. [106]

Klapper, J. (1992). Preliminary considerations for the teaching of FL reading. *Language Learning Journal, 6,* 53–56. [59, 91, 110]

Klare, G. R. (1984). Readability. In P. D. Pearson (Ed.), *Handbook of reading research* (pp. 681–744). White Plains, NY: Longman. [60, 65]

Krashen, S. D. (1985). *The input hypothesis: Issues and implications.* New York: Longman. [16]

Krashen, S. D. (1988). Do we learn to read by reading? The relationship between free reading and reading ability. In D. Tannen (Ed.), *Linguistics in context: Connecting observation and understanding* (pp. 269–298). Norwood, NJ: Ablex. [32, 38]

Krashen, S. D. (1989). We acquire vocabulary and spelling by reading: Additional evidence for the input hypothesis. *The Modern Language Journal, 73*(4), 440–464. [37, 39]

Krashen, S. D. (1991). The input hypothesis: An update. In J. Alatis (Ed.), *Georgetown University round table on language and linguistics, 1991* (pp. 427–431). Washington, DC: Georgetown University Press. [16]

Krashen, S. D. (1993a). The case for free voluntary reading. *The Canadian Modern Language Review, 50*(1), 72–82. [39, 47]

Krashen, S. D. (1993b). *The power of reading: Insights from the research.* Englewood, CO: Libraries Unlimited. [7, 33, 38, 39]

Kuhara-Kojima, K., Hatano, G., Saito, H., & Haebara, T. (1996). Vocalization latencies of skilled and less skilled comprehenders for words written in hiragana and kanji. *Reading Research Quarterly, 31*(2), 158–171. [13–14]

Lai, F.-K. (1993a). Effect of extensive reading on English learning in Hong Kong. *CUHK (Chinese University of Hong Kong) Education Journal, 21*(1), 23–36. [34, 35, 37, 46]

Lai, F.-K. (1993b). The effect of a summer reading course on reading and writing skills. *System, 21*(1), 87–100. [34, 35]

Laidlaw, C. (1988). *Countdown to midnight.* Oxford: Heinemann. [144, 145]

Laird, E. (1978). *The house on the hill.* London: Heinemann. [144, 146, 152]

Laird, E. (1991). *The earthquake.* Harlow, Essex: Longman. [152]

Lee, N. G., & Neal, J. C. (1992–1993). Reading rescue: Intervention for a student "at promise." *Journal of Reading, 36*(4), 276–282. [100, 130]

Lee, W. R. (1983). Some points about "authenticity." *World Language English, 2*(1), 10–14. [62]

Luppescu, S., & Day, R. R. (1993). Reading, dictionaries, and vocabulary learning. *Language Learning, 43*(2), 263–287. [93, 122]

Maley, A. (1988). Foreword. In J. Greenwood, *Class readers* (p. 3). Oxford: Oxford University Press. [63, 139]

Marzano, R. J. (1992). *A different kind of classroom: Teaching with dimensions of learning.* Alexandria, VA: Association for Supervision and Curriculum Development. [21]

Mason, B., & Krashen, S. (1997). Extensive reading in English as a foreign language. *System, 25*(1), 91–102. [34, 35]

Mason, B., & Pendergast, T. (1993). Taking a cloze look. In R. R. Day (Ed.), *New ways in teaching reading* (pp. 16–17). Alexandria, VA: TESOL. [88–90, 157]

Mathewson, G. C. (1994). Model of attitude influence upon reading and learning to read. In R. B. Ruddell, M. R. Ruddell, & H. Singer (Eds.), *Theoretical models and processes of reading* (4th ed.) (pp. 1131–1161). Newark, DE: International Reading Association. [23]

Mayne, E. (1915). The object of teaching reading. In W. J. Beecher & G. B. Faxon (Eds.), *Methods, aids, and devices for teachers* (pp. 40–41). Dansville, NY: F. A. Owen. [9]

McInness, J. A. (1973). Language prerequisites for reading. In M. M. Clark & A. Milne (Eds.), *Reading and related skills* (pp. 100–104). London: Ward Lock. [163]

McKenna, M. C. (1994). Toward a model of reading attitude acquisition. In E. H. Cramer & M. Castle (Eds.), *Fostering the love of reading: The affective domain in reading education* (pp. 18–40). Newark, DE: International Reading Association. [21, 23, 31]

McRae, J. (1991). *Literature with a small 'l.'* London: Macmillan. [63, 74–75, 77]

Mikulecky, B. S. (1990). *A short course in teaching reading skills.* Reading, MA: Addison-Wesley. [40, 106]

Milne, J. (1977). *Heinemann guided readers handbook.* London: Heinemann. [66, 67, 75, 79]

Modern Language Association of America. (1948). Report of the Committee of Twelve of the Modern Language Association of America: A critical review of methods of teaching. In M. Newmark (Ed.), *Twentieth century modern language teaching: Sources and readings* (pp. 281–294). New York: Philosophical Library. (Original work published in 1901.) [5, 9]

Moran, C., & Williams, E. (1993). Survey review: Recent materials for the teaching of reading at intermediate level and above. *ELT Journal, 47*(1), 64–84. [3, 9]

More teens' favorite books: Young adults' choices 1993–1995. (1996). Newark, DE: International Reading Association. [106]

Morrow, K., & Schocker, M. (1987). Using texts in a communicative approach. *ELT Journal, 41*(4), 248–256. [65, 91, 144]

Murphy, B. M. Z. (1987). Bad books in easy English. *Modern English Teacher, 14*(3), 22–23. [77]

Muzevich, K. (1995–1996). "Capture the flag" captures students' interest. *Reading Today, 13*(3), 16. [155]

Nagy, W. E., & Herman, P. A. (1987). Breadth and depth of vocabulary knowledge: Implications for acquisition and instruction. In M. G. McKeown & M. E. Curtis (Eds.), *The nature of vocabulary acquisition* (pp. 19–35). Hillsdale, NJ: Lawrence Erlbaum. [14–15, 17]

Nation, P., & Coady, J. (1988). Vocabulary and reading. In R. Carter & M. McCarthy (Eds.), *Vocabulary and language teaching* (pp. 97–110). Harlow, Essex: Longman. [18]

Nell, V. (1988). *Lost in a book: The psychology of reading for pleasure.* New Haven: Yale University Press. [31]

Nelson, P. (1984). Towards a more communicative reading course: Motivating students who are not "reading addicts." *Reading in a Foreign Language, 2*(1), 188–196. [126–127]

Newmark, M. (Ed.). (1948). *Twentieth century modern language teaching: Sources and readings.* New York: Philosophical Library. [9]

New York City Board of Education. (1948). Syllabus of minima in modern foreign languages: Classroom technic in reading. In M. Newmark (Ed.), *Twentieth century modern language teaching: Sources and readings* (pp. 299–302). New York: Philosophical Library. (Original work published in 1931.) [6]

Nuttall, C. (1982). *Teaching reading skills in a foreign language.* London: Heinemann. [40, 117]

Nuttall, C. (1996). *Teaching reading skills in a foreign language* (2nd ed.). Oxford: Heinemann. [40, 54–55, 57, 83, 107, 115–116, 117, 136, 139]

Otto, W. (1991). Ten best ideas for reading teachers. In E. Fry (Ed.), *Ten best ideas for reading teachers* (pp. 93–97). Reading, MA: Addison-Wesley. [127]

Palmer, H. E. (1964). *The principles of language-study.* Oxford: Oxford University Press. (Original work published in 1921.) [5]

Palmer, H. E. (1968). *The scientific study and teaching of languages.* Oxford: Oxford University Press. (Original work published in 1917.) [5]

Paulston, C. B., & Bruder, M. N. (1976). *Teaching English as a second language: Techniques and procedures.* Cambridge, MA: Winthrop. [85]

Pegolo, C. (1985). The role of rhythm and intonation in the silent reading of French as a foreign language. *Reading in a Foreign Language, 3*(1), 313–327. [130]

Pennink, B. (1981). *This is Washington.* London: Heinemann. [144, 146]

Perfetti, C. A. (1985). *Reading ability.* New York: Oxford University Press. [12, 14]

Pitts, M., White, H., & Krashen, S. (1989). Acquiring second language vocabulary through reading: A replication of the Clockwork Orange study using second language acquirers. *Reading in a Foreign Language, 5*(2), 271–275. [34]

Polak, J., & Krashen, S. (1988). Do we need to teach spelling? The relationship between spelling and voluntary reading among community college ESL students. *TESOL Quarterly, 22*(1), 141–146. [37–38]

Pratkanis, A. R. (1989). The cognitive representation of attitudes. In A. R. Pratkanis, S. J. Breckler, & A. G. Greenwald (Eds.), *Attitude structure and function* (pp. 71–98). Hillsdale, NJ: Lawrence Erlbaum. [22]

Rayner, K. (Ed.). (1983). *Eye movements in reading: Perceptual and language processes.* New York: Academic Press. [13]

Rayner, K., & Pollatsek, A. (1989). *The psychology of reading.* Englewood Cliffs, NJ: Prentice Hall. [13, 20]

Richards, J. C., Platt, J., & Platt, H. (1992). *Longman dictionary of language teaching and applied linguistics* (2nd ed.). Harlow, Essex: Longman. [6, 58, 60]

Rivers, W. M. (1981). *Teaching foreign-language skills* (2nd ed.). Chicago: University of Chicago Press. [55]

Robb, T. N., & Susser, B. (1989). Extensive reading vs. skills building in an EFL context. *Reading in a Foreign Language, 5*(2), 239–251. [34]

Robinson, R., & Hulett, J. (1991). Ten best ideas for elementary reading teachers. In E. Fry (Ed.), *Ten best ideas for reading teachers* (pp. 106–107). Reading, MA: Addison-Wesley. [128]

Rodrigo, V. (1995, March). Does a reading program work in a foreign language classroom? Paper presented at the Extensive Reading Colloquium, American Association of Applied Linguistics, Long Beach, CA. [34, 36]

Rönnqvist, L., & Sell, R. D. (1994). Teenage books for teenagers: Reflections on literature in language education. *ELT Journal, 48*(2), 125–132. [104]

Ruddell, M. R. (1994). Vocabulary knowledge and comprehension: A comprehension-process view of complex literacy relationships. In R. B. Ruddell, M. R. Ruddell, & H. Singer (Eds.), *Theoretical models and processes of reading* (4th ed.) (pp. 414–447). Newark, DE: International Reading Association. [14]

Saint-Exupéry, A. de. (1943). *The little prince.* Trans. K. Woods. San Diego, CA: Harcourt-Brace. [105, 132]

Samuels, S. J. (1979). The method of repeated readings. *The Reading Teacher, 32*(4), 403–408. (Reprinted with update by the author in *The Reading Teacher, 50*(5), 376–381 [1997]). [132]

Samuels, S. J. (1994). Toward a theory of automatic information processing in reading, revisited. In R. B. Ruddell, M. R. Ruddell, & H. Singer (Eds.),

Theoretical models and processes of reading (4th ed.) (pp. 816–837). Newark, DE: International Reading Association. [12, 15, 16]

Scarcella, R. C., & Oxford, R. L. (1992). *The tapestry of language learning: The individual in the communicative classroom.* Boston: Heinle & Heinle. [54]

Schell, L. M. (1991). Ten best ideas for reading teachers. In E. Fry (Ed.), *Ten best ideas for reading teachers* (pp. 115–116). Reading, MA: Addison-Wesley. [46]

Schumann, F. M., & Schumann, J. H. (1977). Diary of a language learner: An introspective study of second language learning. In H. D. Brown, C. A. Yorio, & R. H. Crymes (Eds.), *On TESOL '77. Teaching and learning English as a second language: Trends in research and practice* (pp. 241–249). Washington, DC: TESOL. [99]

Science Research Associates. (1969). *SRA reading laboratory 1a, 1b, 1c, 2a, 2b, 2c, 3a, 3b.* New York: McGraw-Hill. [134]

Silberstein, S. (1994). *Techniques and resources in teaching reading.* New York: Oxford University Press. [59, 60]

Simensen, A. M. (1987). Adapted readers: How are they adapted? *Reading in a Foreign Language, 4*(1), 41–57. [6]

Smith, F. (1983). *Essays into literacy.* Portsmouth, NH: Heinemann. [24]

Smith, R. (1997). Transforming a non-reading culture. In G. M. Jacobs, C. Davis, & W. A. Renandya (Eds.), *Successful strategies for extensive reading* (pp. 30–43). Singapore: SEAMEO Regional Language Centre. [130]

Stanovich, K. E. (1992). The psychology of reading: Evolutionary and revolutionary developments. In W. Grabe (Ed.), *Annual Review of Applied Linguistics, 12* (pp. 3–30). Cambridge: Cambridge University Press. [12, 13]

Stoll, D. R. (Ed.). (1997). *Magazines for kids and teens* (new ed.). Glassboro, NJ: Educational Press Association, & Newark, DE: International Reading Association. [103]

Stoller, F. (1986). Reading lab: Developing low-level reading skills. In F. Dubin, D. E. Eskey, & W. Grabe (Eds.), *Teaching second language reading for academic purposes* (pp. 51–76). Reading, MA: Addison-Wesley. [40]

Stoller, F. L., & Grabe, W. (1993). Implications for L2 vocabulary acquisition and instruction from L1 vocabulary research. In T. Huckin, M. Haynes, & J. Coady (Eds.), *Second language reading and vocabulary learning* (pp. 24–44). Norwood, NJ: Ablex. [18, 20]

Stone, J. (1994, October). Readers should be accessible . . . *EFL Gazette,* 15. [77]

Susser, B., & Robb, T. N. (1989). Extensive homework. *The Language Teacher, 13*(8), 7–9. [84–86, 95]

Susser, B., & Robb, T. N. (1990). EFL extensive reading instruction: Research and procedure. *JALT Journal, 12*(2), 161–185. [84–85]

Swaffar, J. K. (1985). Reading authentic texts in a foreign language: A cognitive model. *The Modern Language Journal, 69*(1), 15–34. [60]

Taylor, B. (1991). Ten best ideas for reading teachers. In E. Fry (Ed.), *Ten best ideas for reading teachers* (p. 123). Reading, MA: Addison-Wesley. [136]

Teens' favorite books: Young adults' choices 1987–1992. (1992). Newark, DE: International Reading Association. [106]

Thistlethwaite, L. (1994). Literature for all ages in the adult education program. *Reading Research and Instruction, 34*(2), 136–148. [99]

Tudor, I., & Hafiz, F. (1989). Extensive reading as a means of input to L2 learning. *Journal of Research in Reading, 12*(2), 164–178. [34, 35, 37]

Vincent, M. (1986). Simple text and reading text. Part I: Some general issues. In C. J. Brumfit & R. A. Carter (Eds.), *Literature and language teaching* (pp. 208–215). Oxford: Oxford University Press. [74]

Wallace, C. (1992). *Reading.* Oxford: Oxford University Press. [16, 118]

Walter, C. (1986). *Genuine articles: Authentic reading texts for intermediate students of American English.* Cambridge: Cambridge University Press. [54]

Welch, R. A. (1986, October). Personal communication. [114]

Welch, R. A. (1997). Introducing extensive reading. *The Language Teacher, 21*(5), 51–53. [122–123]

West, M. (1931). *Robinson Crusoe.* London: Longmans, Green. (Adapted from the original book by Daniel Defoe.) [169]

West, M. (1936). *The new method readers for teaching English reading to foreign children: Reader IV.* London: Longmans, Green. [171]

West, M. (1955). Learning to read a foreign language. In M. West, *Learning to read a foreign language and other essays on language-teaching* (2nd ed.) (pp. 1–46). London: Longmans, Green. (Original work published in 1926.) [6]

West, M. (1960). *Teaching English in difficult circumstances.* London: Longmans, Green. [67]

West, M., & Swan, D. K. (1976). *Robinson Crusoe.* Harlow, Essex: Longman. (Adapted from the original book by Daniel Defoe.) [169]

Widdowson, H. G. (1976). The authenticity of language data. In J. F. Fanselow & R. H. Crymes (Eds.), *On TESOL '76* (pp. 261–270). Washington, DC: TESOL. [53, 54, 62]

Widdowson, H. G. (1978). *Teaching language as communication.* Oxford: Oxford University Press. [57, 62, 79]

Widdowson, H. G. (1979). *Explorations in applied linguistics.* Oxford: Oxford University Press. [59, 61, 62, 65, 140, 141, 142]

Widdowson, H. G. (1984a). *Explorations in applied linguistics 2.* Oxford: Oxford University Press. [62]

Widdowson, H. G. (1984b). Reading and communication. In J. C. Alderson & A. H. Urquhart (Eds.), *Reading in a foreign language* (pp. 213–226). Harlow, Essex: Longman. [62]

Williams, E. (1983). Communicative reading. In K. Johnson & D. Porter (Eds.), *Perspectives in communicative language teaching* (pp. 171–183). London: Academic Press. [55]

Williams, E. (1984). *Reading in the language classroom.* London: Macmillan. [54]

Williams, E., & Moran, C. (1989). Reading in a foreign language at intermediate and advanced levels with particular reference to English. *Language Teaching, 22*(4), 217–228. [6]

Williams, R. (1986). "Top ten" principles for teaching reading. *ELT Journal, 40*(1), 42–45. [29]

Yano, Y., Long, M. H., & Ross, S. (1994). The effects of simplified and elaborated texts on foreign language reading comprehension. *Language Learning, 44*(2), 189–219. [59–60, 65]

Yong, T. H., & Idamban, S. (1997). Reading aloud to students as part of extensive reading. In G. M. Jacobs, C. Davis, & W. A. Renandya (Eds.), *Successful strategies for extensive reading* (pp. 109–119). Singapore: SEAMEO Regional Language Centre. [130]

Yopp, R., & Yopp, H. (1991). Ten best ideas for reading teachers. In E. Fry (Ed.), *Ten best ideas for reading teachers* (pp. 132–134). Reading, MA: Addison-Wesley. [96]

Yorio, C. A. (1985). The ESL reading class: Reality or unreality. In C. N. Hedley & A. N. Baratta (Eds.), *Contexts of reading* (pp. 151–164). Norwood, NJ: Ablex. [4, 9, 135–136]

Index

A few authors cited in the text are listed in the Index if the reference is either detailed or not connected to a specific work. For a listing of all authors and works mentioned in the book, refer to the References.